Teach Yourself
VISUALLY™
Windows® XP

Visual

From
maranGraphics®

&

Wiley Publishing, Inc.

Teach Yourself VISUALLY™ Windows® XP

Published by
Wiley Publishing, Inc.
909 Third Avenue
New York, NY 10022

Published simultaneously in Canada

Copyright©2001 by maranGraphics Inc.
  5755 Coopers Avenue
  Mississauga, Ontario, Canada
  L4Z 1R9

Library of Congress Control Number: 2001093187

ISBN: 0-7645-3619-2

Manufactured in the United States of America

10   9   8

1K/QR/RQ/QS/MG

Trademark Acknowledgments

Important Numbers

For U.S. corporate orders, please call maranGraphics at 800-469-6616
or fax 905-890-9434.

For general information on our other products and services or
to obtain technical support, please contact our Customer Care
Department within the U.S. at 800-762-2974, outside the U.S. at
317-572-3993 or fax 317-572-4002.

Permissions

U.S. Corporate Sales	**U.S. Trade Sales**
Contact maranGraphics at (800) 469-6616 or fax (905) 890-9434.	Contact Wiley at (800) 762-2974 or fax (317) 572-4002.

Some comments from our readers...

"I have to praise you and your company on the fine products you turn out. I have twelve of the *Teach Yourself VISUALLY* and *Simplified* books in my house. They were instrumental in helping me pass a difficult computer course. Thank you for creating books that are easy to follow."

–Gordon Justin (Brielle, NJ)

"I commend your efforts and your success. I teach in an outreach program for the Dr. Eugene Clark Library in Lockhart, TX. Your *Teach Yourself VISUALLY* books are incredible and I use them in my computer classes. All my students love them!"

–Michele Schalin (Lockhart, TX)

"Thank you so much for helping people like me learn about computers. The Maran family is just what the doctor ordered. Thank you, thank you, thank you."

–Carol Moten (New Kensington, PA)

"I would like to take this time to compliment maranGraphics on creating such great books. Thank you for making it clear. Keep up the good work."

–Kirk Santoro (Burbank, CA)

"I write to extend my thanks and appreciation for your books. They are clear, easy to follow, and straight to the point. Keep up the good work!"

–Seward Kollie (Dakar, Senegal)

"What fantastic teaching books you have produced! Congratulations to you and your staff. You deserve the Nobel prize in Education in the Software category. Thanks for helping me to understand computers."

–Bruno Tonon (Melbourne, Australia)

"Over time, I have bought a number of your 'Read Less-Learn More' books. For me, they are THE way to learn anything easily."

–José A. Mazón (Cuba, NY)

"I was introduced to maranGraphics about four years ago and YOU ARE THE GREATEST THING THAT EVER HAPPENED TO INTRODUCTORY COMPUTER BOOKS!"

–Glenn Nettleton (Huntsville, AL)

"Compliments To The Chef!! Your books are extraordinary! Or, simply put, Extra-Ordinary, meaning way above the rest! THANK YOU THANK YOU THANK YOU! for creating these."

–Christine J. Manfrin (Castle Rock, CO)

"I'm a grandma who was pushed by an 11-year-old grandson to join the computer age. I found myself hopelessly confused and frustrated until I discovered the Visual series. I'm no expert by any means now, but I'm a lot further along than I would have been otherwise. Thank you!"

–Carol Louthain (Logansport, IN)

"Thank you, thank you, thank you...for making it so easy for me to break into this high-tech world. I now own four of your books. I recommend them to anyone who is a beginner like myself. Now... if you could just do one for programming VCRs, it would make my day!"

–Gay O'Donnell (Calgary, Alberta, Canada)

"You're marvelous! I am greatly in your debt."

–Patrick Baird (Lacey, WA)

maranGraphics is a family-run business
located near Toronto, Canada.

At **maranGraphics**, we believe in producing great computer books–one book at a time.

Each maranGraphics book uses the award-winning communication process that we have been developing over the last 25 years. Using this process, we organize screen shots, text and illustrations in a way that makes it easy for you to learn new concepts and tasks.

We spend hours deciding the best way to perform each task, so you don't have to! Our clear, easy-to-follow screen shots and instructions walk you through each task from beginning to end.

Our detailed illustrations go hand-in-hand with the text to help reinforce the information. Each illustration is a labor of love–some take up to a week to draw!

We want to thank you for purchasing what we feel are the best computer books money can buy. We hope you enjoy using this book as much as we enjoyed creating it!

Sincerely,

The Maran Family

Please visit us on the Web at:
www.maran.com

CREDITS

Author:
Ruth Maran

Copy Editors:
Roxanne Van Damme
Raquel Scott

Technical Consultant:
Paul Whitehead

Project Manager:
Judy Maran

Editorial Review:
Kelleigh Johnson

Editors:
Wanda Lawrie
Roxanne Van Damme
Roderick Anatalio
Teri Lynn Pinsent
Norm Schumacher
Megan Kirby
Cathy Lo
Stacey Morrison

Screen Captures:
Jill Maran

Layout Artist:
Treena Lees

Illustrators:
Russ Marini
Steven Schaerer
Suzana G. Miokovic
Paul Baker
Hee-Jin Park

Screen Artist and Illustrator:
Darryl Grossi

Indexer:
Raquel Scott

Permissions Coordinator:
Jennifer Amaral

**Wiley Vice President and
Executive Group Publisher:**
Richard Swadley

**Wiley Vice President
and Publisher:**
Barry Pruett

Wiley Editorial Support:
Jennifer Dorsey
Sandy Rodrigues
Lindsay Sandman

Post Production:
Robert Maran

ACKNOWLEDGMENTS

Thanks to the dedicated staff of maranGraphics, including
Jennifer Amaral, Roderick Anatalio, Paul Baker, Darryl Grossi,
Kelleigh Johnson, Megan Kirby, Wanda Lawrie, Treena Lees,
Cathy Lo, Jill Maran, Judy Maran, Robert Maran, Ruth Maran,
Russ Marini, Suzana G. Miokovic, Stacey Morrison, Hee-Jin Park,
Teri Lynn Pinsent, Steven Schaerer, Norm Schumacher, Raquel Scott,
Roxanne Van Damme and Paul Whitehead.

Finally, to Richard Maran who originated the easy-to-use graphic
format of this guide. Thank you for your inspiration and guidance.

TABLE OF CONTENTS

Chapter 1

WINDOWS BASICS

Chapter 2

CREATE DOCUMENTS

Chapter 3

CREATE PICTURES

Chapter 4

VIEW FILES

Chapter 5

WORK WITH FILES

TABLE OF CONTENTS

Chapter 6

CUSTOMIZE WINDOWS

Chapter 7

WORK WITH MUSIC AND VIDEOS

Chapter 8

CREATE MOVIES

Chapter 9

SHARE YOUR COMPUTER

Chapter 10

OPTIMIZE COMPUTER PERFORMANCE

TABLE OF CONTENTS

Chapter 11

WORK ON A NETWORK

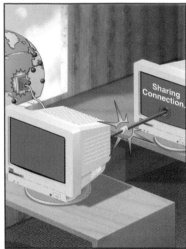

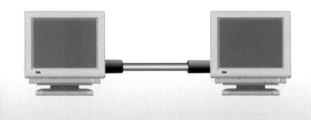

Chapter 12

BROWSE THE WEB

Chapter 13

EXCHANGE E-MAIL

Chapter 14

EXCHANGE INSTANT MESSAGES

INTRODUCTION TO WINDOWS

Microsoft® Windows® XP is a program that controls the overall activity of your computer.

Microsoft Windows XP ensures that all parts of your computer work together smoothly and efficiently. **XP** stands for e**xp**erience.

Work with Files

Windows provides ways to manage the files stored on your computer. You can sort, open, rename, print, delete, move and search for files. You can also e-mail a file, publish a file to the Web and copy files to a floppy disk or recordable CD. Windows includes the WordPad and Paint programs to help you quickly start creating files.

Customize Windows

You can customize Windows to suit your preferences. You can add a colorful picture to your screen, have sound effects play when certain events occur on your computer and change the way your mouse works. Windows also allows you to set up a screen saver to appear when you do not use your computer for a period of time.

Work with Multimedia

Windows allows you to play music CDs and listen to radio stations that broadcast on the Internet. Windows also helps you find the latest music and movies on the Internet, organize your media files and copy songs from your computer to a recordable CD. You can also transfer your home movies to your computer so you can organize and edit the movies before sharing them with friends and family.

Share Your Computer

If you share your computer with other people, you can create user accounts to keep the personal files and settings for each person separate. You can assign a password to each user account and easily share files with other users.

Optimize Computer Performance

Windows provides tools to help you optimize your computer's performance. You can install new programs, update Windows, remove unnecessary files to free up disk space and restore your computer to an earlier time if you experience problems. You can also allow a friend or colleague at another computer to view your computer screen and take control of your computer to help you solve a computer problem.

Work on a Network

Windows allows you to share information and equipment with other people on a network. You can share folders stored on your computer as well as a printer that is directly connected to your computer. Windows also provides a wizard to help you set up a network.

Access the Internet

Windows allows you to browse through the information on the World Wide Web. You can search for Web pages of interest and create a list of your favorite Web pages so you can quickly access the pages in the future. Windows also allows you to exchange electronic mail with people around the world. You can read, send, reply to, forward, print and delete e-mail messages. Windows also includes the Windows Messenger program that allows you to exchange instant messages and files over the Internet with friends and family.

USING THE START MENU

You can use the Start menu to access programs, files, computer settings and help with Windows.

The programs available on the Start menu depend on the software installed on your computer.

USING THE START MENU

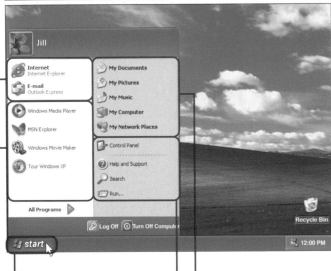

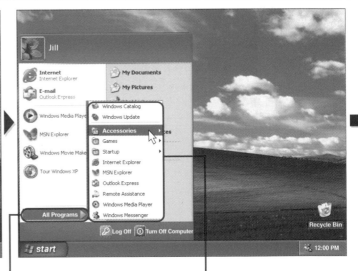

1 Click **start** to display the Start menu.

■ These items start your Web browser and e-mail program.

■ These items allow you to quickly start the programs you have most recently used.

■ These items allow you to quickly access commonly used locations.

■ These items allow you to change your computer's settings, get help, search for information and run programs.

■ If the Start menu displays the item you want to use, click the item.

2 If the item you want to use is not displayed on the Start menu, click **All Programs**.

■ A list of the programs on your computer appears. A menu item with an arrow (▸) will display another menu.

3 To display another menu, position the mouse ⁀ over the menu item with an arrow (▸).

Which programs does Windows provide?

Windows comes with many useful programs. Here are some examples.

Disk Cleanup is a program that helps you remove unnecessary files from your computer to free up disk space.

Windows Media Player is a program that allows you to find and play media files, play music CDs and listen to radio stations that broadcast on the Internet.

WordPad is a word processing program that allows you to create documents, such as letters and memos.

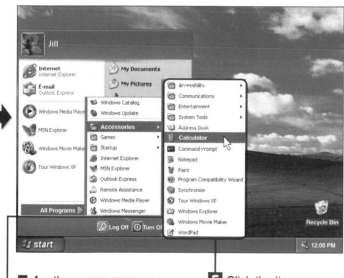

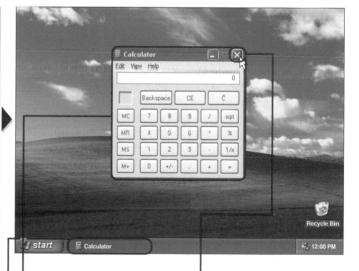

■ Another menu appears.

4 You can repeat step **3** until the item you want to use appears.

5 Click the item you want to use.

Note: To close the Start menu without selecting an item, click outside the menu area.

■ In this example, the Calculator window appears.

■ A button for the open window appears on the taskbar.

6 When you finish working with the window, click ⊠ to close the window.

SCROLL THROUGH A WINDOW

You can use a scroll bar to browse through the information in a window. Scrolling is useful when a window is not large enough to display all the information it contains.

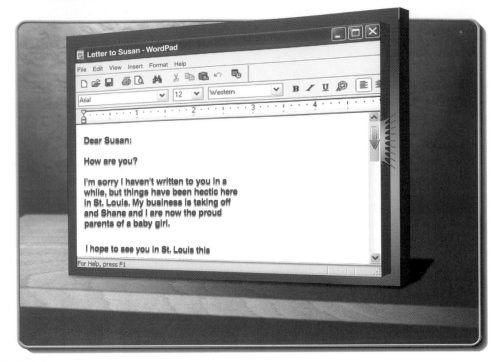

SCROLL THROUGH A WINDOW

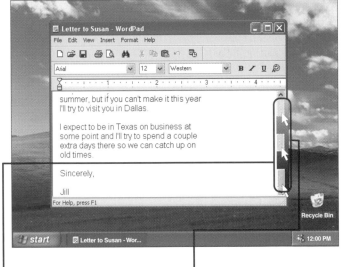

SCROLL UP

1 Click ⬆ to scroll up through the information in a window.

SCROLL DOWN

1 Click ⬇ to scroll down through the information in a window.

SCROLL TO ANY POSITION

1 Position the mouse ⬉ over the scroll box.

2 Drag the scroll box along the scroll bar until the information you want to view appears.

■ The location of the scroll box indicates which part of the window you are viewing. For example, when the scroll box is halfway down the scroll bar, you are viewing information from the middle of the window.

CLOSE A WINDOW

When you finish working with a window, you can close the window to remove it from your screen.

CLOSE A WINDOW

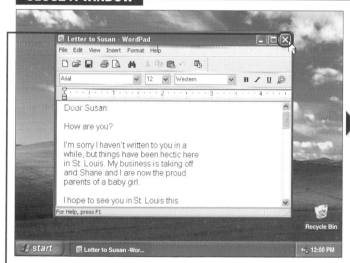

1 Click ☒ in the window you want to close.

■ The window disappears from your screen.

■ The button for the window disappears from the taskbar.

MOVE A WINDOW

If a window covers items on your screen, you can move the window to a different location.

You may want to move several windows to see the contents of multiple windows at once.

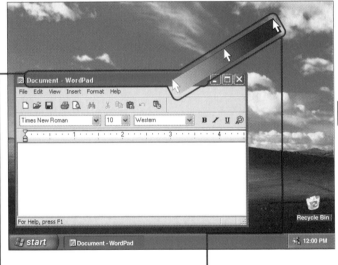

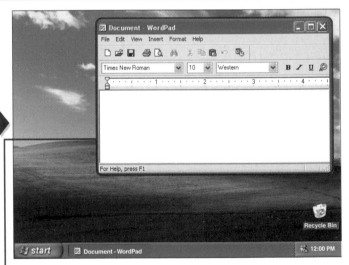

1 Position the mouse ↳ over the title bar of the window you want to move.

2 Drag the mouse ↳ to where you want to place the window.

■ The window moves to the new location.

Note: You cannot move a maximized window. For information on maximizing a window, see page 10.

RESIZE A WINDOW

You can easily change the size of a window displayed on your screen.

Enlarging the size of a window allows you to view more information in the window. Reducing the size of a window allows you to view items covered by the window.

RESIZE A WINDOW

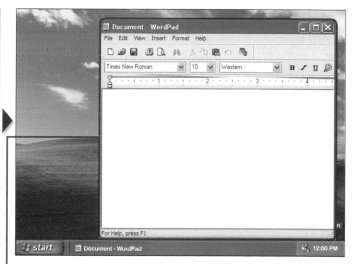

1 Position the mouse ℝ over an edge of the window you want to resize (ℝ changes to ↕, ↔, ↖ or ↗).

2 Drag the mouse ↕ until the window displays the size you want.

■ The window displays the new size.

Note: You cannot resize a maximized window. For information on maximizing a window, see page 10.

MAXIMIZE A WINDOW

You can maximize a window to fill your entire screen. This allows you to view more of the window's contents.

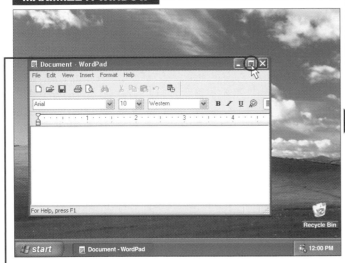

1 Click  in the window you want to maximize.

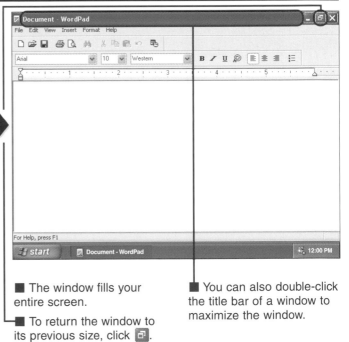

■ The window fills your entire screen.

■ To return the window to its previous size, click 🗗.

■ You can also double-click the title bar of a window to maximize the window.

If you are not using
a window, you can
minimize the window
to temporarily remove
it from your screen.
You can redisplay the
window at any time.

Minimizing a
window allows you
to temporarily put
a window aside so
you can work on
other tasks.

MINIMIZE A WINDOW

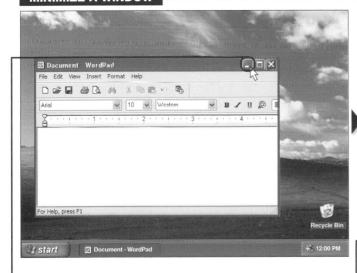

1 Click ■ in the window
you want to minimize.

■ The window reduces
to a button on the taskbar.

■ To redisplay the
window, click its button
on the taskbar.

*Note: If a menu appears,
displaying the names of
several open windows when
you click a button on the
taskbar, click the name of the
window you want to redisplay.*

SWITCH BETWEEN WINDOWS

If you have more than one window open on your screen, you can easily switch between the windows.

Each window is like a separate piece of paper. Switching between windows is like placing a different piece of paper at the top of the pile.

You can work in only one window at a time. The active window appears in front of all other windows and displays a dark title bar.

SWITCH BETWEEN WINDOWS

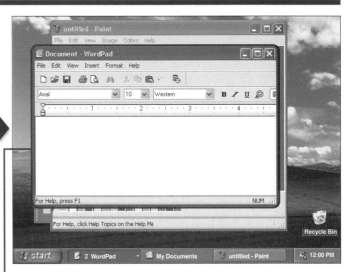

■ The taskbar displays a button for each open window. If you have many windows open, all the buttons for a program may appear as a single button on the taskbar.

1 To display the window you want to work with, click its button on the taskbar.

■ A menu may appear, displaying the name of each open window in the program.

2 Click the name of the window you want to display.

■ The window appears in front of all other windows. You can now clearly view the contents of the window.

Note: You can also click anywhere inside a window to display the window in front of all other windows.

You can close a
program that is no
longer responding
without having to
shut down Windows.

When you close a
misbehaving program,
you will lose any
information you did not
save in the program.

Closing a
misbehaving
program should
not affect other
open programs.

CLOSE A MISBEHAVING PROGRAM

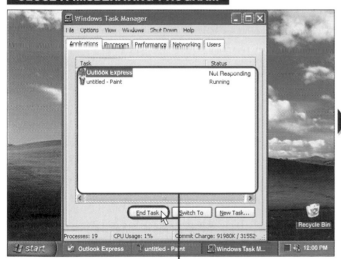

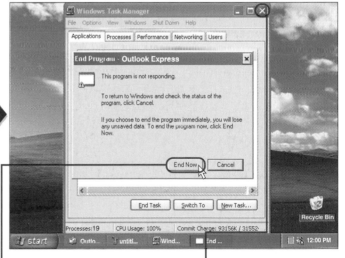

1 To close a misbehaving
program, press and hold
down the `Ctrl` and `Alt`
keys as you press the
`Delete` key.

■ The Windows Task
Manager window appears.

■ This area lists the
programs that are currently
running. The phrase **Not
Responding** appears
beside the name of a
misbehaving program.

2 Click the program
that is misbehaving.

3 Click **End Task**.

■ The End Program
dialog box appears,
stating that the program
is not responding.

4 Click **End Now** to
close the program.

5 Click ⊠ to close the
Windows Task Manager
window.

PLAY GAMES

Windows includes several games that you can play on your computer. Games are a fun way to improve your mouse skills and hand-eye coordination.

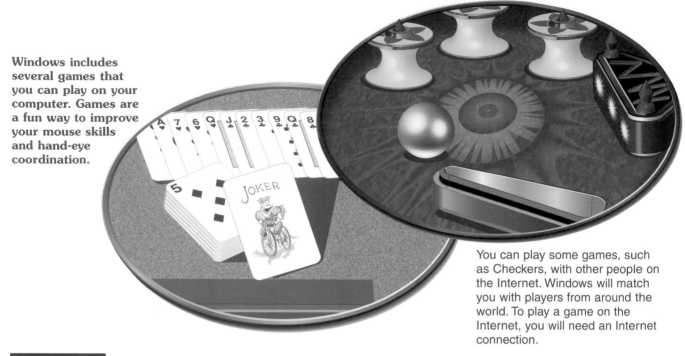

You can play some games, such as Checkers, with other people on the Internet. Windows will match you with players from around the world. To play a game on the Internet, you will need an Internet connection.

PLAY GAMES

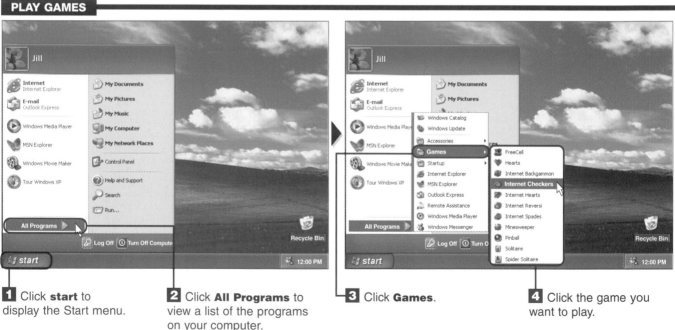

1 Click **start** to display the Start menu.

2 Click **All Programs** to view a list of the programs on your computer.

3 Click **Games**.

4 Click the game you want to play.

What games are included with Windows?

Here are some popular games included with Windows.

Minesweeper

Minesweeper is a strategy game in which you try to avoid being blown up by mines.

Pinball

Pinball is similar to a pinball game you would find at an arcade. You launch a ball and then try to score as many points as possible.

Solitaire

Solitaire is a classic card game that you play on your own. The object of the game is to place all the cards in order from ace to king in four stacks—one stack for each suit.

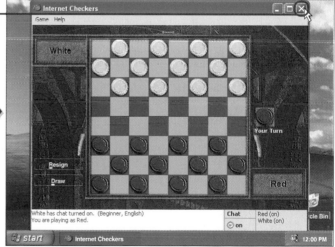

■ If you selected an Internet game, a dialog box appears that displays information about playing games on the Internet.

Note: If you selected a non-Internet game, skip to step 6.

5 Click **Play** to continue.

Note: If you are not currently connected to the Internet, a dialog box will appear that allows you to connect.

■ A window appears, displaying the game. In this example, the Internet Checkers window appears.

6 When you finish playing the game, click ☒ to close the window.

■ A message may appear, confirming that you want to leave the game. Click **Yes** to leave the game.

USING THE CALCULATOR

Windows provides a calculator that you can use to perform calculations.

You can use the Calculator to perform the same calculations you can perform on a handheld calculator.

USING THE CALCULATOR

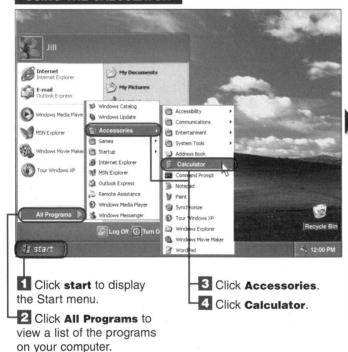

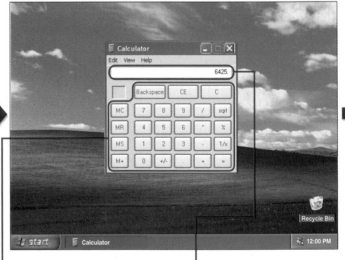

1 Click **start** to display the Start menu.

2 Click **All Programs** to view a list of the programs on your computer.

3 Click **Accessories**.

4 Click **Calculator**.

■ The Calculator window appears.

5 To enter information into the Calculator, click each button as you would press the buttons on a handheld calculator.

Note: You can also use the keys on your keyboard to enter information into the Calculator.

■ This area displays the numbers you enter and the result of each calculation.

Can I enter numbers using the keys on the right side of my keyboard?

To use the number keys on the right side of your keyboard to enter information into the Calculator, the Num Lock light must be on. To turn the light on, press the Num Lock key on your keyboard.

What are some useful buttons on the Calculator?

Button	Description
Backspace	Removes the last digit of the displayed number.
CE	Clears the displayed number.
C	Clears the current calculation.
MC, MR, MS	Clears, recalls and stores the number in memory.
M+	Adds the displayed number to the number in memory.
sqrt	Calculates the square root of the displayed number.
1/x	Calculates the reciprocal of the displayed number.

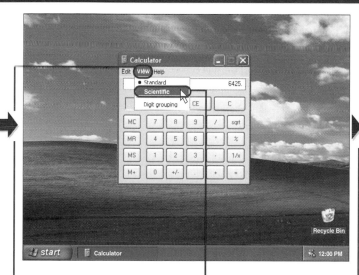

6 To change to the Scientific view of the Calculator, click **View**.

7 Click **Scientific**.

■ The Scientific view of the Calculator appears. This view offers additional features that allow you to perform advanced scientific and statistical calculations.

Note: To return to the Standard view, repeat steps 6 and 7, selecting Standard in step 7.

8 When you finish using the Calculator, click ☒ to close the Calculator window.

SHUT DOWN WINDOWS

When you finish using your computer, you should shut down Windows before turning off your computer.

■ Do not turn off your computer until this message appears on your screen. Many computers will not display this message and will turn off automatically.

Before shutting down Windows, make sure you close all the programs you have open.

SHUT DOWN WINDOWS

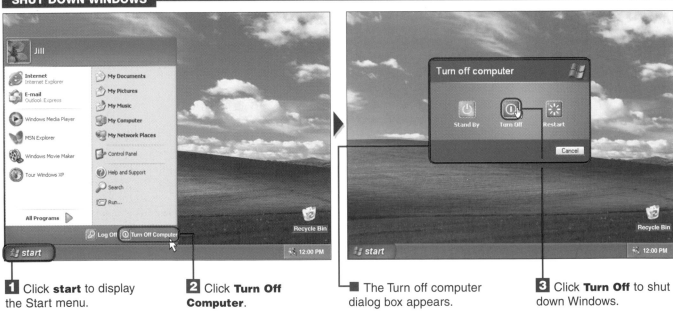

1 Click **start** to display the Start menu.

2 Click **Turn Off Computer**.

■ The Turn off computer dialog box appears.

3 Click **Turn Off** to shut down Windows.

RESTART YOUR COMPUTER

If your computer is not operating properly, you can restart your computer to try to fix the problem.

Before restarting your computer, make sure you close all the programs you have open.

RESTART YOUR COMPUTER

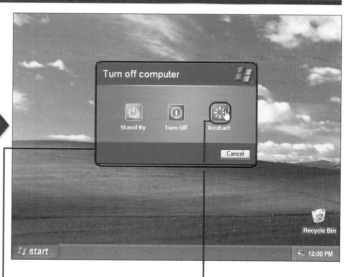

1 Click **start** to display the Start menu.

2 Click **Turn Off Computer**.

■ The Turn off computer dialog box appears.

3 Click **Restart** to restart your computer.

FIND HELP INFORMATION

If you do not know how to perform a task in Windows, you can use the Help feature to find information on the task.

FIND HELP INFORMATION

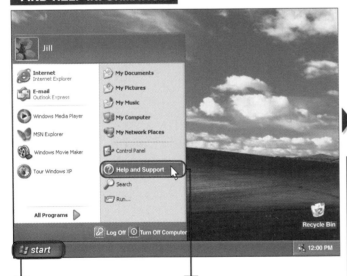

1 Click **start** to display the Start menu.

2 Click **Help and Support**.

■ The Help and Support Center window appears.

■ This area displays a list of common help topics, ways that you can ask for assistance and tasks for which you can receive help. You can click an item of interest to display information about the item.

3 To search for specific help information, click this area and then type a word or phrase that describes the topic of interest.

4 Press the Enter key to start the search.

Why do some help topics display colored text?

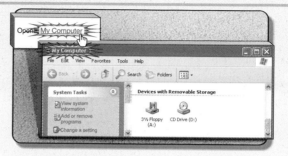

Display a Definition

You can click a word or phrase that appears in green to display a definition of the word or phrase. To hide the definition, click the definition.

Obtain Additional Help

You can click a word or phrase that appears in blue to obtain additional help. Windows may display another help topic or open a window that allows you to perform a task. If you click the phrase "Related Topics" at the bottom of a help topic, a list of related help topics appears. You can click the help topic of interest in the list.

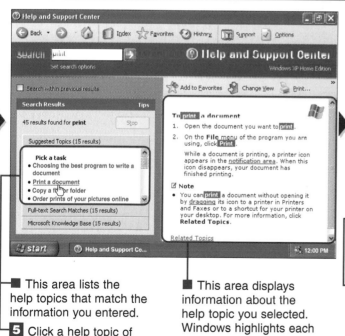

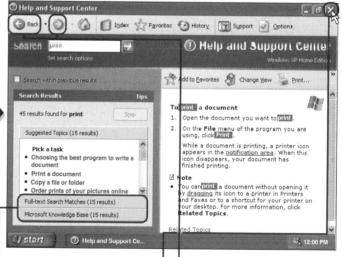

■ This area lists the help topics that match the information you entered.

5 Click a help topic of interest.

■ This area displays information about the help topic you selected. Windows highlights each occurrence of the word or phrase you searched for.

Note: You can repeat step 5 to display information for another help topic.

■ If you want to view a list of help topics under a different heading, click the heading of interest.

Note: To view a list of help topics under the Microsoft Knowledge Base heading, you must be connected to the Internet.

■ To browse through the help topics you have viewed, you can click **Back** or ➡.

6 When you finish reviewing help information, click ✕ to close the Help and Support Center window.

CHAPTER 2

Create Documents

Read this chapter to learn how to create and edit documents quickly and efficiently using the WordPad program.

Dear Kevin:

hool celebrates its 30th
ar! We will be celebrating

START WORDPAD

You can use WordPad to create and edit documents, such as letters and memos.

Annual Staff Picnic

Saturday, August 11, 2001
10:30 am - 6:00 pm
Garden Gate Park

All employees are invited to bring their families out for a fun-filled day at the park. There will be plenty of food and lots of exciting games.

RSVP

M _____

_____ will attend

_____ is unable to attend

Please reply before Friday, July 27, 2001

If you need more advanced features than WordPad provides, you may want to obtain a more sophisticated word processor, such as Microsoft Word or Corel WordPerfect.

START WORDPAD

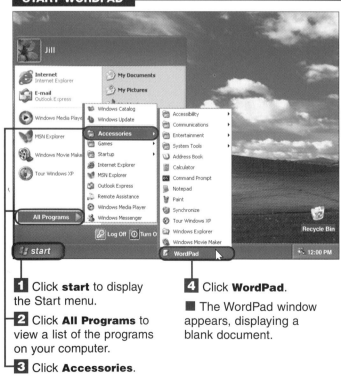

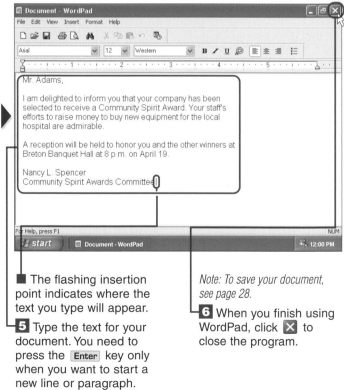

1 Click **start** to display the Start menu.

2 Click **All Programs** to view a list of the programs on your computer.

3 Click **Accessories**.

4 Click **WordPad**.

■ The WordPad window appears, displaying a blank document.

■ The flashing insertion point indicates where the text you type will appear.

5 Type the text for your document. You need to press the Enter key only when you want to start a new line or paragraph.

Note: To save your document, see page 28.

6 When you finish using WordPad, click ☒ to close the program.

EDIT TEXT

You can easily edit the text in your document. You can insert new text or remove text you no longer need.

EDIT TEXT

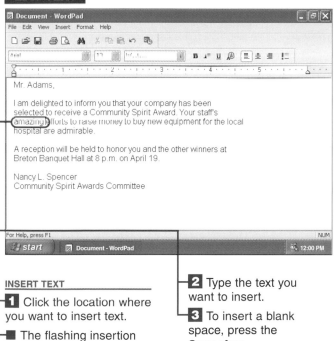

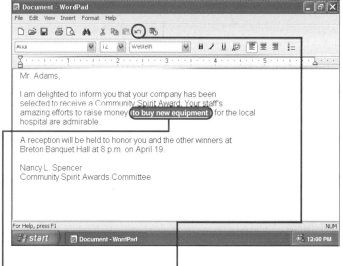

INSERT TEXT

1 Click the location where you want to insert text.

■ The flashing insertion point indicates where the text you type will appear.

2 Type the text you want to insert.

3 To insert a blank space, press the **Spacebar**.

DELETE TEXT

1 To select the text you want to delete, drag the mouse I over the text until the text is highlighted.

2 Press the Delete key to remove the text.

■ To delete one character at a time, click to the left of the first character you want to delete. Then press the Delete key for each character you want to remove.

■ To immediately undo a change, click ↶ .

CHANGE FONT OF TEXT

You can change the font of text to enhance the appearance of your document.

CHANGE FONT OF TEXT

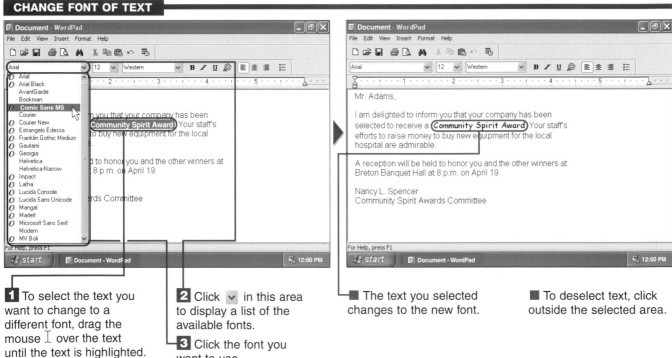

1 To select the text you want to change to a different font, drag the mouse I over the text until the text is highlighted.

2 Click ⌄ in this area to display a list of the available fonts.

3 Click the font you want to use.

■ The text you selected changes to the new font.

■ To deselect text, click outside the selected area.

You can increase or decrease the size of text in your document.

Larger text is easier to read, but smaller text allows you to fit more information on a page.

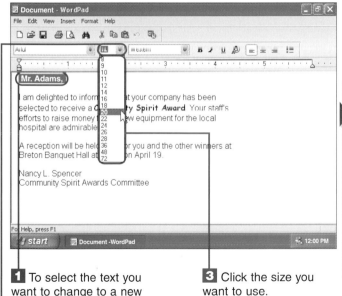

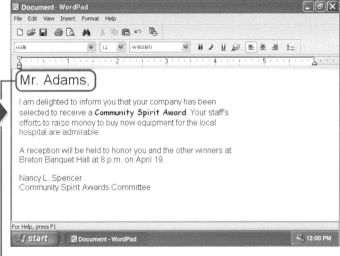

1 To select the text you want to change to a new size, drag the mouse I over the text until the text is highlighted.

2 Click ⌄ in this area to display a list of the available sizes.

3 Click the size you want to use.

Note: WordPad measures the size of text in points. There are approximately 72 points in one inch.

■ The text you selected changes to the new size.

■ To deselect text, click outside the selected area.

SAVE A DOCUMENT

You should save your document to store the document for future use. This allows you to later review and make changes to the document.

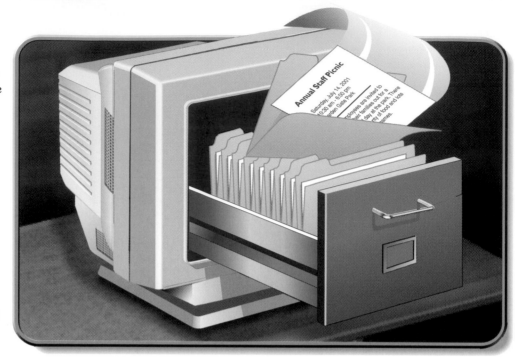

You should regularly save changes you make to a document to avoid losing your work.

SAVE A DOCUMENT

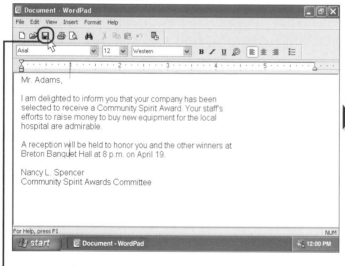

1 Click 💾 to save your document.

■ The Save As dialog box appears.

Note: If you previously saved your document, the Save As dialog box will not appear since you have already named the document.

2 Type a name for your document.

■ This area shows the location where WordPad will store your document. You can click this area to change the location.

3 Click **Save** to save your document.

OPEN A DOCUMENT

You can open a saved document to display the document on your screen. This allows you to review and make changes to the document.

WordPad allows you to work with only one document at a time. If you are currently working with a document, make sure you save the document before opening another document. To save a document, see page 28.

OPEN A DOCUMENT

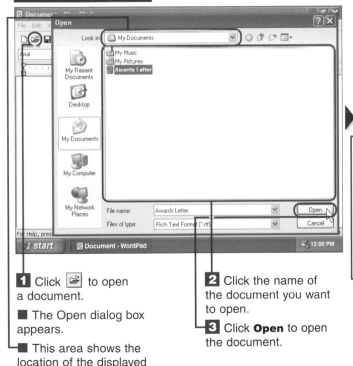

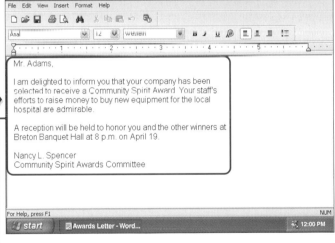

1 Click 🖼 to open a document.

■ The Open dialog box appears.

■ This area shows the location of the displayed documents. You can click this area to change the location.

2 Click the name of the document you want to open.

3 Click **Open** to open the document.

■ The document opens and appears on your screen. You can now review and make changes to the document.

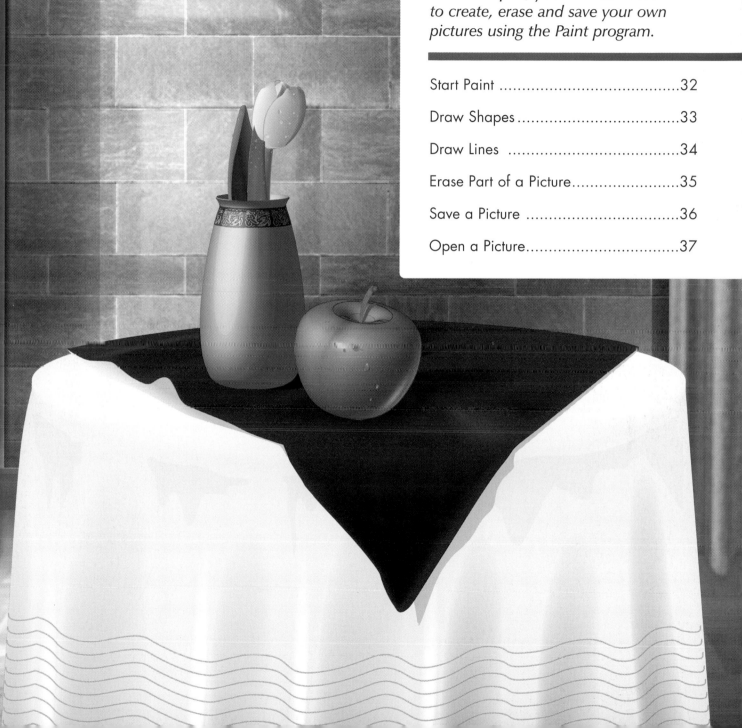

CHAPTER 3

Create Pictures

In this chapter, you will learn how to create, erase and save your own pictures using the Paint program.

Paint is a simple program you can use to draw pictures on your computer.

You can place the pictures you draw in other programs. For example, you can add a picture you draw in Paint to a WordPad document.

If you need more advanced features than Paint provides, you may want to obtain a more sophisticated image editing program, such as Jasc Paint Shop Pro or Adobe Photoshop.

START PAINT

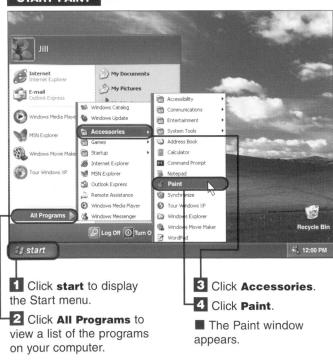

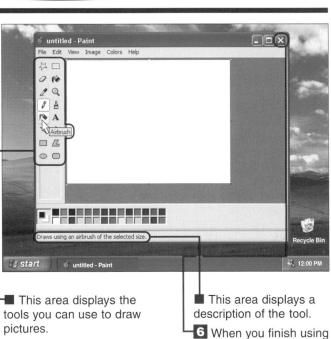

1 Click **start** to display the Start menu.

2 Click **All Programs** to view a list of the programs on your computer.

3 Click **Accessories**.

4 Click **Paint**.

■ The Paint window appears.

■ This area displays the tools you can use to draw pictures.

5 To display a description of a tool, position the mouse over the tool. After a moment, the name of the tool appears in a yellow box.

■ This area displays a description of the tool.

6 When you finish using Paint, click ☒ to close the program.

DRAW SHAPES

You can draw shapes such as circles, squares and polygons in various colors.

You can use these Paint tools to draw shapes.

☐ Rectangle or square

◪ Polygon

◯ Ellipse or circle

☐ Rounded rectangle or square

DRAW SHAPES

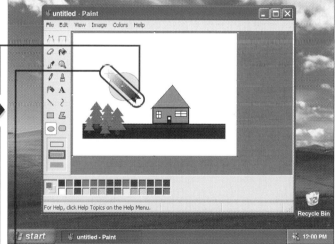

1 Click the tool for the type of shape you want to draw.

2 Click an option to draw the shape with an outline, an inside color or both.

3 To select a color for the outline of the shape, click the color.

4 To select a color for the inside of the shape, right-click the color.

5 Position the mouse ⌖ where you want to begin drawing the shape (⌖ changes to ✛).

6 Drag the mouse ✛ until the shape is the size you want.

■ If you selected ◪ in step **1**, repeat steps **5** and **6** until you finish drawing all the lines for the shape. Then immediately double-click the mouse to complete the shape.

33

DRAW LINES

You can draw straight, wavy and curved lines in various colors.

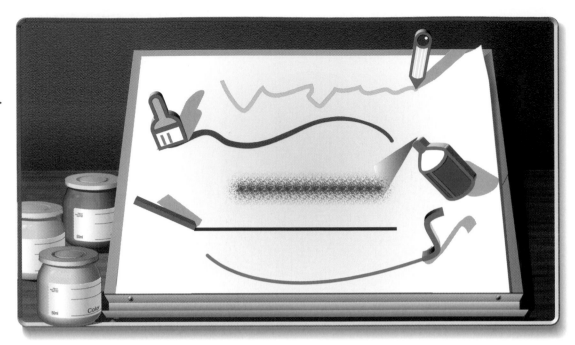

You can use these Paint tools to draw lines.

- ✎ Pencil
- 🖌 Brush
- ✒ Airbrush
- ＼ Straight line
- ⟨ Curved line

DRAW LINES

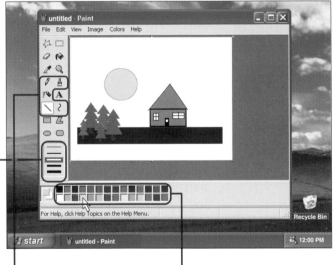

1 Click the tool for the type of line you want to draw.

2 Click the thickness you want to use for the line.

Note: The ✎ tool does not provide any line thickness options.

3 Click the color you want to use for the line.

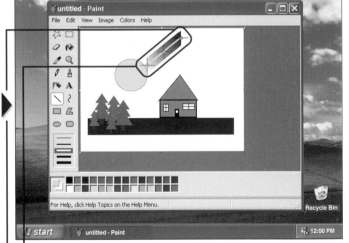

4 Position the mouse ⌕ where you want to begin drawing the line (⌕ changes to ┼, ┼, 🖌 or ✎).

5 Drag the mouse ┼ until the line is the length you want.

■ If you selected ⟨ in step **1**, position the mouse ┼ over the line and then drag the mouse until the line curves the way you want. Then immediately click the mouse to complete the curved line.

ERASE PART OF A PICTURE

You can use
the Eraser tool
to remove part
of your picture.

ERASE PART OF A PICTURE

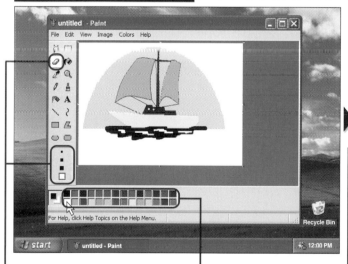

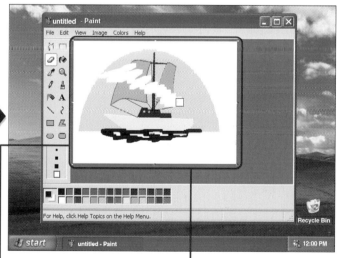

1 Click 🖉 to erase
part of your picture.

2 Click the size of
eraser you want to use.

3 Right-click the color
you want to use for the
eraser.

*Note: Make sure you select
the color that matches the
background color of your
picture.*

4 Position the mouse ▷
where you want to begin
erasing (▷ changes to □).

5 Drag the mouse □ over
the area you want to erase.

*Note: To immediately undo your
change, press and hold down the
Ctrl key as you press the Z key.*

SAVE A PICTURE

You should save your picture to store the picture for future use. This allows you to later review and make changes to the picture.

You should regularly save changes you make to a picture to avoid losing your work.

SAVE A PICTURE

1 Click **File**.

2 Click **Save**.

■ The Save As dialog box appears.

Note: If you previously saved the picture, the Save As dialog box will not appear since you have already named the picture.

3 Type a name for your picture.

■ This area shows the location where Paint will store your picture. You can click this area to change the location.

4 Click **Save** to save your picture.

You can open a saved picture to display the picture on your screen. This allows you to review and make changes to the picture.

Paint allows you to work with only one picture at a time. If you are currently working with a picture, make sure you save the picture before opening another picture. To save a picture, see page 36.

OPEN A PICTURE

1 Click **File**.

2 Click **Open**.

■ The Open dialog box appears.

■ This area shows the location of the displayed pictures. You can click this area to change the location.

3 Click the picture you want to open.

4 Click **Open** to open the picture.

■ The picture opens and appears on your screen.

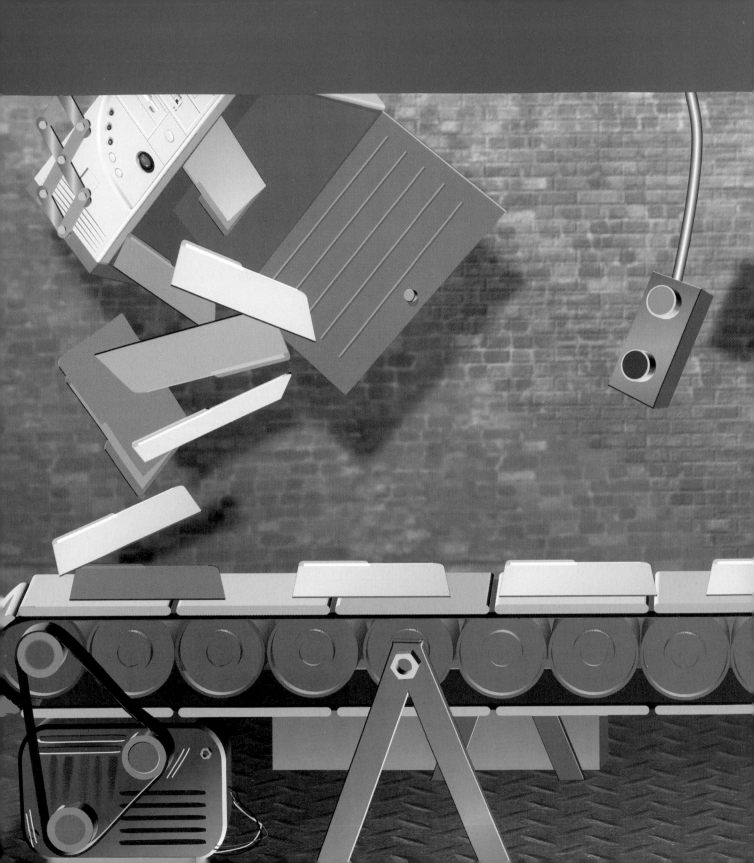

CHAPTER 4

View Files

Read this chapter to learn how to view the files and folders stored on your computer.

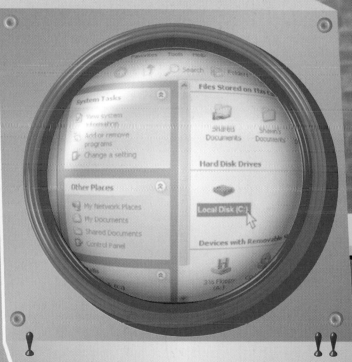

VIEW YOUR PERSONAL FOLDERS

Windows provides personal folders that offer a convenient place for you to store and manage your files. You can view the contents of your personal folders at any time.

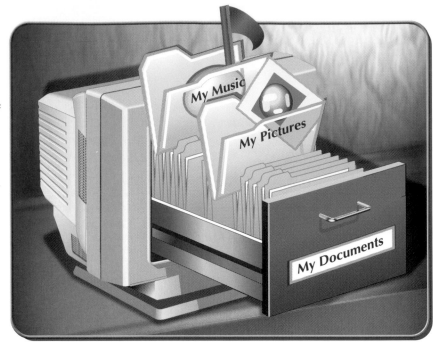

Many programs automatically store files in your personal folders.

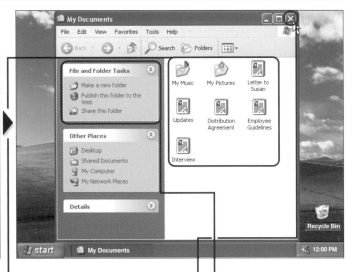

1 Click **start** to display the Start menu.

2 Click **My Documents** to view your documents.

■ A window appears, displaying the contents of the My Documents folder. This folder is useful for storing documents such as letters, reports and memos.

■ The My Documents folder contains the My Music and My Pictures folders.

■ This area displays options you can select to work with the documents in the folder.

3 When you finish viewing the contents of the My Documents folder, click ⊠ to close the folder.

40

What tasks can I perform with the files in my personal folders?

The My Pictures and My Music folders offer several specialized options that you can select to work with your pictures and music. Here are some tasks you can perform.

MY PICTURES

View as a slide show

Displays all the pictures in the My Pictures folder as a full-screen slide show.

Order prints online

Sends the pictures you select to a Web site that allows you to order prints of the pictures.

MY MUSIC

Play all

Plays all the music in the My Music folder.

Shop for music online

Displays the WindowsMedia.com Web site, which allows you to listen to and purchase music.

VIEW THE MY PICTURES OR MY MUSIC FOLDER

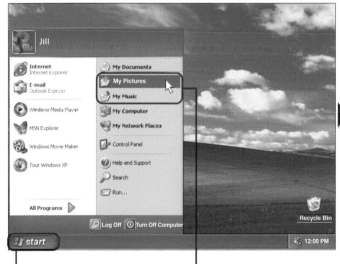

1 Click **start** to display the Start menu.

2 Click **My Pictures** or **My Music** to view your pictures or music.

■ A window appears, displaying the contents of the folder you selected.

■ In this example, the contents of the My Pictures folder appear. This folder displays a miniature version of each picture in the folder.

■ This area displays options you can select to work with the files in the folder.

3 When you finish viewing the contents of the folder, click ⊠ to close the folder.

You can easily browse through the drives, folders and files on your computer.

Windows uses folders to organize the information stored on your computer.

VIEW CONTENTS OF YOUR COMPUTER

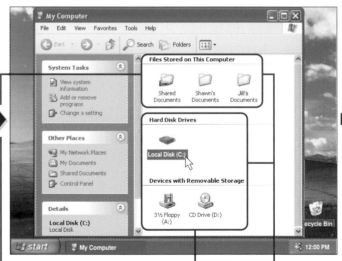

1 Click **start** to display the Start menu.

2 Click **My Computer** to view the contents of your computer.

■ The My Computer window appears.

Note: To view the contents of a floppy or CD-ROM drive, make sure you insert the floppy disk or CD-ROM disc into the appropriate drive before continuing.

■ The folders in this area contain files that all users set up on your computer can access. For more information on these folders, see pages 184 and 185.

■ The items in this area represent your hard drive, floppy drive, CD-ROM drive and any other drives available on your computer.

3 To display the contents of a drive or folder, double-click the item.

What do the icons in a window represent?

Each item in a window displays an icon to help you distinguish between the different types of items. Common types of items include:

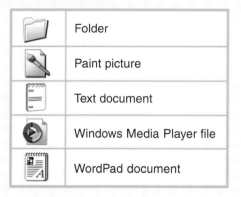

Folder	
Paint picture	
Text document	
Windows Media Player file	
WordPad document	

How can I view information about a folder or file in a window?

To display information about a folder or file in a window, position the mouse over the folder or file. A yellow box appears, displaying information about the folder or file.

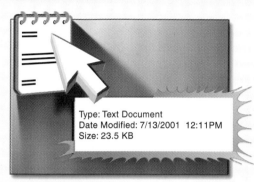

Type: Text Document
Date Modified: 7/13/2001 12:11PM
Size: 23.5 KB

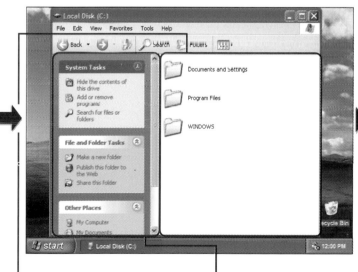

■ The contents of the drive or folder you selected appear.

Note: If the contents of the drive you selected do not appear, click **Show the contents of this folder** *in the window.*

■ This area displays options that you can select to perform common tasks and access commonly used locations on your computer. The available options depend on the selected item.

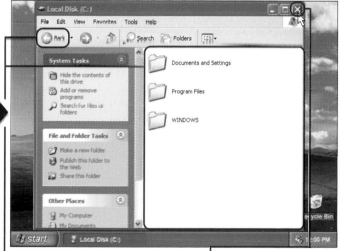

4 To continue browsing through the contents of your computer, you can double-click a folder to display its contents.

■ To return to a window you have previously viewed, click **Back**.

5 When you finish viewing the contents of your computer, click ⊠ to close the window.

CHANGE VIEW OF ITEMS

You can change the view of items in a window. The view you select determines the way files and folders will appear in the window.

CHANGE VIEW OF ITEMS

1 Click **View** to change the view of items in a window.

■ A bullet (●) appears beside the current view of the items.

2 Click the way you want to view the items.

■ In this example, the items appear in the Details view.

Filmstrip

The Filmstrip view displays pictures in a single row that you can scroll through. This view is only available in some windows, such as the My Pictures window. You can click a picture to display a larger version of the picture above the other pictures.

Thumbnails

The Thumbnails view displays a miniature version of each picture and some other types of files.
If a miniature version of a file cannot be shown, an icon is displayed to indicate the type of file, such as a WordPad document ( ). In this view, miniature versions of a few pictures within a folder are shown on the folder's icon.

Tiles

The Tiles view displays items as large icons and displays information about each item below the item's file name.
You can sort the items to change the information that each item displays. To sort items, see page 46.

Icons

The Icons view displays items as small icons with the file name appearing below each icon.

List

The List view displays items as small icons arranged in a list. This view is useful if you want to find a particular item in a long list of items.

Details

The Details view displays information about each item, including the name, size, type and date the items were last changed.

SORT ITEMS

You can sort the items displayed in a window to help you find files and folders more quickly.

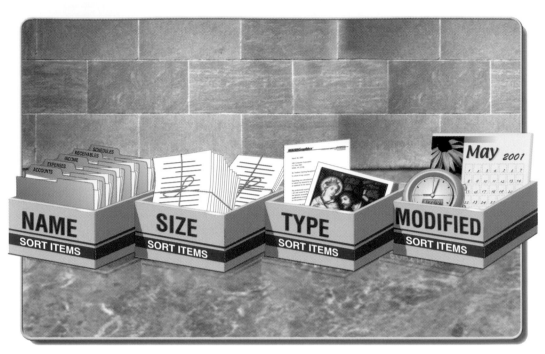

You can sort items by name, size, type or the date the items were last changed. Some windows allow you to sort items in other ways. For example, the My Music window allows you to sort items by artist, album title and track number.

SORT ITEMS

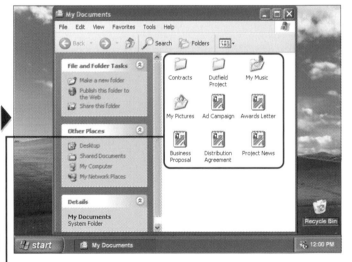

1 Click **View**.

2 Click **Arrange Icons by**.

3 Click the way you want to sort the items in the window.

■ The items appear in the new order. In this example, the items are sorted by type.

■ To sort the items in the reverse order, repeat steps **1** to **3**.

Note: You can only sort the items in the reverse order when viewing items in the List or Details view. To change the view of items, see page 44.

GROUP ITEMS

You can group items to better organize the files and folders in a window.

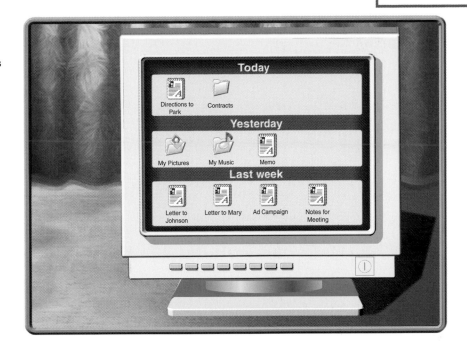

GROUP ITEMS

■ **1** Click **View**.

■ **2** Click **Arrange Icons by**.

■ **3** Click **Show in Groups**.

Note: The Show in Groups option is not available when viewing items in the List or Filmstrip view. To change the view of items, see page 44.

■ Windows groups the items in the window.

■ You can sort the items to change the way the items are grouped in the window. For example, sorting the items by size will group the items by size. To sort items, see page 46.

■ If you no longer want to group the items in a window, repeat steps **1** to **3**.

USING WINDOWS EXPLORER

Windows Explorer shows the organization of all the files and folders on your computer.

You can work with the files in Windows Explorer as you would work with files in any window. For example, you can move, rename and delete files in Windows Explorer. To work with files, see pages 52 to 93.

USING WINDOWS EXPLORER

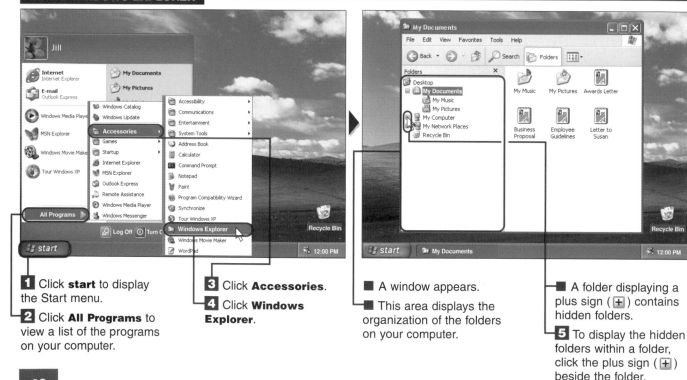

1 Click **start** to display the Start menu.

2 Click **All Programs** to view a list of the programs on your computer.

3 Click **Accessories**.

4 Click **Windows Explorer**.

■ A window appears.

■ This area displays the organization of the folders on your computer.

■ A folder displaying a plus sign (⊞) contains hidden folders.

5 To display the hidden folders within a folder, click the plus sign (⊞) beside the folder.

How can I quickly perform tasks with the files and folders displayed in Windows Explorer?

To quickly perform tasks in Windows Explorer, click the **Folders** button to display a list of options that you can select. The options that appear depend on the file or folder that is currently selected. To return to the organization of the folders, click the **Folders** button again.

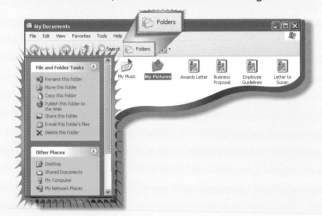

How can I view information about a file or folder displayed in Windows Explorer?

Position the mouse ⌖ over a file or folder. After a few seconds, a yellow box appears, displaying information about the file or folder.

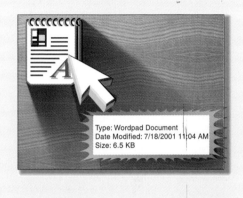

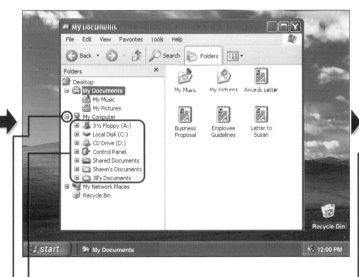

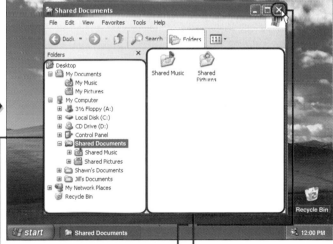

■ The hidden folders appear.

■ The plus sign (⊞) beside the folder changes to a minus sign (⊟). This indicates that all the folders within the folder are displayed.

Note: You can click the minus sign (⊟) to once again hide the folders within the folder.

6 To display the contents of a folder, click the name of the folder.

■ This area displays the contents of the folder.

7 When you finish using Windows Explorer, click ⊠ to close the window.

CHAPTER 5

Work With Files

This chapter teaches you how to manage your files efficiently. Learn how to print files, move files, search for files, copy files to a floppy disk or CD and much more.

SELECT FILES

Before working with files, you often need to select the files you want to work with. Selected files appear highlighted on your screen.

You can select folders the same way you select files. Selecting a folder will select all the files in the folder.

SELECT FILES

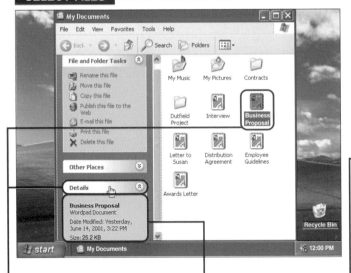

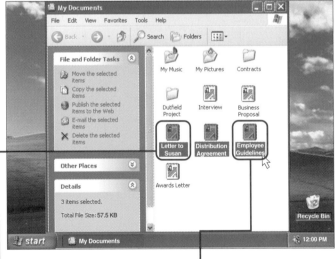

SELECT ONE FILE

1 Click the file you want to select. The file is highlighted.

2 If you want to display information about the file, click **Details**.

■ Information about the file appears, including the file type and the date and time the file was last changed.

*Note: To hide the information, click **Details** again.*

SELECT A GROUP OF FILES

1 Click the first file you want to select.

2 Press and hold down the Shift key as you click the last file you want to select.

How do I deselect files?

To deselect all the files in a window, click a blank area in the window.

To deselect one file from a group of selected files, press and hold down the Ctrl key as you click the file you want to deselect.

Note: You can deselect folders the same way you deselect files.

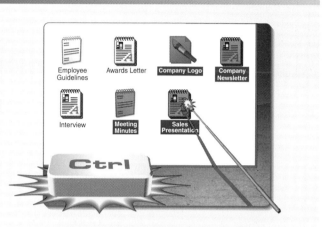

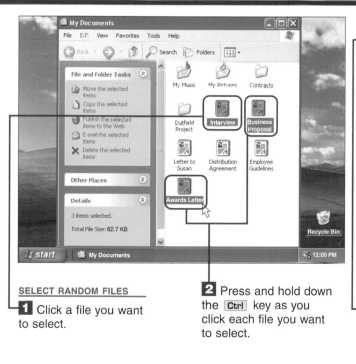

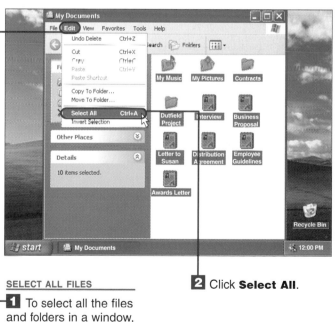

SELECT RANDOM FILES

1 Click a file you want to select.

2 Press and hold down the Ctrl key as you click each file you want to select.

SELECT ALL FILES

1 To select all the files and folders in a window, click **Edit**.

2 Click **Select All**.

OPEN A FILE

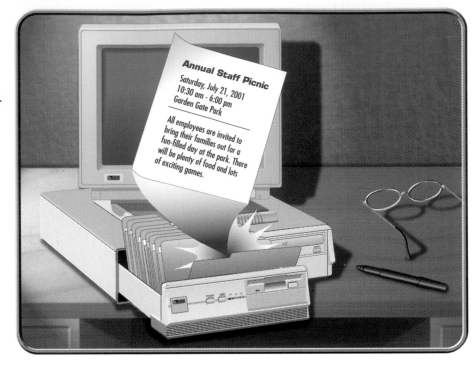

You can open a file to display its contents on your screen. Opening a file allows you to review and make changes to the file.

You can open folders the same way you open files.

OPEN A FILE

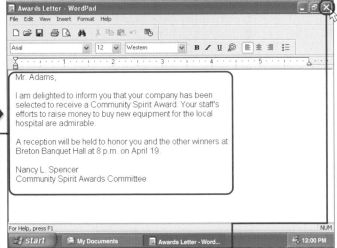

1 Double-click the file you want to open.

■ The file opens. You can review and make changes to the file.

Note: If you opened a picture, the picture appears in the Windows Picture and Fax Viewer window. To make changes to the picture, you will need to open the picture within the program you used to create the picture or in another image editing program.

2 When you finish working with the file, click ☒ to close the file.

You can rename a file to better describe the contents of the file. Renaming a file can help you more quickly locate the file in the future.

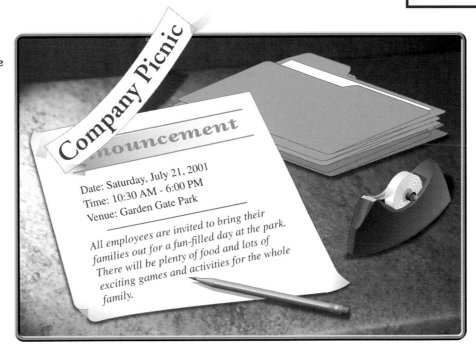

You can rename folders the same way you rename files. You should not rename folders that Windows or other programs require to operate.

RENAME A FILE

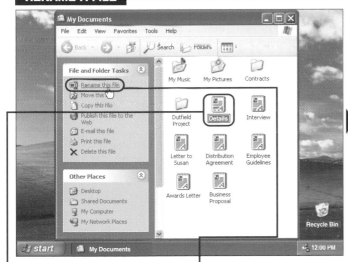

1 Click the name of the file you want to rename.

Note: You should not rename files that Windows or other programs require to operate.

2 Click **Rename this file** or press the `F2` key.

■ A box appears around the file name.

3 Type a new name for the file and then press the `Enter` key.

*Note: A file name cannot contain the \ / : * ? " < > or | characters.*

■ If you change your mind while typing a new file name, you can press the `Esc` key to return to the original file name.

PRINT A FILE

You can produce a paper copy of a file stored on your computer.

Before printing a file, make sure your printer is turned on and contains paper.

PRINT A FILE

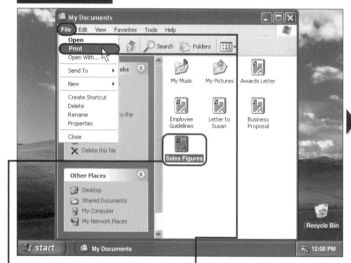

1 Click the file you want to print.

■ To print more than one file, select all the files you want to print. To select multiple files, see page 52.

2 Click **File**.

3 Click **Print**.

Note: If you selected a picture, the Photo Printing Wizard appears. For information on using the Photo Printing Wizard to print pictures, see page 58.

■ Windows quickly opens, prints and then closes the file.

■ When you print a file, a printer icon (🖨) appears in this area. The printer icon disappears when the file has finished printing.

How can I stop a file from printing?

You may want to stop a file from printing if you accidentally selected the wrong file or if you want to make last-minute changes to the file.

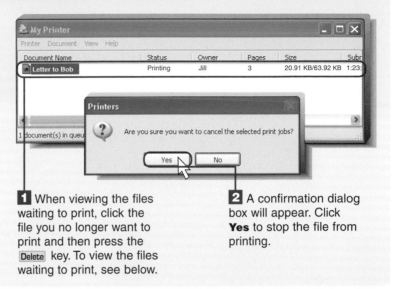

1 When viewing the files waiting to print, click the file you no longer want to print and then press the Delete key. To view the files waiting to print, see below.

2 A confirmation dialog box will appear. Click **Yes** to stop the file from printing.

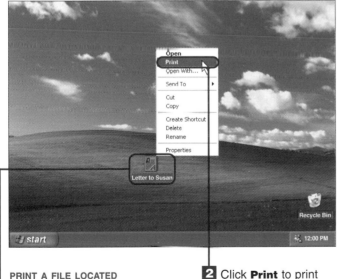

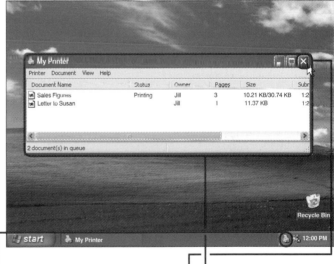

PRINT A FILE LOCATED ON THE DESKTOP

1 Right-click the file you want to print. A menu appears.

2 Click **Print** to print the file.

■ Windows quickly opens, prints and then closes the file.

VIEW FILES WAITING TO PRINT

1 Double-click the printer icon ( ) to view information about the files waiting to print.

Note: If the printer icon is not displayed, the files have finished printing.

■ A window appears, displaying information about each file waiting to print. The file at the top of the list will print first.

2 When you finish viewing the information, click ☒ to close the window.

PRINT PICTURES

You can use the
Photo Printing
Wizard to print
your pictures.

You can obtain pictures
on the Internet, use a
scanner or digital camera
to copy pictures into your
computer, purchase
pictures at computer
stores or use a drawing
program, such as Paint,
to create your own
pictures. Windows also
includes a few sample
pictures.

PRINT PICTURES

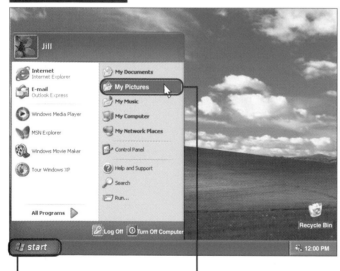

1 Click **start** to
display the Start menu.

2 Click **My Pictures** to
view the pictures stored
in your My Pictures
folder.

■ The contents of the
My Pictures folder
appear.

3 Click **Print pictures**
to print the pictures in
the folder.

*Note: To print the pictures in a
subfolder within the My Pictures
folder, click the subfolder before
performing step 3.*

How can I get the best results when printing pictures?

Use High-Quality Paper

Your printer may allow you to use high-quality, glossy paper that is specifically designed for printing pictures. This type of paper will produce the best results when printing pictures.

Select a High Resolution

Make sure your printer is set to the highest possible resolution. A higher resolution will usually result in higher-quality pictures, but the pictures may take longer to print.

Can I use the Photo Printing Wizard to print pictures that are not stored in the My Pictures folder?

Yes. When you print a picture stored in another location on your computer, the Photo Printing Wizard will automatically appear to help you print the picture. You can print a picture stored in another location on your computer as you would print any file. For information on printing a file, see page 56.

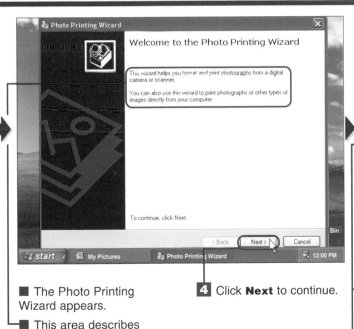

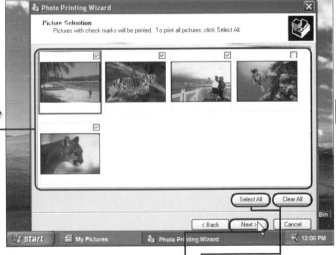

■ The Photo Printing Wizard appears.

■ This area describes the wizard.

4 Click **Next** to continue.

■ This area displays a miniature version of each picture in the folder. Windows will print each picture that displays a check mark (✔).

5 To add (☑) or remove (☐) a check mark from a picture, click the check box (☐) for the picture.

■ To quickly select or deselect all the pictures, click **Select All** or **Clear All**.

6 Click **Next** to continue.

CONTINUED ▶

The Photo Printing Wizard allows you to select the layout you want to use for the printed pictures.

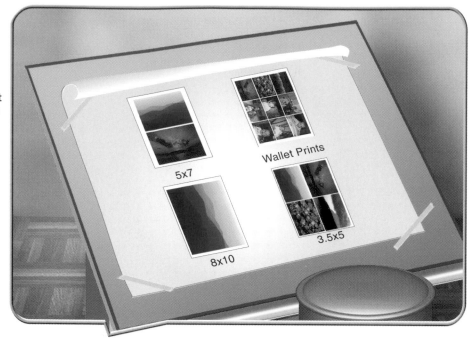

You can select a layout that prints more than one picture on a page. Some layouts may crop part of a large picture so the picture will fit better on a page.

PRINT PICTURES (CONTINUED)

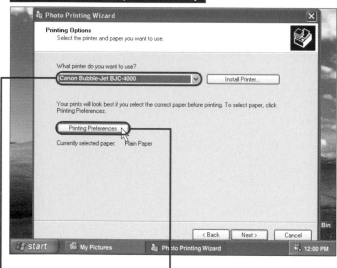

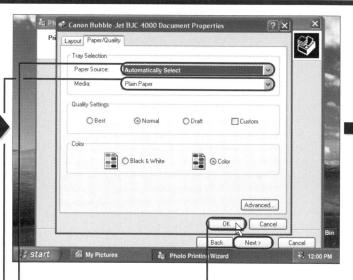

■ This area displays the printer you will use to print the pictures. You can click this area to select a different printer.

7 Click **Printing Preferences** to select the paper you want to use to print the pictures.

■ A Properties dialog box for the printer appears.

■ This area indicates where the paper you will use is located in the printer. You can click this area to change the paper source.

■ This area displays the type of paper you will use to print your pictures. You can click this area to change the type of paper.

Note: The available settings depend on your printer.

8 Click **OK** to confirm your changes.

9 Click **Next** to continue.

What other tasks can I perform with my pictures?

The My Pictures folder offers several options that you can select to perform tasks with your pictures.

View as a slide show

Displays all the pictures in the My Pictures folder as a full-screen slide show.

Order prints online

Sends the pictures you select to a Web site that allows you to order prints of the pictures.

Set as desktop background

Uses the picture you select as your desktop background. For information on changing the desktop background, see page 104.

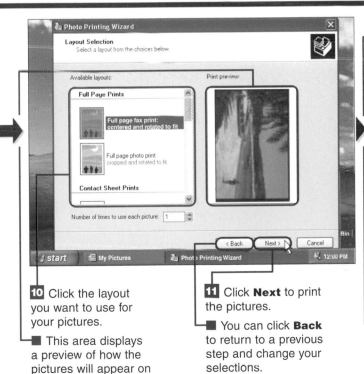

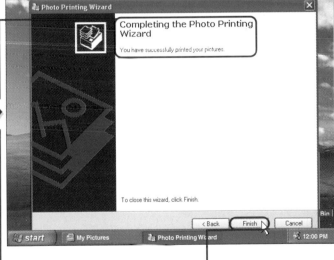

10 Click the layout you want to use for your pictures.

■ This area displays a preview of how the pictures will appear on a printed page.

11 Click **Next** to print the pictures.

■ You can click **Back** to return to a previous step and change your selections.

■ Windows prints the pictures.

■ This area indicates that you have successfully completed the Photo Printing Wizard.

12 Click **Finish** to close the wizard.

DELETE A FILE

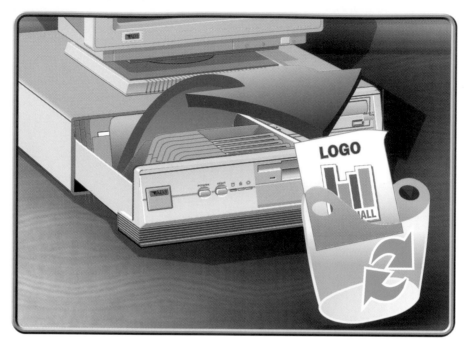

You can delete a file you no longer need.

Before you delete a file, make sure you will no longer need the file. You should also make sure you do not delete a file that Windows or other programs require to operate.

DELETE A FILE

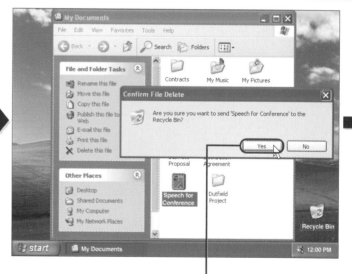

1 Click the file you want to delete.

■ To delete more than one file, select all the files you want to delete. To select multiple files, see page 52.

2 Click **Delete this file** or press the Delete key.

*Note: If you selected multiple files, click **Delete the selected items** in step **2**.*

■ The Confirm File Delete dialog box appears.

3 Click **Yes** to delete the file.

**How can I permanently delete
a file from my computer?**

When you delete a file,
Windows places the file in the
Recycle Bin in case you later
want to restore the file. If you do
not want to place a deleted file
in the Recycle Bin, such as
when deleting a confidential file,
you can permanently delete the
file from your computer.

To permanently delete a
file from your computer,
perform steps **1** to **3** on
page 62, except press and
hold down the `Shift` key
as you perform step **2**.

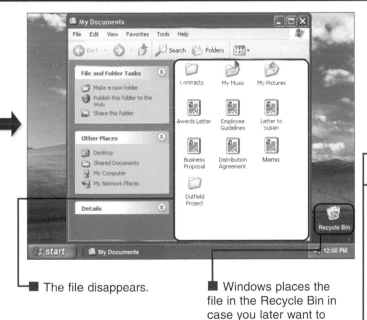

■ The file disappears.

■ Windows places the
file in the Recycle Bin in
case you later want to
restore the file.

*Note: To restore a file from the
Recycle Bin, see page 64.*

DELETE A FOLDER

**You can delete a folder and
all the files it contains.**

1 Click the folder you want
to delete.

2 Click **Delete this folder**
or press the `Delete` key.

■ The Confirm Folder
Delete dialog box
appears.

3 Click **Yes** to delete
the folder.

RESTORE A DELETED FILE

The Recycle Bin stores all the files you have deleted. You can easily restore any file in the Recycle Bin to its original location on your computer.

You can restore folders the same way you restore files. When you restore a folder, Windows restores all the files in the folder.

RESTORE A DELETED FILE

■ The appearance of the Recycle Bin indicates whether or not the bin contains deleted files.

🗑 Contains deleted files.

🗑 Does not contain deleted files.

1 Double-click **Recycle Bin**.

■ The Recycle Bin window appears, displaying all the files you have deleted.

2 Click the file you want to restore.

■ To restore more than one file, select all the files you want to restore. To select multiple files, see page 52.

3 Click **Restore this item**.

*Note: If you selected multiple files, click **Restore the selected items** in step 3.*

Why is the file I want to restore not in the Recycle Bin?

The Recycle Bin does not store files you deleted from your network or from removable storage media such as a floppy disk. Files deleted from these locations are permanently deleted and cannot be restored. Files that are larger than the storage capacity of the Recycle Bin are also permanently deleted.

Can I permanently remove one file from the Recycle Bin?

You may want to permanently remove one file from the Recycle Bin, such as a file that contains confidential information. You can permanently remove a file from the Recycle Bin by deleting the file in the Recycle Bin as you would delete any file on your computer. To delete a file, see page 62.

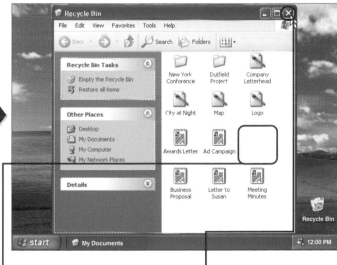

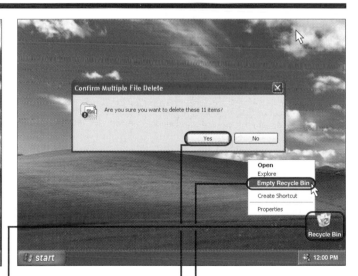

■ The file disappears from the Recycle Bin window and returns to its original location on your computer.

4 Click ✖ to close the Recycle Bin window.

EMPTY THE RECYCLE BIN

You can empty the Recycle Bin to create more free space on your computer. When you empty the Recycle Bin, the files are permanently removed and cannot be restored.

1 Right-click **Recycle Bin**. A menu appears.

2 Click **Empty Recycle Bin**.

■ The Confirm Multiple File Delete dialog box appears.

3 Click **Yes** to permanently delete all the files in the Recycle Bin.

MOVE A FILE

You can move a file to a new location on your computer to re-organize your files.

When you move a file, the file will disappear from its original location and appear in the new location.

You can move a folder the same way you move a file. When you move a folder, all the files in the folder are also moved.

MOVE A FILE

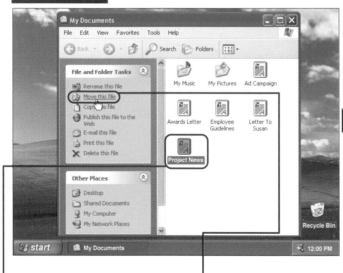

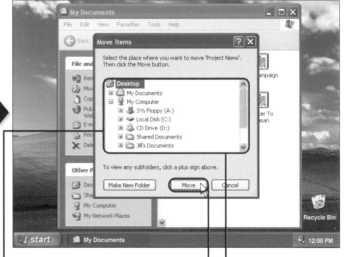

1 Click the file you want to move.

■ To move more than one file at once, select all the files you want to move. To select multiple files, see page 52.

2 Click **Move this file**.

*Note: If you selected multiple files, click **Move the selected items** in step 2.*

■ The Move Items dialog box appears.

■ This area displays the locations where you can move the file. A location displaying a plus sign (⊞) contains hidden items.

■ To display the hidden items within a location, click the plus sign (⊞) beside the location (⊞ changes to ⊟).

3 Click the location where you want to move the file.

4 Click **Move** to move the file.

Why would I want to move a file?

You may want to move a file to a different folder to keep files of the same type in one location on your computer. For example, you can move all your documents to the My Documents folder provided by Windows. Windows also includes the My Pictures and My Music folders that you can use to store your pictures and music files. To open one of these folders, see page 40.

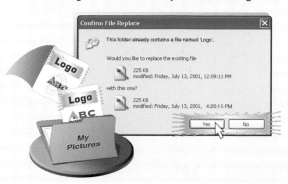

Why does a dialog box appear when I try to move a file?

If you try to move a file to a folder that contains a file with the same name, a dialog box appears, confirming the move. You can click **Yes** or **No** in the dialog box to specify if you want to replace the existing file with the file you are moving.

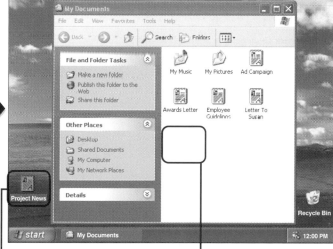

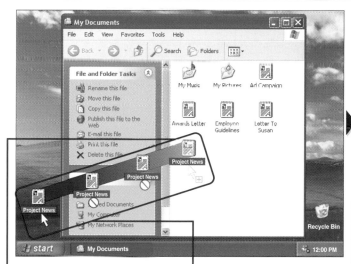

USING DRAG AND DROP

■ Before moving a file, make sure you can clearly see the location where you want to move the file.

1 Position the mouse ⌖ over the file you want to move.

■ To move more than one file at once, select all the files you want to move. Then position the mouse ⌖ over one of the files. To select multiple files, see page 52.

2 Drag the file to a new location.

■ The file moves to the new location.

■ The file disappears from its original location.

COPY A FILE

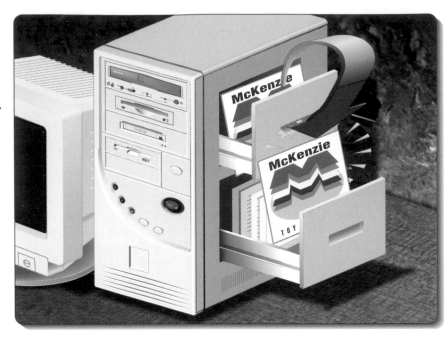

You can copy a file to a new location on your computer.

When you copy a file, the file appears in both the original and new locations.

You can copy a folder the same way you copy a file. When you copy a folder, all the files in the folder are also copied.

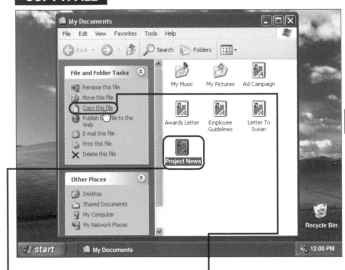

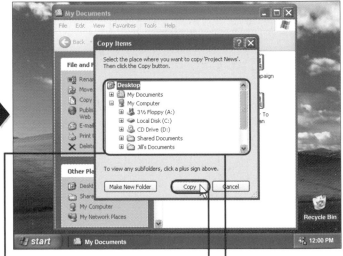

1 Click the file you want to copy.

■ To copy more than one file at once, select all the files you want to copy. To select multiple files, see page 52.

2 Click **Copy this file**.

Note: If you selected multiple files, click **Copy the selected items** *in step 2.*

■ The Copy Items dialog box appears.

■ This area displays the locations where you can copy the file. A location displaying a plus sign (⊞) contains hidden items.

3 To display the hidden items within a location, click the plus sign (⊞) beside the location (⊞ changes to ⊟).

4 Click the location where you want to copy the file.

5 Click **Copy** to copy the file.

Can I copy a file to the same folder that contains the file?

Yes. If you copy a file to the same folder that contains the file, Windows will add "Copy of" to the new file name. Copying a file to the same folder is useful if you plan to make major changes to a file, but you want to keep the original copy of the file. This gives you two copies of the file—the original file and a file that you can change.

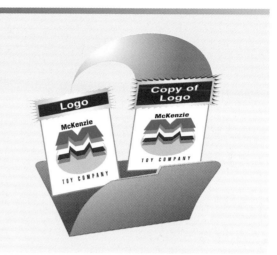

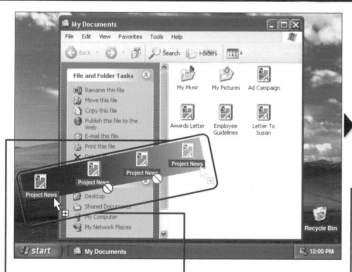

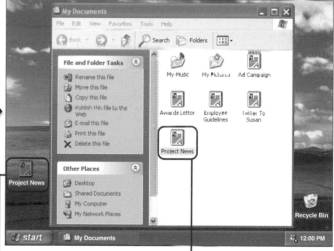

USING DRAG AND DROP

■ Before copying a file, make sure you can clearly see the location where you want to copy the file.

1 Position the mouse ⍾ over the file you want to copy.

■ To copy more than one file at once, select all the files you want to copy. Then position the mouse ⍾ over one of the files. To select multiple files, see page 52.

2 Press and hold down the **Ctrl** key as you drag the file to a new location.

■ A copy of the file appears in the new location.

■ The original file remains in the original location.

E-MAIL A FILE

You can e-mail a file to a friend, colleague or family member. You must have an e-mail account set up on your computer to be able to e-mail a file.

You can e-mail many types of files, including documents, pictures, videos and sounds. The computer receiving the file must have the necessary hardware and software installed to display or play the file.

E-MAIL A FILE

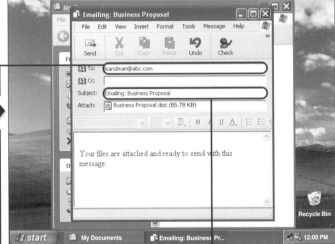

1 Click the file you want to send in an e-mail message.

■ To send more than one file in an e-mail message, select all the files you want to send. To select multiple files, see page 52.

2 Click **E-mail this file**.

*Note: If you selected multiple files, click **E-mail the selected items** in step 2.*

■ A window appears that allows you to compose a message.

3 Type the e-mail address of the person you want to receive the message.

Note: To send the message to more than one person, separate each e-mail address with a semicolon (;).

4 Windows uses the name of the file as the subject. To specify a different subject, drag the mouse I over the subject and then type a new subject.

**Why does a dialog box appear
when I try to e-mail a picture?**

Windows can change the file
size and dimensions of a picture
you are sending in an e-mail
message so the picture will
transfer faster over the Internet
and fit better on a recipient's
computer screen. Reducing the
file size of a picture is useful
when you are e-mailing a large
picture, since most companies
that provide e-mail accounts do
not allow you to send messages
larger than 2 MB.

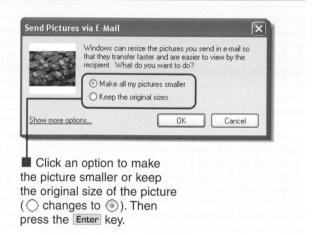

■ Click an option to make
the picture smaller or keep
the original size of the picture
(○ changes to ◉). Then
press the Enter key.

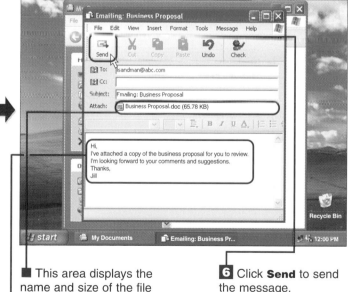

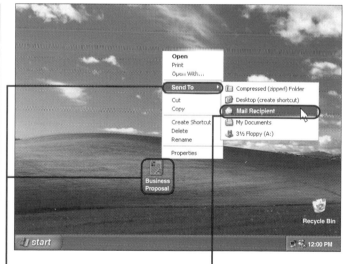

■ This area displays the
name and size of the file
you selected.

5 Windows includes a
message that indicates that
your files are attached. To use
a different message, drag the
mouse I over the message
and then type a new message.

6 Click **Send** to send
the message.

*Note: If you are not currently
connected to the Internet, a
dialog box will appear that
allows you to connect.*

**E-MAIL A FILE LOCATED
ON THE DESKTOP**

1 Right-click the file you
want to send in an e-mail
message. A menu appears.

2 Click **Send To**.

3 Click **Mail Recipient**.

4 Perform steps **3** to **6**
starting on page 70 to
compose and send the
message.

PUBLISH A FILE TO THE WEB

You can publish files, such as documents and pictures, to the Web to allow friends, family and colleagues to view the files.

If you have just one or two small files that you want to share with another person, you may want to send the files in an e-mail message instead. To send files in an e-mail message, see page 274.

PUBLISH A FILE TO THE WEB

1 Click the file you want to publish to the Web.

■ To publish more than one file, select all the files you want to publish. To select multiple files, see page 52.

2 Click **Publish this file to the Web**.

*Note: If you selected multiple files, click **Publish the selected items to the Web** in step **2**.*

■ The Web Publishing Wizard appears.

■ This area describes the wizard.

3 Click **Next** to continue.

Why does the Web Publishing Wizard ask me to set up an account after I choose a service provider?

The first time you publish a file to the Web, you will need to set up an account with a service provider. Follow the instructions on your screen to set up an account. When you set up an account, you may be required to obtain a Passport, which allows you to access many services on the Internet using a single user name and password. If you have previously set up an account, you may be asked to log in to your account to continue.

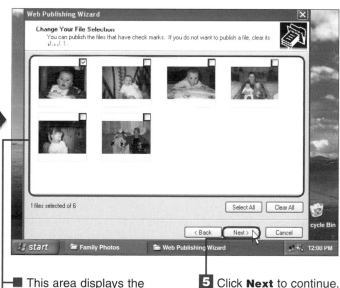

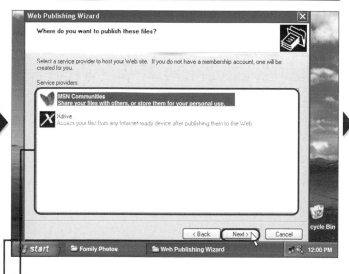

■ This area displays the contents of the folder that stores the file you selected to publish. Windows will publish each file that displays a check mark (✔).

4 To add (☑) or remove (☐) a check mark from a file, click the check box (☐) for the file.

5 Click **Next** to continue.

Note: If you are not currently connected to the Internet, a dialog box will appear, allowing you to connect.

6 Click the service provider you want to publish the file.

7 Click **Next** to continue.

Note: The following screens depend on the service provider you selected. A service provider may occasionally change the options displayed in the screens to make the wizard easier to use or to provide different options.

CONTINUED

PUBLISH A FILE TO THE WEB

If you selected the MSN service provider to publish your file, you can choose to share the file with other people or publish the file for your own private use.

PUBLISH A FILE TO THE WEB (CONTINUED)

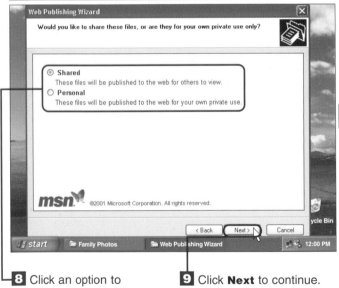

8 Click an option to specify if you want to publish the file for others to view or for your own private use (⊙ changes to ⊙).

9 Click **Next** to continue.

*Note: If you selected **Personal** in step **8**, skip to step **16**.*

10 To create a community on the Web where you want to publish the file, click this option.

11 Click **Next** to continue.

*Note: If you have previously created a community on the Web, click the name of the community in step **10** and then skip to step **16**.*

Why would I publish a file for my own private use?

You can publish a file for your own private use to store a backup copy of an important file in case your computer fails or you accidentally erase the file. You can also publish a file so you can access the file from many locations. For example, you can publish a presentation that you plan to deliver so you can access the presentation from any location.

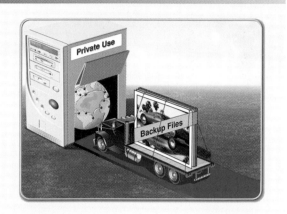

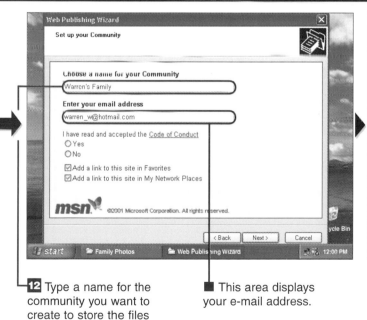

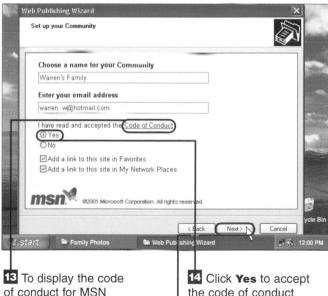

12 Type a name for the community you want to create to store the files you publish.

■ This area displays your e-mail address.

13 To display the code of conduct for MSN Web communities, click **Code of Conduct**.

■ When you finish reviewing the code of conduct, click **X** to close the MSN Code of Conduct window.

14 Click **Yes** to accept the code of conduct (○ changes to ◉).

15 Click **Next** to continue.

CONTINUED

PUBLISH A FILE TO THE WEB

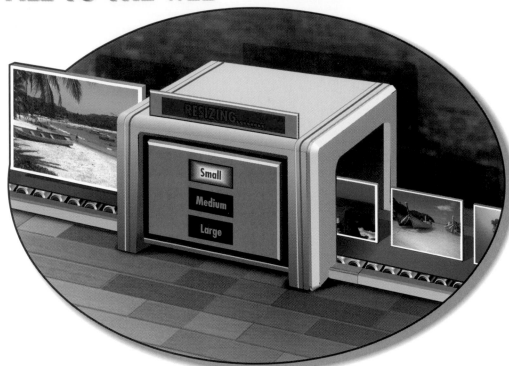

If you are publishing a picture, the Web Publishing Wizard can adjust the size of the picture so it will transfer faster and be easier to view on a computer screen.

PUBLISH A FILE TO THE WEB (CONTINUED)

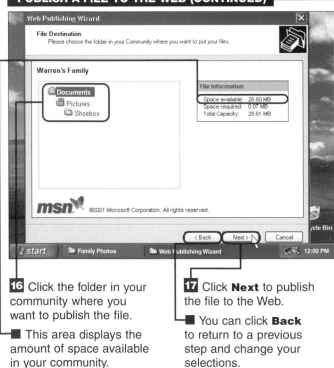

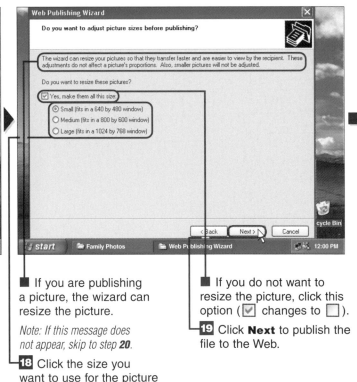

16 Click the folder in your community where you want to publish the file.

■ This area displays the amount of space available in your community.

17 Click **Next** to publish the file to the Web.

■ You can click **Back** to return to a previous step and change your selections.

■ If you are publishing a picture, the wizard can resize the picture.

Note: If this message does not appear, skip to step 20.

18 Click the size you want to use for the picture (○ changes to ◉).

■ If you do not want to resize the picture, click this option (☑ changes to ☐).

19 Click **Next** to publish the file to the Web.

How can I manage the files I published to the Web?

My Network Places

After you publish files to the Web, the My Network Places window may contain a folder that stores links to the files you have published. When you are connected to the Internet, you can add or delete files in the folder to add or delete the files on the Web. To open the My Network Places window, see page 228.

Web Page Favorites

Your list of favorite Web pages may also display a link to the Web site where you published the files. You can use this link to quickly display your published files. To view your list of favorite Web pages, see page 261.

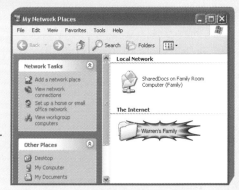

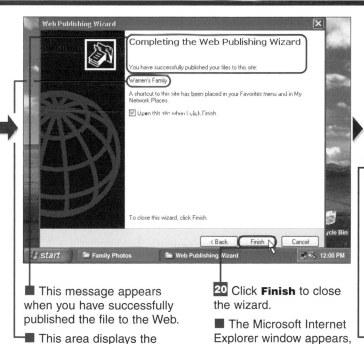

■ This message appears when you have successfully published the file to the Web.

■ This area displays the MSN Web community where the file can be accessed.

20 Click **Finish** to close the wizard.

■ The Microsoft Internet Explorer window appears, displaying the Web site where you published the file.

■ This area displays the Web page address where the file can be accessed.

21 Click the folder where you published the file.

■ The name of the file you published appears in this area. To view the file, click the name of the file.

Note: If you published the file to a photo album, you need to click the name of the album to view the file name.

CREATE A NEW FILE

You can instantly create, name and store a new file in the location you want without starting a program.

Creating a new file without starting a program allows you to focus on the organization of your files rather than the programs you need to accomplish your tasks.

CREATE A NEW FILE

1 Display the contents of the folder you want to contain a new file.

Note: To browse through the folders on your computer, see pages 40 to 43.

2 Click **File**.

3 Click **New**.

4 Click the type of file you want to create.

What types of files can I create?

The types of files you can create depend on the programs installed on your computer. By default, Windows allows you to create the following types of files.

File Type	Description
Briefcase	Stores copies of files that you want to work with on another computer.
Bitmap Image	Creates an image file.
Wordpad Document	Creates a WordPad document.
Rich Text Document	Creates a document that can contain formatting.
Text Document	Creates a document that cannot contain any formatting.
Wave Sound	Creates a sound file.
Compressed (zipped) Folder	Creates a folder that compresses its contents to save storage space.

■ The new file appears with a temporary name.

5 Type a name for the new file and then press the Enter key.

*Note: A file name cannot contain the \ / : * ? " < > or | characters.*

CREATE A NEW FILE ON THE DESKTOP

1 Right-click a blank area on your desktop. A menu appears.

2 Click **New**.

3 Click the type of file you want to create.

4 Type a name for the new file and then press the Enter key.

CREATE A NEW FOLDER

You can create a new folder to help you organize the files stored on your computer.

Creating a folder is like placing a new folder in a filing cabinet.

CREATE A NEW FOLDER

1 Display the contents of the folder you want to contain a new folder.

Note: To browse through the folders on your computer, see pages 40 to 43.

2 Click **Make a new folder**.

Note: If the Make a new folder option is not available, click a blank area in the window to display the option.

■ The new folder appears, displaying a temporary name.

3 Type a name for the new folder and then press the Enter key.

*Note: A folder name cannot contain the \ / : * ? " < > or | characters.*

How can creating a new folder help me organize the files on my computer?

You can create a new folder to store files you want to keep together, such as files for a particular project. This allows you to quickly locate the files. For example, you can create a folder named "Reports" that stores all of your reports. You can create as many folders as you need to set up a filing system that makes sense to you.

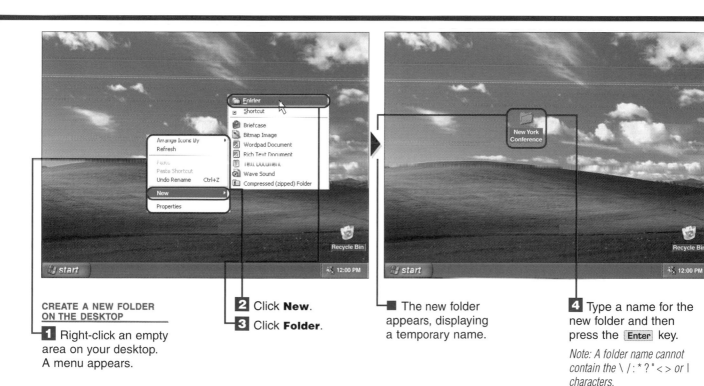

**CREATE A NEW FOLDER
ON THE DESKTOP**

1 Right-click an empty area on your desktop. A menu appears.

2 Click **New**.

3 Click **Folder**.

■ The new folder appears, displaying a temporary name.

4 Type a name for the new folder and then press the Enter key.

*Note: A folder name cannot contain the \ / : * ? " < > or | characters.*

CREATE A COMPRESSED FOLDER

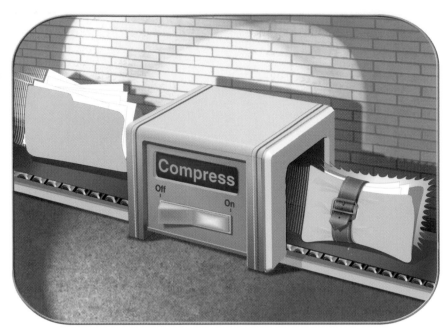

You can create a new, compressed folder that you can use to store files.

Creating compressed folders can help you save storage space on your computer and on removable storage media, such as floppy disks. Compressed folders also transfer quickly over the Internet.

The amount of space a compressed folder saves depends on the types of files you add to the folder. For example, text files will compress significantly more than pictures.

CREATE A COMPRESSED FOLDER

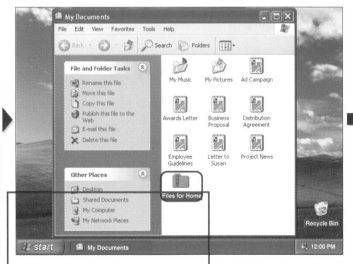

1 Display the contents of the folder you want to contain a compressed folder.

Note: To browse through the folders on your computer, see pages 40 to 43.

2 Click **File**.

3 Click **New**.

4 Click **Compressed (zipped) Folder**.

■ A compressed folder appears, displaying a temporary name. A compressed folder displays a zipper in its icon ( ).

5 Type a name for the compressed folder and then press the Enter key.

*Note: A compressed folder name cannot contain the \ / : * ? " < > or | characters.*

How do I decompress a file stored in a compressed folder?

To decompress a file stored in a compressed folder, move the file to a location outside the folder. Windows will create a decompressed copy of the file in the new location. To move a file, see page 66. Decompressing a file allows you to work with the file as you would work with any file on your computer.

6 To add a file to the compressed folder, position the mouse ⬧ over the file and then drag the file to the folder.

■ Windows will add a compressed copy of the file to the folder. The original file will remain in its original location.

Note: You can open the files in a compressed folder as you would open any file on your computer. You cannot make changes to the files in a compressed folder.

CREATE A COMPRESSED FOLDER ON THE DESKTOP

1 Right-click an empty area on your desktop. A menu appears.

2 Click **New**.

3 Click **Compressed (zipped) Folder**.

■ A compressed folder appears, displaying a temporary name.

4 Type a name for the compressed folder and then press the Enter key.

SEARCH FOR FILES

If you cannot remember the exact name or location of a file you want to work with, you can have Windows search for the file on your computer.

SEARCH FOR FILES

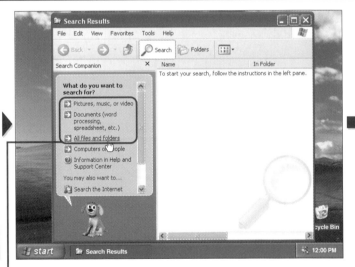

1 Click **start** to display the Start menu.

2 Click **Search** to search for files on your computer.

■ The Search Results window appears.

3 Click the type of file you want to search for.

*Note: The following options depend on the type of file you select. In this example, **All files and folders** is selected.*

What other options does Windows offer to help me find a file?

Windows offers different options, depending on the type of file you select in step **3** on page 84.

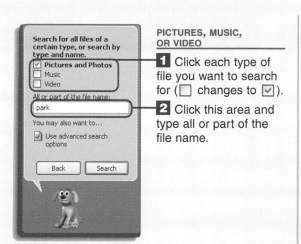

PICTURES, MUSIC, OR VIDEO

1 Click each type of file you want to search for (☐ changes to ☑).

2 Click this area and type all or part of the file name.

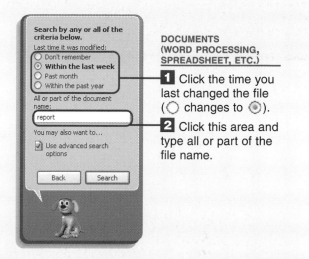

DOCUMENTS (WORD PROCESSING, SPREADSHEET, ETC.)

1 Click the time you last changed the file (◯ changes to ◉).

2 Click this area and type all or part of the file name.

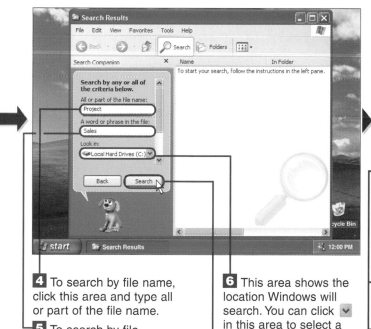

4 To search by file name, click this area and type all or part of the file name.

5 To search by file contents, click this area and type a word or phrase that appears within the file.

6 This area shows the location Windows will search. You can click ⌄ in this area to select a different location.

7 Click **Search** to start the search.

■ This area displays the matching files that Windows found.

■ To open a file, double-click the file.

8 When you finish viewing the results of your search, click ☒ to close the Search Results window.

ADD A SHORTCUT TO THE DESKTOP

You can add a shortcut to the desktop that will provide a quick way of opening a file you regularly use.

ADD A SHORTCUT TO THE DESKTOP

1 Click the file you want to create a shortcut to.

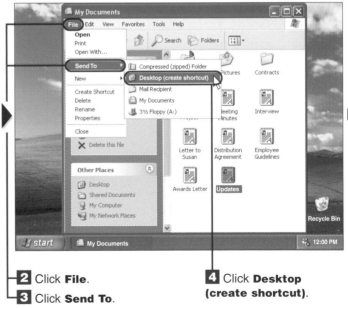

2 Click **File**.

3 Click **Send To**.

4 Click **Desktop (create shortcut)**.

How do I rename or delete a shortcut?

You can rename or delete a shortcut the same way you would rename or delete any file. Renaming or deleting a shortcut will not affect the original file. To rename a file, see page 55. To delete a file, see page 62.

Can I move a shortcut to a different location?

Yes. If you do not want a shortcut to appear on your desktop, you can move the shortcut to a different location on your computer. You can move a shortcut the same way you would move any file. To move a file, see page 66.

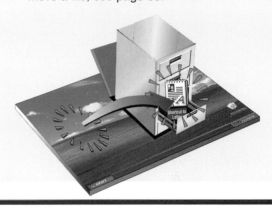

■ The shortcut appears on your desktop.

■ You can tell the difference between the shortcut and the original file because the shortcut icon displays an arrow ( ).

■ You can double-click the shortcut to open the file at any time.

Note: You can create a shortcut to a folder the same way you create a shortcut to a file. Creating a shortcut to a folder will give you quick access to all the files in the folder.

COPY A FILE TO A FLOPPY DISK

You can copy
a file stored on
your computer
to a floppy disk.
This is useful if
you want to give
a friend, family
member or
colleague a
copy of the file.

When copying
a file to a floppy
disk, you must
use a formatted
floppy disk. To
format a floppy
disk, see page 206.

COPY A FILE TO A FLOPPY DISK

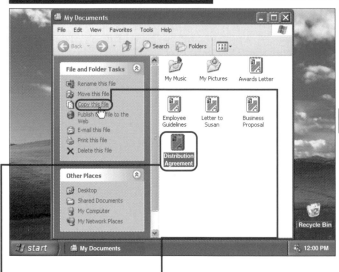

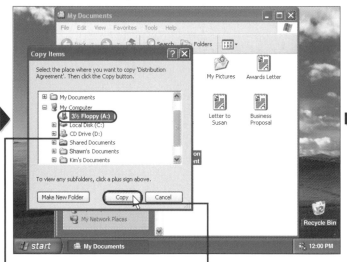

1 Insert a floppy disk
into your floppy drive.

2 Click the file you
want to copy to the
floppy disk.

■ To copy more than one
file, select all the files you
want to copy. To select
multiple files, see page 52.

3 Click **Copy this file**.

*Note: If you selected multiple
files, click **Copy the selected
items** in step 3.*

■ The Copy Items dialog
box appears.

4 Click the drive that
contains the floppy disk.

5 Click **Copy** to copy
the file to the floppy disk.

How can I protect the information on my floppy disks?

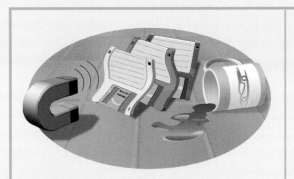

not write-protected

write-protected

Store in a Safe Location

You should keep floppy disks away from moisture, heat and magnets, which can damage the information stored on the disks.

Write-protect

You can prevent people from making changes to information on floppy disks by sliding the tab on the disks to the write-protected position.

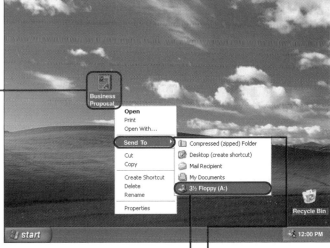

■ Windows places a copy of the file on the floppy disk.

Note: To view the contents of a floppy disk, see page 42.

■ You can copy a folder to a floppy disk the same way you copy a file. When you copy a folder, Windows copies all the files in the folder.

COPY A FILE ON YOUR DESKTOP

1 Insert a floppy disk into your floppy drive.

2 Right-click the file you want to copy to the floppy disk. A menu appears.

3 Click **Send To**.

4 Click the drive that contains the floppy disk.

COPY FILES TO A CD

You can copy files, such as documents and pictures, from your computer to a CD.

You will need a recordable CD drive to copy files to a CD. For information on recordable CD drives, see the top of page 153.

If you only want to copy songs to a CD, see page 152 for information on using Windows Media Player to copy the songs.

A CD can typically store 650 MB of information.

COPY FILES TO A CD

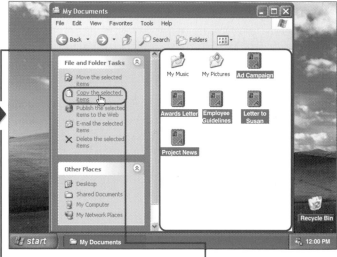

SELECT FILES TO COPY

1 Insert a CD into your recordable CD drive.

■ A dialog box may appear, asking what you want Windows to do.

2 Click **Take no action**.

3 Click **OK**.

Note: A window displaying the contents of the CD may appear instead of the dialog box. You can click ☒ in the window to close the window.

4 Select the files you want to copy to the CD. To select multiple files, see page 52.

5 Click **Copy the selected items**.

*Note: If you selected only one file, click **Copy this file** in step 5.*

Why would I copy files to a CD?

You can copy files to a CD to transfer large amounts of information between computers or make backup copies of the files stored on your computer. Making backup copies of your files will provide you with extra copies of your files in case you accidentally erase the files or your computer fails.

Can I copy a folder to a CD?

Yes. You can copy a folder to a CD the same way you copy files to a CD. When you copy a folder to a CD, Windows will copy all the files in the folder. To copy a folder to a CD, perform steps **1** to **7** starting on page 90, except select **Copy this folder** in step **5**. Then perform steps **1** to **8** starting on page 91.

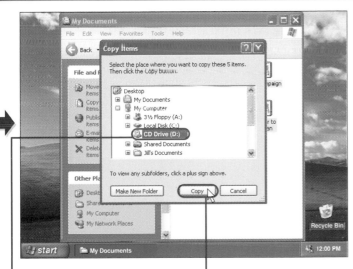

■ The Copy Items dialog box appears.

6 Click the recordable CD drive that contains the CD you want to copy the files to.

7 Click **Copy** to place a copy of the files in a temporary storage area on your computer where the files will be held until you copy them to the CD.

■ You can repeat steps **4** to **7** for each set of files you want to copy to the CD.

COPY SELECTED FILES TO A CD

1 Click **start** to display the Start menu.

2 Click **My Computer** to view the contents of your computer.

CONTINUED

COPY FILES TO A CD

Before copying the files you selected to a CD, Windows stores the files in a temporary storage area on your computer. This allows you to review the files you selected before copying the files to a CD.

■ The My Computer window appears.

3 Double-click the recordable CD drive that contains the CD you want to copy the files to.

■ A window appears, displaying the files being held in a temporary storage area on your computer and any files currently stored on the CD.

Note: If the window displays a file you no longer want to copy to the CD, you can delete the file. To delete a file, see page 62.

4 Click **Write these files to CD** to copy the files to the CD.

Can I copy files to a CD at different times?

Yes. Each time you copy files to a CD, however, approximately 20 MB of extra information is stored on the CD. To make the best use of the storage space on the CD, you may want to copy all the files to the CD at one time.

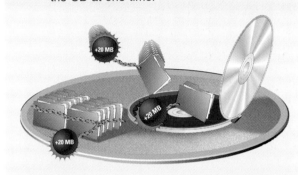

How do I erase a CD-RW disc?

You can erase a CD-RW disc to permanently delete all the files on the disc. You cannot erase a CD-R disc.

2 Click **Erase this CD-RW**.

■ The CD Writing Wizard appears. Follow the instructions in the wizard to erase the disc.

1 Display the contents of your CD-RW disc. To view the contents of a CD, see page 42.

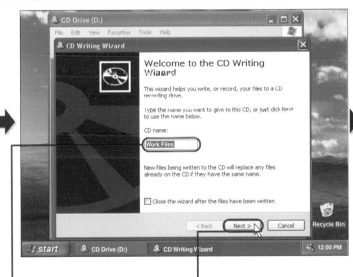

■ The CD Writing Wizard appears.

5 Type a name for the CD.

Note: The name you specify for the CD will appear in the My Computer window when the CD is in a CD drive. To view the My Computer window, see page 42.

6 Click **Next** to copy the files to the CD.

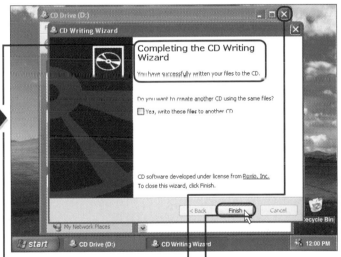

■ This message appears when Windows has successfully copied files to the CD.

Note: Windows will automatically eject the CD from your recordable CD drive when the copy is complete.

7 Click **Finish** to close the wizard.

8 Click ✕ to close the window for the recordable CD drive.

Note: To display the contents of a CD to confirm that the files were copied, see page 42.

COPY PICTURES FROM A DIGITAL CAMERA

You can use the Scanner and Camera Wizard to copy pictures stored on a digital camera to your computer.

To copy pictures from a digital camera, the camera must be installed, connected to your computer and turned on. You may also need to set your camera to a specific mode, such as the Connect mode.

COPY PICTURES FROM A DIGITAL CAMERA

1 Click **start** to display the Start menu.

2 Click **All Programs** to view a list of the programs on your computer.

3 Click **Accessories**.

4 Click **Scanner and Camera Wizard**.

Note: The Scanner and Camera Wizard option is only available after you connect and install a Windows Image Acquisition (WIA) compatible digital camera on your computer. The wizard may start automatically for many digital cameras.

■ The Scanner and Camera Wizard appears.

■ This area displays the name of the digital camera installed on your computer.

5 Click **Next** to continue.

What are the advantages of using a digital camera?

Cost Effective

You can print your own pictures, which allows you to avoid paying a company to develop your pictures. You also do not have to purchase film since digital cameras store pictures on re-usable media.

Obtain Better Pictures

Digital cameras allow you to preview your pictures and immediately retake pictures that are unsatisfactory. When printing pictures, you can choose to print only the pictures you want.

Easily Share Pictures

After you transfer pictures from a digital camera to your computer, you can use the pictures in documents, publish the pictures to the Web or send the pictures in e-mail messages to your friends and family.

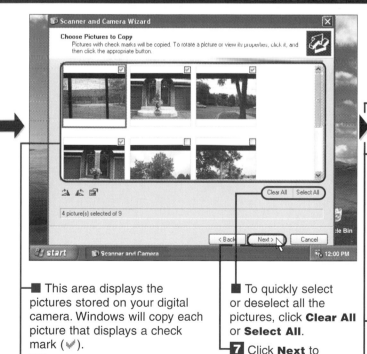

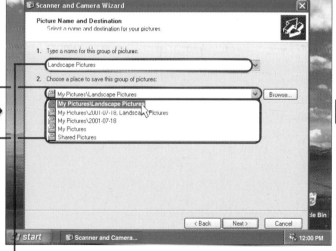

■ This area displays the pictures stored on your digital camera. Windows will copy each picture that displays a check mark (✔).

6 To add (☑) or remove (☐) a check mark from a picture, click the check box (☐) for the picture.

■ To quickly select or deselect all the pictures, click **Clear All** or **Select All**.

7 Click **Next** to continue.

8 Type a name for the group of pictures.

9 Click this area to list the folders where you can store the pictures.

10 Click the folder you want to store the pictures.

Note: You can store the pictures in the My Pictures folder, in a subfolder within the My Pictures folder or in the Shared Pictures folder. For information on these folders, see the top of page 101.

CONTINUED

You can choose to delete the pictures stored on your digital camera after the pictures are copied to your computer.

If you choose to delete the pictures stored on your digital camera, you will not be able to recover the pictures.

COPY PICTURES FROM A DIGITAL CAMERA (CONTINUED)

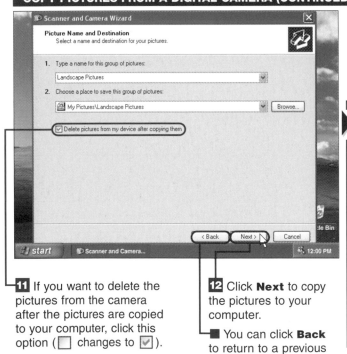

11 If you want to delete the pictures from the camera after the pictures are copied to your computer, click this option (☐ changes to ☑).

12 Click **Next** to copy the pictures to your computer.

■ You can click **Back** to return to a previous step and change your selections.

■ This message appears when your pictures have been successfully copied to your computer.

13 Click an option to specify if you want to publish the pictures to a Web site or order prints of the pictures from a photo printing Web site (○ changes to ◉).

14 Click **Next** to continue.

Note: If you chose to publish the pictures or order prints in step **13**, follow the instructions in the wizard. For information on publishing files to the Web, see page 72.

What tasks can I perform with my pictures?

When viewing your pictures, Windows provides several options you can select to perform tasks with the pictures.

View as a slide show

Displays your pictures as a full-screen slide show.

Print the selected pictures

Prints the pictures you select using the Photo Printing Wizard. For information on using the Photo Printing Wizard to print pictures, see page 58.

E-mail this file

E-mails a picture you select to a friend, colleague or family member. For information on e-mailing files, see page 70.

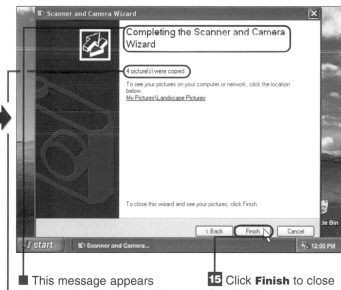

■ This message appears when you have completed the Scanner and Camera Wizard.

■ This area displays the number of pictures the wizard copied to your computer.

15 Click **Finish** to close the wizard.

■ The folder containing your pictures appears.

■ Each picture displays the name you specified in step **8** and is sequentially numbered.

16 When you finish viewing the pictures, click ⊠ to close the folder.

SCAN A DOCUMENT

You can use the Scanner and Camera Wizard to scan paper documents into your computer.

You can scan documents such as photographs, drawings, reports, newsletters, newspaper articles and forms into your computer.

SCAN A DOCUMENT

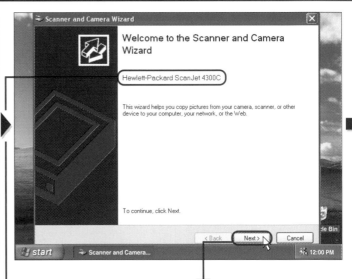

1 Click **start** to display the Start menu.

2 Click **All Programs** to view a list of the programs on your computer.

3 Click **Accessories**.

4 Click **Scanner and Camera Wizard**.

Note: The Scanner and Camera Wizard option is only available after you connect and install a Windows Image Acquisition (WIA) compatible scanner on your computer.

■ The Scanner and Camera Wizard appears.

■ This area displays the name of the scanner installed on your computer.

5 Click **Next** to continue.

What types of documents can I scan?

The Scanner and Camera Wizard allows you to specify the type of document you are scanning. You can scan a color, grayscale, black and white or text document. For example, if you are scanning a document that contains only shades of gray, select the **Grayscale picture** option in step **6** below.

Color   **Grayscale**   **Black and White**   **Text Document**

Which file format should I select for my scanned document?

The file format you should select depends on how you plan to use the document. The BMP and TIF file formats are useful for producing high-quality pictures. The JPG and PNG file formats are useful for pictures you plan to publish to the Web.

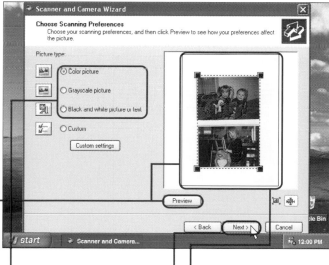

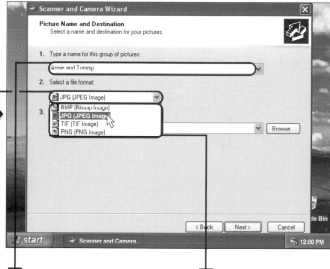

6 Click the type of document you are scanning (○ changes to ◉).

7 Click **Preview** to preview the document.

■ This area displays the preview. A dashed line appears around the area that Windows will scan.

8 To change the area that Windows will scan, position the mouse ↖ over a handle (■) and then drag the handle until the dashed line surrounds the area you want to scan.

9 Click **Next** to continue.

10 Type a name for the scanned document.

11 Click this area to list the available file formats that Windows can use to save the document.

12 Click the file format you want to use.

CONTINUED

SCAN A DOCUMENT

You can select the folder on your computer where you want to store the scanned document.

SCAN A DOCUMENT (CONTINUED)

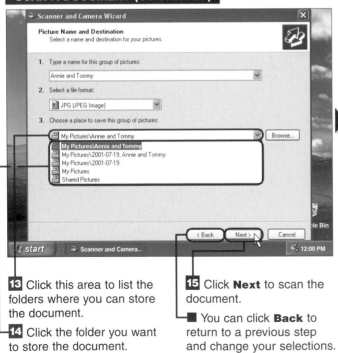

13 Click this area to list the folders where you can store the document.

14 Click the folder you want to store the document.

15 Click **Next** to scan the document.

■ You can click **Back** to return to a previous step and change your selections.

■ This message appears when the scan is complete.

16 Click an option to specify if you want to publish the document to a Web site or order prints of the document from a photo printing Web site (○ changes to ◉).

17 Click **Next** to continue.

*Note: If you chose to publish the document or order prints in step **16**, follow the instructions in the wizard. For information on publishing files to the Web, see page 72.*

Which folder should I use to store my scanned document?

My Pictures

If you want to be able to quickly access the scanned document in the future, store the document in the My Pictures folder. To open the My Pictures folder, see page 41.

Subfolder within My Pictures

To keep the scanned document separate from other pictures in the My Pictures folder, store the document in a subfolder within the My Pictures folder. To name the subfolder, you can select the name you gave the scanned document (Corvette), the current date (2001-01-01) or both (2001-01-01, Corvette).

Shared Pictures

If you want other users set up on your computer to be able to access the scanned document, store the document in the Shared Pictures folder. The Shared Pictures folder is stored in the Shared Documents folder on your computer. To open the Shared Documents folder, see page 184.

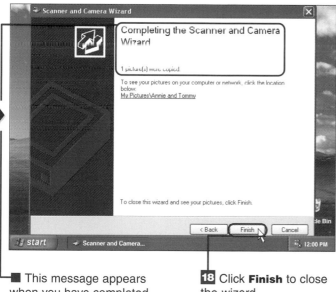

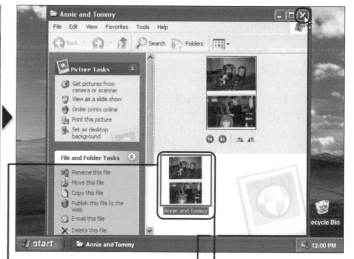

■ This message appears when you have completed the Scanner and Camera Wizard.

18 Click **Finish** to close the wizard.

■ The folder containing the scanned document appears.

■ The scanned document is selected. The document displays the name you specified in step **10**.

■ To open the scanned document, double-click the document.

19 When you finish viewing the scanned document, click ☒ to close the folder.

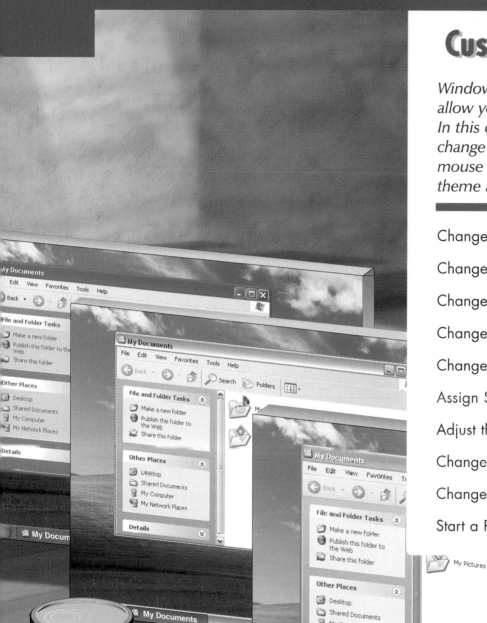

CHAPTER 6

Customize Windows

Windows XP includes several features that allow you to personalize your computer. In this chapter, you will learn how to change the screen saver, adjust your mouse settings, change your desktop theme and more.

CHANGE THE DESKTOP BACKGROUND

You can select a picture, background color or both to decorate your desktop.

When selecting a picture to decorate your desktop, you can use a picture that Windows provides or your own picture.

CHANGE THE DESKTOP BACKGROUND

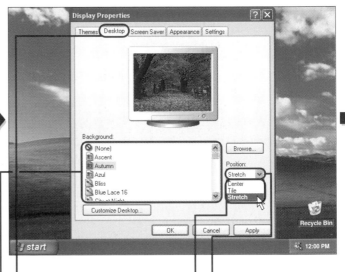

1 Right-click a blank area on your desktop. A menu appears.

2 Click **Properties**.

■ The Display Properties dialog box appears.

3 Click the **Desktop** tab.

4 To display a picture on your desktop, click the picture you want to use.

Note: Pictures stored in your My Pictures folder appear in the list.

5 To select how you want to display the picture on your desktop, click this area.

6 Click the way you want to display the picture.

How can I display a picture on my desktop?

Windows offers three ways that you can display a picture on your desktop.

Center

Displays the picture in the middle of your desktop.

Tile

Repeats the picture until it fills your entire desktop.

Stretch

Stretches the picture to cover your entire desktop.

Note: If you select a large picture that fills your entire desktop, selecting one of these options will have no effect on the way the picture will appear on your desktop.

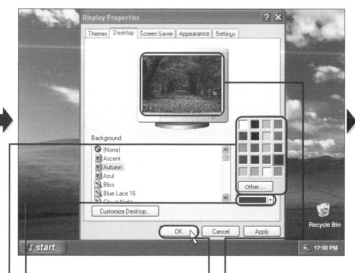

7 To select a color for your desktop, click this area to display a list of the available colors.

8 Click the color you want to use.

Note: If you selected a picture in step 4, the color you select will fill any space not covered by the picture.

■ This area displays how the picture and/or color will appear on your desktop.

9 Click **OK** to add the picture and/or color to your desktop.

■ The picture and/or color appear on your desktop.

■ To remove a picture from your desktop, perform steps **1** to **4**, selecting **(None)** in step **4**. Then perform step **9**.

CHANGE THE SCREEN APPEARANCE

You can change the
style and colors that
Windows uses to
display windows and
other items on your
screen.

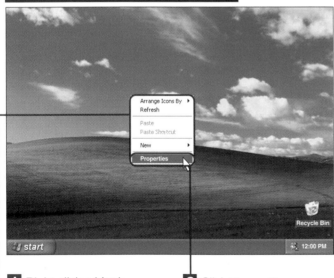

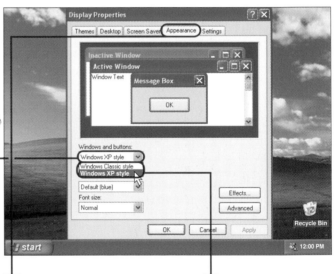

1 Right-click a blank
area on your desktop.
A menu appears.

2 Click **Properties**.

■ The Display Properties
dialog box appears.

3 Click the **Appearance** tab.

4 Click this area to display
the available styles.

5 Click the style you
want to use.

*Note: The available styles
depend on the current theme.
For information on themes,
see page 126.*

How can I change the appearance of my screen?

Windows XP style

Windows Classic style

Windows and buttons

By default, you can choose between the Windows XP style, which is the default style of Windows XP, and the Windows Classic style, which is the style used in previous versions of Windows.

Color scheme

You can change the colors used in items such as windows, dialog boxes and the Start menu.

Font size

You can change the size of text shown in items such as menus, icons and the title bars of windows. Changing the font size will also change the size of some buttons such as the Close button (). Increasing the font size is useful if you have trouble reading the text on your screen or clicking small buttons.

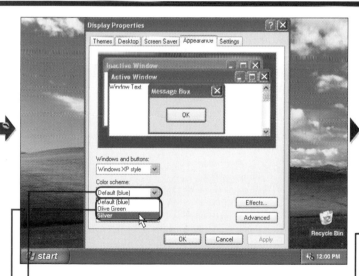

6 Click this area to display the available color schemes.

7 Click the color scheme you want to use.

Note: The available color schemes depend on the style you selected in step 5.

8 Click this area to display the available font sizes.

9 Click the font size you want to use.

Note: The available font sizes depend on the color scheme you selected in step 7.

■ This area displays a preview of how your screen will appear.

10 Click **OK** to change the appearance of your screen.

CHANGE THE SCREEN SAVER

A screen saver is a moving picture or pattern that appears on the screen when you do not use your computer for a period of time.

You can use a screen saver to hide your work while you are away from your desk.

By default, Windows will display a screen saver when you do not use your computer for ten minutes.

CHANGE THE SCREEN SAVER

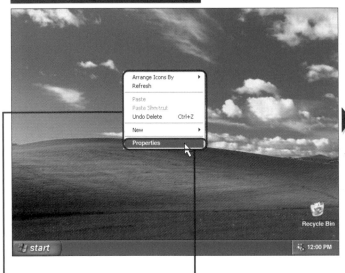

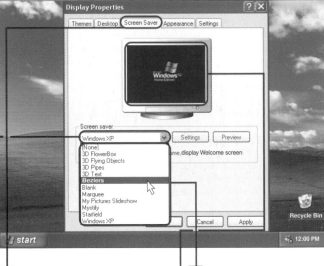

1 Right-click a blank area on your desktop. A menu appears.

2 Click **Properties**.

■ The Display Properties dialog box appears.

3 Click the **Screen Saver** tab.

4 Click this area to display a list of the available screen savers.

5 Click the screen saver you want to use.

■ This area will display a preview of how the screen saver will appear on your screen.

Do I need to use a screen saver?

Screen savers were originally designed to prevent screen burn, which occurs when an image appears in a fixed position on the screen for a period of time. Today's monitors are less susceptible to screen burn, but people still use screen savers for their entertainment value.

What does the My Pictures Slideshow screen saver do?

You can select the My Pictures Slideshow screen saver to have the pictures stored in your My Pictures folder appear as your screen saver. Windows will rotate through all the pictures in the folder, displaying each picture on your screen for six seconds at a time. To view the contents of your My Pictures folder, see page 41.

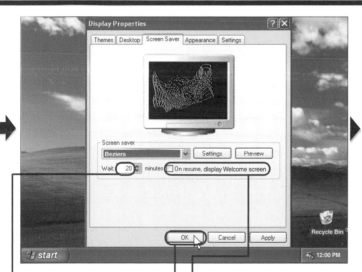

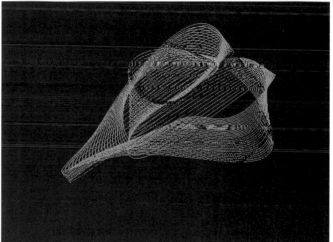

6 To specify the number of minutes your computer must be inactive before the screen saver will appear, double-click this area. Then type the number of minutes.

7 If multiple users are set up on your computer, this option requires you to log on to Windows each time you remove the screen saver. You can click this option to turn the option off (☑ changes to ☐).

Note: For information on logging on to Windows, see page 183.

8 Click **OK**.

■ The screen saver appears when you do not use your computer for the number of minutes you specified.

■ You can move the mouse or press a key on the keyboard to remove the screen saver from your screen.

■ To stop a screen saver from appearing, perform steps **1** to **5**, selecting **(None)** in step **5**. Then perform step **8**.

CHANGE THE DATE AND TIME

You should make sure the correct date and time are set in your computer. Windows uses the date and time to determine when you create and update your files.

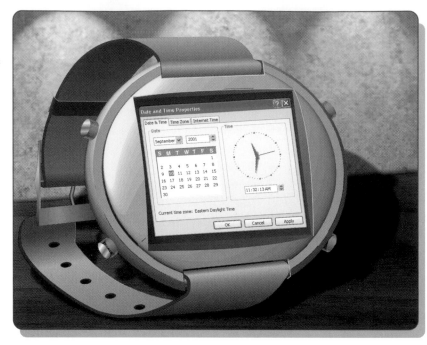

Your computer has a built-in clock that keeps track of the date and time even when you turn off your computer.

CHANGE THE DATE AND TIME

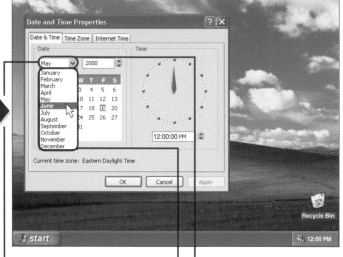

■ This area displays the time set in your computer.

1 To display the date set in your computer, position the mouse ⍩ over the time. After a moment, the date appears.

2 To change the date or time set in your computer, double-click this area.

■ The Date and Time Properties dialog box appears.

■ This area displays the month set in your computer.

3 To change the month, click this area.

4 Click the correct month.

110

Will Windows ever change the time automatically?

Windows will change the time automatically to compensate for daylight saving time. When you turn on your computer after daylight saving time occurs, Windows will have automatically changed the time.

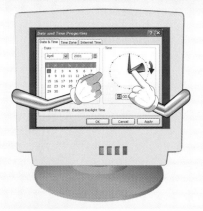

Can Windows ensure that my computer's clock is accurate?

Windows automatically synchronizes your computer's clock with a time server on the Internet approximately once a week. You must be connected to the Internet for the synchronization to occur. If you are on a network that uses a firewall to protect against unauthorized access, Windows will not be able to synchronize your computer's clock.

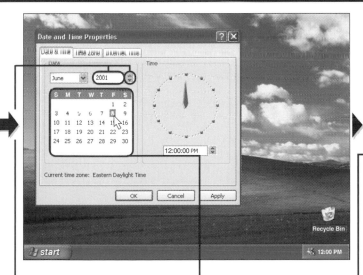

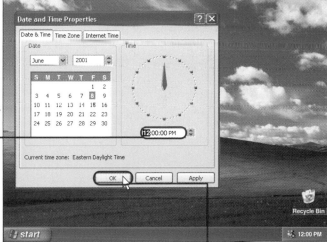

■ This area displays the year set in your computer.

5 To change the year, click ▲ or ▼ in this area until the correct year appears.

■ This area displays the days in the month. The current day is highlighted.

6 To change the day, click the correct day.

■ This area displays the time set in your computer.

7 To change the time, double-click the part of the time you want to change. Then type the correct information.

8 Click **OK** to confirm your changes.

CHANGE THE SCREEN RESOLUTION

You can change the
screen resolution to
adjust the amount
of information that
can fit on your
screen.

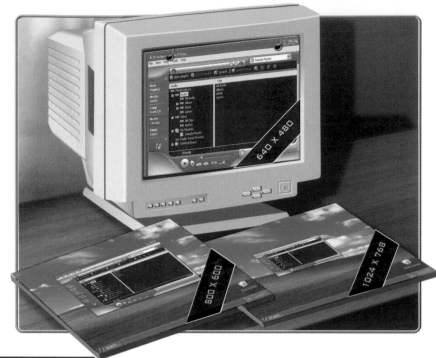

Your monitor and
video adapter
determine which
screen resolutions
are available on
your computer.

CHANGE THE SCREEN RESOLUTION

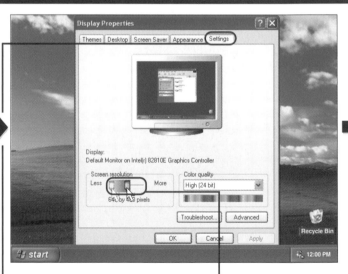

1 Right-click a blank
area on your desktop.
A menu appears.

2 Click **Properties**.

■ The Display Properties
dialog box appears.

3 Click the **Settings** tab.

4 To change the
screen resolution, drag
the slider (⬇) to select
the resolution you want
to use.

Which screen resolution should I use?

The screen resolution is measured by the number of horizontal and vertical pixels displayed on a screen. A pixel is the smallest point on a screen. The screen resolution you should choose depends on the size of your monitor and the amount of information you want to view on your screen at once.

Lower screen resolutions display larger images so you can see the information on your screen more clearly.

Higher screen resolutions display smaller images so you can display more information on your screen at once.

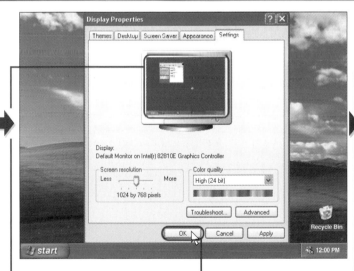
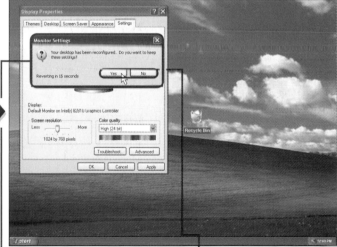

■ This area displays how your screen will look at the new screen resolution.

5 Click **OK** to confirm your change.

■ Your screen will turn black for a moment.

■ Windows resizes the information on your screen.

■ The Monitor Settings dialog box may appear, asking if you want to keep the new screen resolution.

6 Click **Yes** or **No** to specify if you want to keep the new screen resolution.

Note: If you do not perform step 6 within 15 seconds, Windows will automatically restore your original screen resolution.

ASSIGN SOUNDS TO PROGRAM EVENTS

Windows can play sound effects when certain program events occur on your computer. For example, you can hear a short tune when you start Windows.

You can change the sounds assigned to many events at once by selecting a sound scheme. A sound scheme consists of a set of related sounds.

ASSIGN SOUNDS TO PROGRAM EVENTS

1 Click **start** to display the Start menu.

2 Click **Control Panel** to change your computer's settings.

■ The Control Panel window appears.

3 Click **Sounds, Speech, and Audio Devices**.

What program events can Windows assign sounds to?

Windows can assign sounds to over 30 events on your computer. Here are some examples.

Exit Windows

A sound will play each time you exit Windows.

tjones@abc.com

New Mail Notification

A sound will play each time you receive a new e-mail message.

Empty Recycle Bin

A sound will play each time you empty the Recycle Bin.

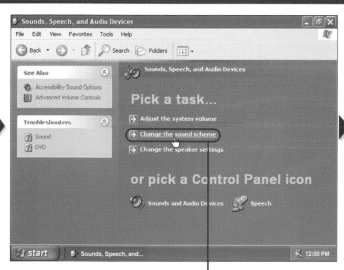

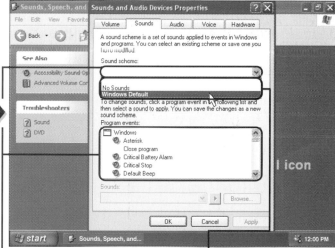

■ The Sounds, Speech, and Audio Devices window appears.

4 Click **Change the sound scheme** to assign sounds to program events on your computer.

■ The Sounds and Audio Devices Properties dialog box appears.

■ This area lists the events that you can assign sounds to.

5 Click this area to display a list of the available sound schemes.

6 Click the sound scheme you want to use.

Note: If you do not want sounds to play for any events, select ***No Sounds****.*

CONTINUED

ASSIGN SOUNDS TO PROGRAM EVENTS

When assigning sounds to program events, you can test the sound that Windows will play for each event.

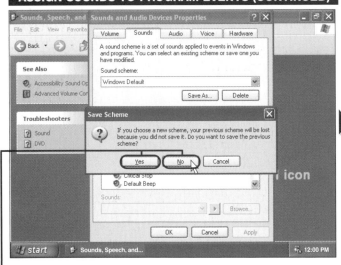

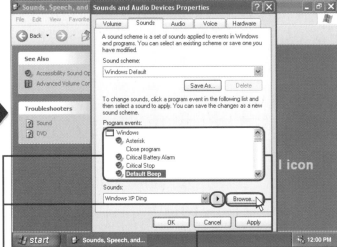

■ The Save Scheme dialog box may appear, asking if you want to save the previous sound scheme.

7 Click **Yes** or **No** to specify if you want to save the previous sound scheme.

*Note: If you selected **Yes**, a dialog box will appear, allowing you to name the sound scheme. Type a name for the sound scheme and then press the ⟨Enter⟩ key. The sound scheme will appear in the list of available sound schemes.*

■ A speaker icon (🔊) appears beside each event that will play a sound.

8 To play the sound for an event, click the event.

9 Click ▶ to play the sound.

ASSIGN SOUNDS TO SPECIFIC EVENTS

10 To assign a sound to a specific event, click the event.

11 Click **Browse** to search for the sound you want to use.

Where can I obtain sounds that I can assign to specific program events?

You can use the sounds included with Windows, purchase collections of sounds at computer stores or obtain sounds on the Internet. The sounds you use must be in the Wave format. Wave files have the .wav extension, such as chimes.wav. You can obtain sounds at the following Web sites.

www.favewavs.com

www.wavlist.com

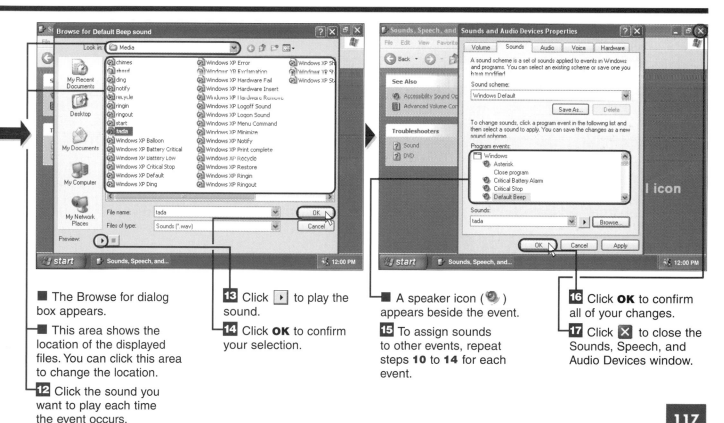

■ The Browse for dialog box appears.

■ This area shows the location of the displayed files. You can click this area to change the location.

12 Click the sound you want to play each time the event occurs.

13 Click ▶ to play the sound.

14 Click **OK** to confirm your selection.

■ A speaker icon (🔊) appears beside the event.

15 To assign sounds to other events, repeat steps **10** to **14** for each event.

16 Click **OK** to confirm all of your changes.

17 Click ✕ to close the Sounds, Speech, and Audio Devices window.

ADJUST THE VOLUME

You can adjust
the volume of
sound on your
computer.

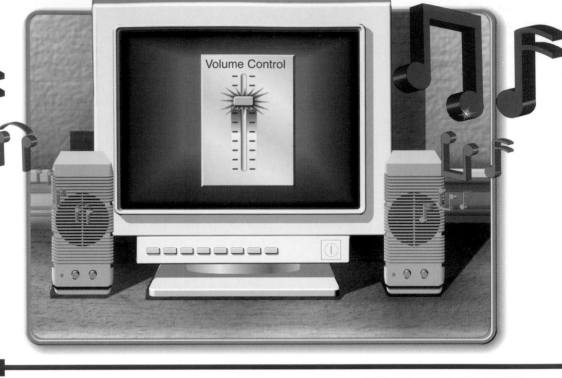

You can adjust the
volume of all the devices
on your computer at
once. You can also adjust
the volume of specific
devices without affecting
the volume of other
devices.

ADJUST THE VOLUME

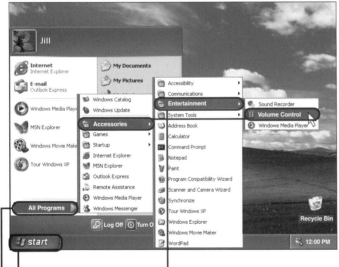

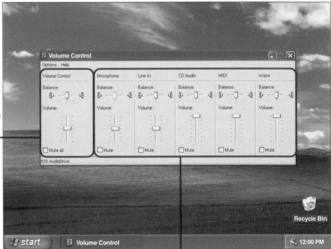

1 Click **start** to display
the Start menu.

2 Click **All Programs** to
view a list of the programs
on your computer.

3 Click **Accessories**.

4 Click **Entertainment**.

5 Click **Volume Control**.

■ A window appears that
allows you to change the
sound volume on your
computer.

■ This area displays the
control that allows you
to change the volume
of all the devices on your
computer at once.

■ This area displays controls
that allow you to change the
volume of individual devices
on your computer.

*Note: The available devices depend
on the sound capabilities of your
computer.*

Is there a quick way to adjust the speaker volume?

Many speakers have a volume dial that you can use to adjust the volume. Your speakers may also have a power button that you can use to turn the sound on or off.

What devices can I adjust the volume for?

Windows allows you to adjust the volume of many devices on your computer. Here are some common devices for which you can adjust the volume.

Device	Controls
Microphone	Recording volume when using a microphone to record sounds.
Line In	Recording volume of devices, such as a CD player or tape player, that connect to the Line In port. The Line In port is usually located at the back of a computer.
CD Audio	Playback volume of audio CDs.
MIDI	Playback volume of MIDI sounds.
Wave	Playback volume of Wave sounds.

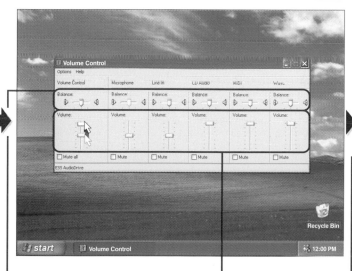

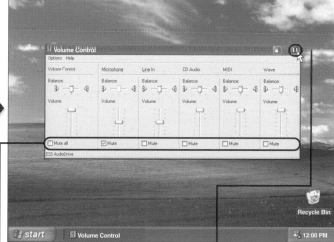

6 To change the balance between the left and right speakers for a device, drag the balance slider ( ) for the device.

Note: Changing the balance between the left and right speakers is useful when one speaker is farther away than the other and you want to make that speaker louder.

7 To increase or decrease the volume for a device, drag the volume slider ( ) for the device.

8 To turn off the sound for a device, click **Mute** for the device (changes to).

Note: To once again turn on the sound for a device, repeat step 8.

9 When you finish adjusting the volume, click to close the window.

CHANGE THE MOUSE SETTINGS

You can change the way your mouse works to make the mouse easier to use.

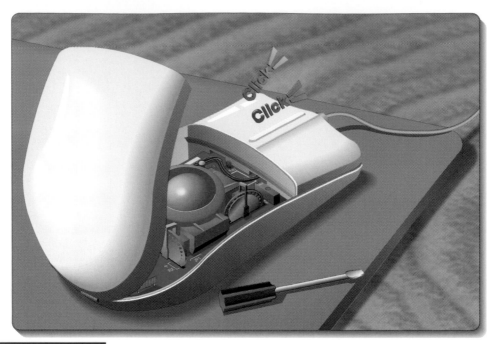

CHANGE THE MOUSE SETTINGS

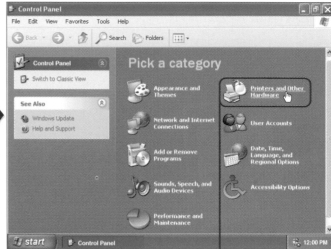

1 Click **start** to display the Start menu.

2 Click **Control Panel** to change your computer's settings.

■ The Control Panel window appears.

3 Click **Printers and Other Hardware**.

Should I use a mouse pad?

A mouse pad provides a smooth surface for moving the mouse on your desk. You should use a mouse pad to reduce the amount of dirt that enters the mouse and protect your desk from scratches. Hard plastic mouse pads attract less dirt and provide a smoother surface than fabric mouse pads.

My mouse pointer does not move smoothly on my screen. What can I do?

You may need to clean the inside of your mouse. Turn the mouse over and remove and clean the roller ball. Then use a cotton swab to remove the dirt from the rollers inside the mouse.

■ The Printers and Other Hardware window appears.

4 Click **Mouse** to change your mouse settings.

■ The Mouse Properties dialog box appears.

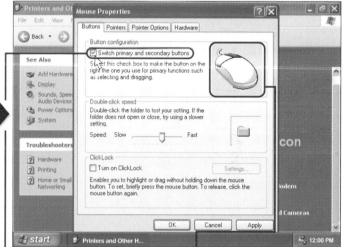

SWITCH MOUSE BUTTONS

5 If you are left-handed and want to use the right mouse button to perform most tasks, click this option to switch the functions of the left and right mouse buttons (☐ changes to ☑).

■ This area displays which mouse button you will use to perform most tasks.

Note: When you change some mouse settings, Windows immediately changes the way your mouse works.

CONTINUED

CHANGE THE MOUSE SETTINGS

You can personalize the way your mouse works by changing the double-click speed. You can also change the appearance of the mouse pointers that Windows displays.

Double-click Speed

Pointer Appearance

If you are a new mouse user or you have difficulty double-clicking the mouse, you may find a slower double-click speed easier to use.

CHANGE THE MOUSE SETTINGS (CONTINUED)

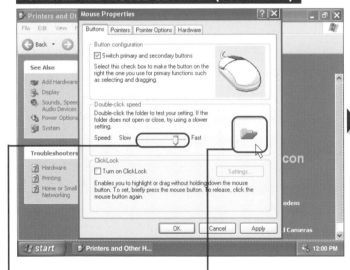

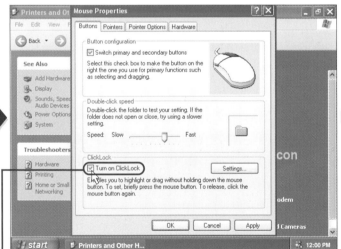

DOUBLE-CLICK SPEED

6 To change the amount of time that can pass between two clicks of the mouse button for Windows to recognize a double-click, drag this slider (⬇) to a new position.

7 To test the new double-click speed, double-click the folder in this area.

■ The folder opens or closes when you double-click at the correct speed.

CLICKLOCK

8 To select information or drag items without having to continuously hold down the mouse button, click this option (☐ changes to ☑).

How can I use the ClickLock mouse setting to select text?

The ClickLock mouse setting allows you to select text without having to continuously hold down the mouse button.

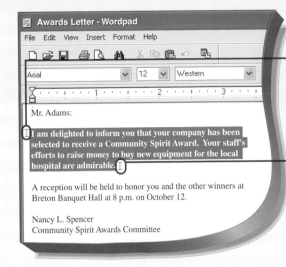

1 To select text using the ClickLock mouse setting, position the mouse I to the left of the text you want to select and then briefly press and hold down the mouse button.

2 Position the mouse I at the end of the text you want to select and then click the mouse button again.

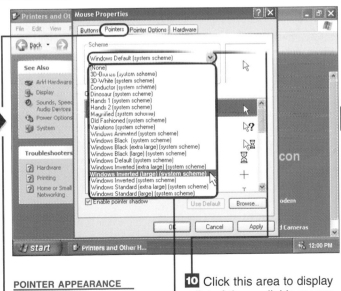

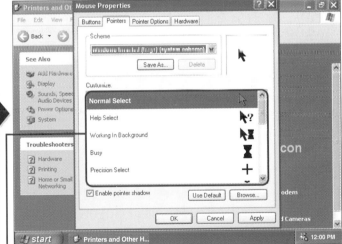

POINTER APPEARANCE

9 To change the appearance of all the mouse pointers that Windows displays, click the **Pointers** tab.

10 Click this area to display a list of the available mouse pointer sets.

11 Click the mouse pointer set you want to use.

■ This area lists the mouse pointers included in the set you selected.

Note: The mouse pointer assumes different shapes. Each shape offers a visual cue to indicate what Windows is doing or the task you can perform.

CONTINUED

CHANGE THE MOUSE SETTINGS

You can change how fast the mouse pointer moves on your screen. You can also have the mouse pointer automatically appear over the default button in most dialog boxes.

Pointer Speed

Snap to Default Button

The default button in most dialog boxes is the **OK** button.

CHANGE THE MOUSE SETTINGS (CONTINUED)

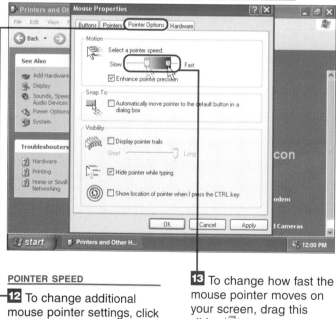

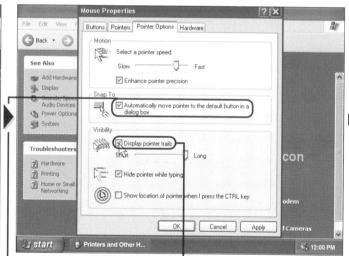

POINTER SPEED

12 To change additional mouse pointer settings, click the **Pointer Options** tab.

13 To change how fast the mouse pointer moves on your screen, drag this slider ( ) to a new position.

SNAP TO DEFAULT BUTTON

14 To have the mouse pointer automatically appear over the default button in most dialog boxes, click this option (changes to).

DISPLAY POINTER TRAILS

15 To leave a trail of mouse pointers as you move the mouse pointer on your screen, click this option (changes to).

How can I make the mouse pointer easier to see on my screen?

Windows offers two mouse settings that can help you more clearly see the mouse pointer on your screen. These settings are especially useful on portable computer screens where the mouse pointer can be difficult to follow.

Display pointer trails

Displays mouse pointer trails to help you follow the movement of the mouse pointer on your screen.

Show location of pointer

Shows the location of the mouse pointer when you press the Ctrl key. Moving circles will briefly appear around the mouse pointer to help you quickly locate the mouse pointer on your screen.

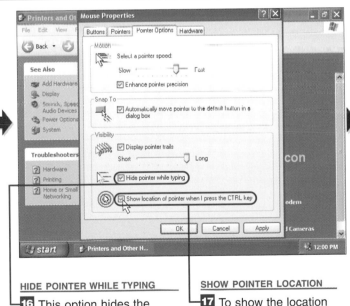

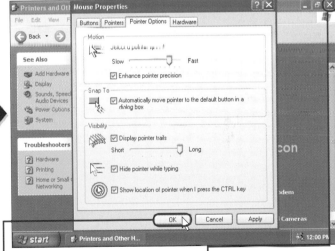

HIDE POINTER WHILE TYPING

■16 This option hides the mouse pointer when you type. You can click this option to turn the option on (☑) or off (☐).

Note: The mouse pointer will re-appear when you move the mouse.

SHOW POINTER LOCATION

■17 To show the location of the mouse pointer when you press the Ctrl key, click this option (☐ changes to ☑).

CONFIRM CHANGES

■18 When you finish changing the mouse settings, click **OK**.

■19 Click ☒ to close the Printers and Other Hardware window.

CHANGE THE DESKTOP THEME

You can use a desktop theme to personalize the overall appearance of Windows.

Each desktop theme contains several coordinated items, including a desktop background, screen saver, colors, sounds, mouse pointers, icons and fonts.

CHANGE THE DESKTOP THEME

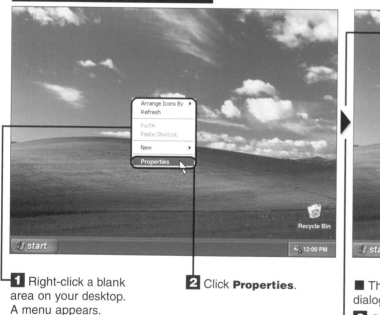

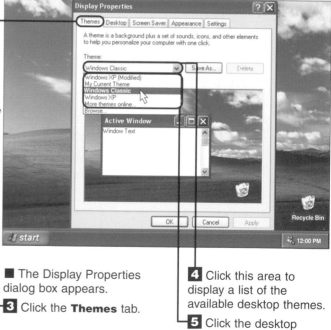

1 Right-click a blank area on your desktop. A menu appears.

2 Click **Properties**.

■ The Display Properties dialog box appears.

3 Click the **Themes** tab.

4 Click this area to display a list of the available desktop themes.

5 Click the desktop theme you want to use.

What desktop themes are available?

My Current Theme
The theme you are currently using.

Windows Classic
This theme resembles the style used in previous versions of Windows.

Windows XP
The theme initially displayed on Windows XP.

More themes online
You can select this option to obtain additional themes on the Internet. The Microsoft Internet Explorer window will appear and display a Web page that allows you to obtain additional themes.

Theme Name (Modified)
If you make changes to a theme, such as changing the desktop background, a new theme appears with the word **Modified** in its name.

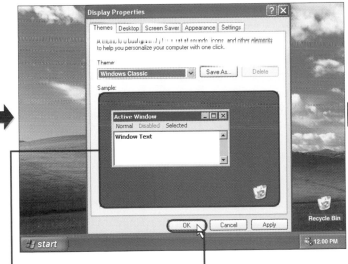

■ This area displays a preview of the desktop theme you selected.

6 Click **OK** to confirm your change.

■ Windows applies the desktop theme you selected.

■ To return to the original desktop theme, perform steps **1** to **6**, selecting **Windows XP** in step **5**.

START A PROGRAM AUTOMATICALLY

If you use the same program every day, you can have the program start automatically each time you turn on your computer.

To have a program start automatically, you need to place a shortcut for the program in the Startup folder. A shortcut is a link to the program.

START A PROGRAM AUTOMATICALLY

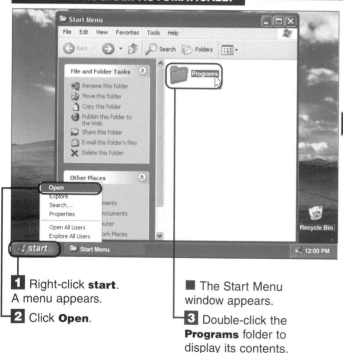

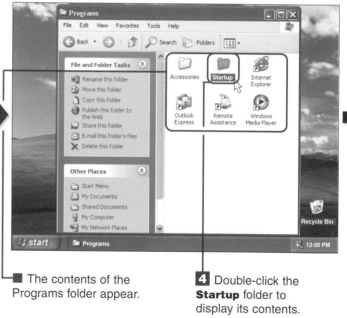

1 Right-click **start**. A menu appears.

2 Click **Open**.

■ The Start Menu window appears.

3 Double-click the **Programs** folder to display its contents.

■ The contents of the Programs folder appear.

4 Double-click the **Startup** folder to display its contents.

**How do I stop a program
from starting automatically?**

To stop a program from
starting automatically,
you must remove the
shortcut for the program
from the Startup folder.
Deleting a shortcut for
a program from the
Startup folder will not
remove the program
from your computer.

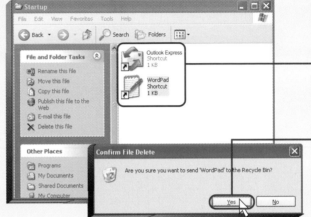

1 Perform steps **1**
to **4** on page 128 to
display the contents
of the Startup folder.

2 Click the shortcut
for the program you
no longer want to start
automatically. Then
press the Delete key.

3 A dialog box will
appear, confirming the
deletion. Click **Yes** to
delete the shortcut for
the program.

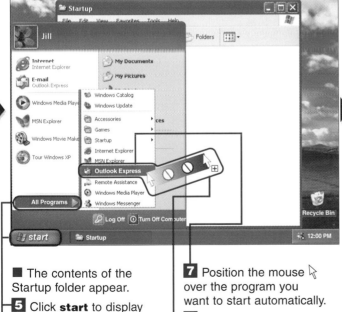

■ The contents of the
Startup folder appear.

5 Click **start** to display
the Start menu.

6 Click **All Programs** to
view a list of the programs
on your computer.

7 Position the mouse ▷
over the program you
want to start automatically.

8 Press and hold down
the Ctrl key as you drag
the program to a blank
area in the Startup
window.

■ A shortcut for the
program appears in
the Startup window.
A shortcut displays an
arrow (⤤) in its icon.

9 Click ✕ to close
the Startup window.

■ The program will now
start automatically each
time you turn on your
computer.

CHAPTER 7

Work With Music and Videos

In this chapter, you will learn how to use the Windows Media Player program. You will learn how to play music CDs, listen to radio stations on the Internet, copy songs to a CD or portable device and more.

PLAY A SOUND OR VIDEO

You can use Windows Media Player to play many types of sound and video files on your computer.

You can obtain sound and video files on the Internet and purchase sound and video files at computer stores.

PLAY A SOUND OR VIDEO

1 Double-click the sound or video file you want to play.

■ The Windows Media Player window appears.

■ If you selected a video file, this area displays the video.

Note: If you selected a sound file, the sound plays. The area may display a graphical representation of the sound.

■ This slider ( ) indicates the progress of the sound or video file.

2 To use the entire screen to view the video that is currently playing, click .

Can I display Windows Media Player in a smaller size?

Yes. You can change the size and appearance of Windows Media Player by switching from the full mode to the skin mode.

Full Mode

The full mode allows you to access all the features that Windows Media Player provides. You can click ⊡ to switch to the skin mode at any time.

Skin Mode

The skin mode takes up less room on your screen, but offers fewer features than the full mode. You can click ⊠ to return to the full mode at any time. To change the appearance of Windows Media Player when displayed in the skin mode, see page 148.

■ The video continues to play using the entire screen.

■ To once again display the video in a window, press the `Esc` key.

3 To adjust the volume, drag this slider (◖) left or right to decrease or increase the volume.

4 To pause or stop the play of the sound or video file, click ⊙ or ⊙ (⊙ changes to ⊙).

■ You can click ⊙ to resume the play of the sound or video file.

5 When you finish playing the sound or video file, click ✕ to close the Windows Media Player window.

PLAY A MUSIC CD

You can use your computer to play music CDs while you work.

You need a computer with sound capabilities and a CD-ROM drive to play music CDs.

PLAY A MUSIC CD

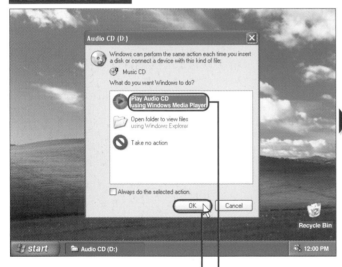

1 Insert a music CD into your CD-ROM drive.

■ The Audio CD dialog box appears, asking what you want Windows to do.

2 Click this option to play the music CD.

3 Click **OK**.

■ The Windows Media Player window appears and the CD begins to play.

■ This area displays a graphical representation of the song that is currently playing.

**How does Windows Media Player know
the name of each song on my music CD?**

If you are connected to the Internet when
you play a music CD, Windows Media
Player attempts to obtain information
about the CD from the Internet. If you
are not connected to the Internet or
information about the CD is unavailable,
Windows Media Player displays the track
number of each song instead. If Windows
Media Player is able to obtain information
about the CD, Windows will recognize
the CD and display the appropriate
information each time you insert the CD.

■ This area displays a list
of the songs on the CD
and the amount of time
that each song will play.
The song that is currently
playing is highlighted.

■ This slider (◉)
indicates the progress
of the current song.

■ This area displays
the amount of time the
current song has been
playing.

ADJUST THE VOLUME

4 To adjust the volume,
drag this slider (◉) left
or right to decrease or
increase the volume.

TURN OFF SOUND

5 Click (◉) to turn off the
sound (◉ changes to ◉).

■ You can click (◉) to once
again turn on the sound.

CONTINUED ▸

PLAY A MUSIC CD

When playing a music CD, you can pause or stop the play of the CD at any time. You can also play a specific song or play the songs in random order.

PLAY A MUSIC CD (CONTINUED)

PAUSE OR STOP PLAY

6 Click ⏸ to pause the play of the CD (⏸ changes to ▶).

7 Click ⏹ to stop the play of the CD.

■ You can click ▶ to resume the play of the CD.

PLAY ANOTHER SONG

■ This area displays a list of the songs on the CD.

8 Click one of the following options to play another song on the CD.

⏮ Play the previous song
⏭ Play the next song

■ To play a specific song in the list, double-click the song.

How can I play a music CD while performing other tasks on my computer?

If you want to perform other tasks on your computer while playing a music CD, minimize the Windows Media Player window to temporarily remove the window from your screen. To minimize the Windows Media Player window, click ▬ in the top right corner of the window.

Can I listen to a music CD privately?

You can listen to a music CD privately by plugging headphones into the jack at the front of your CD-ROM drive or into your speakers. If your CD-ROM drive or speakers do not have a headphone jack, you can plug the headphones into the back of your computer where you normally plug in the speakers.

PLAY SONGS RANDOMLY

9 Click ⦀ to play the songs on the CD in random order (⦀ changes to ⦀).

■ You can click ⦀ to once again play the songs on the CD in order.

CLOSE WINDOWS MEDIA PLAYER

10 When you finish listening to the CD, click ✖ to close the Windows Media Player window.

11 Remove the CD from your CD-ROM drive.

USING THE MEDIA GUIDE

The Media Guide is like
an electronic magazine
that allows you to access
the latest music and
movies on the Internet.
You can also use the
Media Guide to obtain
information on various
topics such as news,
sports and entertainment.

You must have a
connection to the
Internet to use
the Media Guide.

1 Click **start** to display
the Start menu.

2 Click **All Programs** to
view a list of the programs
on your computer.

3 Click **Windows
Media Player**.

■ The Windows Media
Player window appears.

4 Click the **Media
Guide** tab.

*Note: If you are not currently
connected to the Internet, a
message appears, indicating
that you need to be connected.*

■ This area displays the
Media Guide, which is a Web
page that is updated daily to
provide access to the latest
music, movies and information
on the Internet.

*Note: The Media Guide may look
different on your screen.*

Why are different speeds listed for a media file in the Media Guide?

The Media Guide offers files for different connection speeds that you can select to transfer and play a media file such as a music video or movie clip. The connection speed you should select depends on the type of connection you have to the Internet. If problems occur while transferring or playing a media file, try selecting a slower connection speed.

Modem

ISDN Line

Cable Modem or DSL Modem

Type of Connection	Select this Speed
Modem	28k or 56k
Integrated Services Digital Network (ISDN) Line	100k
Cable Modem or Digital Subscriber Line (DSL) Modem	300k or 500k

■ The Media Guide contains links that you can click to display additional information or play media files such as music videos or movie clips. When you position the mouse ⍅ over a link, the mouse ⍅ changes to 🖑.

5 Click a link of interest.

■ In this example, information on the topic you selected appears.

■ You can repeat step **5** to browse through additional information or play other media files.

6 When you finish using the Media Guide, click ✖ to close the Windows Media Player window.

You can use the Media Library to organize and work with all the media files on your computer. A media file can be a sound or video file.

USING THE MEDIA LIBRARY

1 Click **start** to display the Start menu.

2 Click **All Programs** to view a list of the programs on your computer.

3 Click **Windows Media Player**.

■ The Windows Media Player window appears.

4 Click the **Media Library** tab.

■ The first time you visit the Media Library, a dialog box appears, asking if you want to search your computer for media files.

SEARCH COMPUTER FOR MEDIA FILES

5 Click **Yes** to search your computer for media files.

Note: If the dialog box does not appear, press the **F3** *key to search your computer for media files.*

Where can I obtain media files?

Media Guide

You can use the Media Guide that Windows provides to access the latest music, movies and videos on the Internet. For more information on the Media Guide, see page 138.

The Internet

Many Web sites on the Internet offer media files that you can transfer and play on your computer. You can find media files at the following Web sites.
earthstation1.com
www.themez.co.uk

Computer Stores

Many computer stores offer collections of media files that you can purchase.

■ The Search for Media Files dialog box appears.

6 Click **Search** to start the search.

■ Windows searches your computer for media files.

■ This area shows the progress of the search.

7 When the search is complete, click **Close** to close the dialog box.

8 Click **Close** to close the Search for Media Files dialog box.

CONTINUED ▶

USING THE MEDIA LIBRARY

You can play sound and video files that are listed in the Media Library.

USING THE MEDIA LIBRARY (CONTINUED)

VIEW MEDIA FILES

■ The Media Library organizes your media files into categories.

■ A category displaying a plus sign (⊞) contains hidden items.

■ To display the hidden items in a category, click the plus sign (⊞) beside the category (⊞ changes to ⊟).

Note: To once again hide the items in a category, click the minus sign (⊟) beside the category.

1 Click the category that contains the media files of interest.

■ This area displays the media files in the category you selected.

2 To play a media file, double-click the file.

How does the Media Library organize my sound and video files?

The Media Library organizes your sound and video files into the following categories.

AUDIO	
All Audio	Lists all your sound files.
Album	List sound files by album.
Artist	Lists sound files by artist.
Genre	Lists sound files by genre, such as Jazz or Rock.

VIDEO	
All Clips	Lists all your video files.
Author	Lists video files by author.

■ If you selected a video file, the video appears on the **Now Playing** tab.

■ This slider (◯) indicates the progress of the video or sound file.

3 To adjust the volume, drag this slider (◯) left or right to decrease or increase the volume.

4 To stop playing the video or sound file, click ◯.

■ To return to your list of media files, click the **Media Library** tab.

5 When you finish working with your media files, click ✖ to close the Windows Media Player window.

LISTEN TO RADIO STATIONS ON THE INTERNET

You can use Windows Media Player to listen to radio stations from around the world that broadcast on the Internet.

You need a computer with sound capabilities and an Internet connection to listen to radio stations that broadcast on the Internet.

LISTEN TO RADIO STATIONS ON THE INTERNET

1 Click **start** to display the Start menu.

2 Click **All Programs** to view a list of the programs on your computer.

3 Click **Windows Media Player**.

■ The Windows Media Player window appears.

4 Click the **Radio Tuner** tab to listen to radio stations that broadcast on the Internet.

Note: If you are not currently connected to the Internet, a message appears, indicating that you need to be connected.

■ This area displays a list of featured radio stations.

5 Click the name of the radio station you want to play.

How does Windows play radio stations that broadcast on the Internet?

Before Windows plays a radio station, the information is partially transferred and temporarily stored in a section of memory on your computer, called a buffer. While the radio station plays, information continuously transfers from the Internet and is temporarily stored in the buffer. The buffer minimizes the interruptions to the broadcast playing on your computer. Interruptions are caused by disruptions to information or the slowing down of information transferring to your computer.

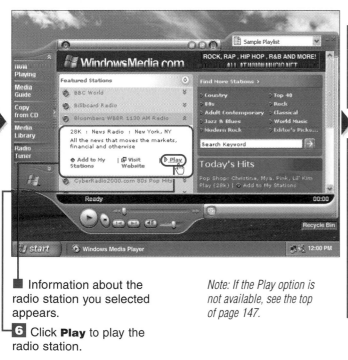

■ Information about the radio station you selected appears.

6 Click **Play** to play the radio station.

Note: If the Play option is not available, see the top of page 147.

■ After a moment, the radio station begins to play.

■ The Microsoft Internet Explorer window opens behind Windows Media Player, displaying the Web page for the radio station. To clearly view the Web page, click the window's button on the taskbar.

7 To adjust the volume, drag the slider (🔘) left or right to decrease or increase the volume.

8 To stop playing the radio station at any time, click 🔘.

CONTINUED ▶

LISTEN TO RADIO STATIONS ON THE INTERNET

You can search for radio stations that broadcast on the Internet.

SEARCH FOR RADIO STATIONS

■ This area displays categories of radio stations you can search for.

1 To search for radio stations in a specific category, click the category of interest.

■ A list of radio stations in the category you selected appears.

■ If the radio station you want to listen to does not appear in the list, you can click this area and type a word or phrase that describes the radio station you want to search for. Then press the `Enter` key.

2 Click the name of the radio station that you want to play in the list.

How do I listen to a radio station if the Play option is not available?

If the Play option does not appear when you click the name of a radio station, you cannot listen to the radio station in Windows Media Player. To listen to the radio station using your Web browser, click the **Visit Website to Play** option. A Web browser window opens, displaying the Web page for the radio station and the radio station begins playing. Some radio stations may require additional information before allowing you to listen to the station in your Web browser.

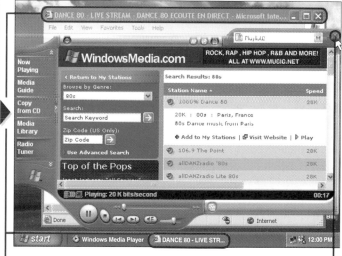

■ Information about the radio station you selected appears.

3 Click **Play** to play the radio station.

Note: If the Play option is not available, see the top of this page.

■ After a moment, the radio station begins to play.

■ The Microsoft Internet Explorer window opens behind Windows Media Player, displaying the Web page for the radio station. To clearly view the Web page, click the window's button on the taskbar.

4 When you finish listening to radio stations, click ✖ to close the Windows Media Player window.

CHANGE SKIN OF WINDOWS MEDIA PLAYER

You can change the skin of Windows Media Player to customize how the player looks and functions.

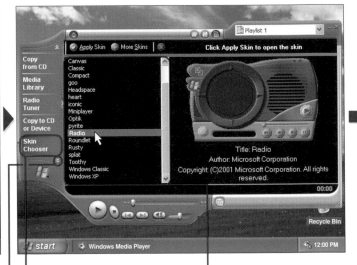

1 Click **start** to display the Start menu.

2 Click **All Programs** to view a list of the programs on your computer.

3 Click **Windows Media Player**.

■ The Windows Media Player window appears.

4 Click the **Skin Chooser** tab to change the skin of Windows Media Player.

■ If the Skin Chooser tab is not displayed, click this arrow (⚡) until the tab appears.

■ This area lists the available skins that you can use with Windows Media Player.

5 Click the skin you want to use.

Where can I obtain more skins for Windows Media Player?

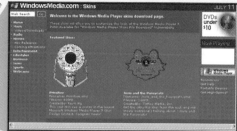

You can obtain more skins for Windows Media Player on the Internet.

When viewing the list of skins in Windows Media Player, click **More Skins**. If you are not currently connected to the Internet, a dialog box will appear that allows you to connect.

Windows will open Microsoft Internet Explorer and display a Web page that offers skins that you can use. When you click the skin you want to use, the skin will transfer to your computer and appear in your list of available skins.

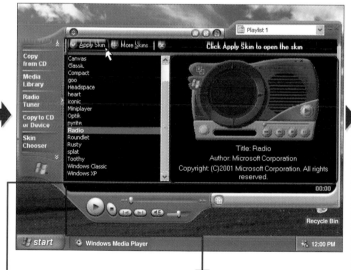

■ This area displays a preview of the skin you selected.

6 Click **Apply Skin** to apply the skin to Windows Media Player.

■ Windows Media Player changes to the skin mode and displays the skin you selected.

Note: Windows Media Player can only display a skin when in the skin mode. For more information on the skin and full modes, see the top of page 133.

■ To once again display Windows Media Player in the full mode, click 🔲.

Note: The location of 🔲 depends on the skin you selected.

COPY SONGS FROM A MUSIC CD

You can copy songs
from a music CD
onto your computer.

Copying songs from a music
CD allows you to play the
songs at any time without
having to insert the CD into
your computer. Copying
songs from a music CD also
allows you to later copy the
songs to a recordable CD or
portable device.

Your CD-ROM drive and
speakers determine whether
you can listen to a music
CD while you copy songs
from the CD.

COPY SONGS FROM A MUSIC CD

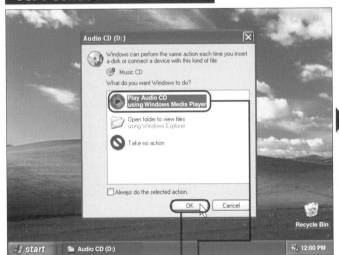

1 Insert the music CD
that contains the songs
you want to copy into
your CD-ROM drive.

■ The Audio CD dialog
box appears, asking what
you want Windows to do.

2 Click this option to
play the music CD.

3 Click **OK**.

■ The Windows Media
Player window appears
and the CD begins to play.

4 Click the **Copy from CD**
tab.

■ This area displays
information about each
song on the CD. Windows
Media Player will copy
each song that displays
a check mark (✔) to your
computer.

5 To add (☑) or
remove (☐) a check
mark beside a song,
click the box (☐)
beside the song.

6 Click **Copy Music**
to start copying the
selected songs to your
computer.

How can I play a song I copied from a music CD?

Windows offers two ways that you can play a song you copied from a music CD.

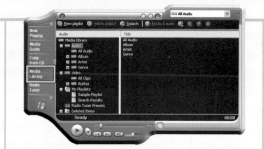

Use the My Music Folder

Songs you copy from a music CD are stored in the My Music folder on your computer. The My Music folder contains a subfolder for each artist whose songs you have copied to your computer. To open the My Music folder, see page 41. You can double-click a song in the folder to play the song.

Use Windows Media Player

Songs you copy from a music CD are listed in the Media Library in Windows Media Player. To play a song in the Media Library, see page 140.

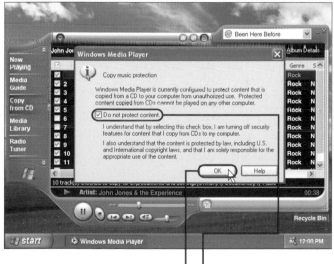

■ The first time you copy songs from a music CD, a dialog box appears, stating that Windows Media Player will protect the songs from unauthorized use. Protected songs cannot be played on another computer.

7 If you want to be able to play the songs on another computer, click this option (☐ changes to ☑).

8 Click **OK** to continue.

■ This column indicates the progress of the copy.

■ To stop the copy at any time, click **Stop Copy**.

9 When you finish copying songs from the music CD, click ✖ to close the Windows Media Player window.

COPY SONGS TO A CD OR PORTABLE DEVICE

You can use Windows Media Player to copy songs on your computer to a CD or to a portable device such as an MP3 player.

When using Windows Media Player to copy songs, you can only copy songs that appear in the Media Library. For information on using the Media Library, see page 140. To add songs to the Media Library from a music CD, see page 150.

You should not perform other tasks on your computer when copying songs to a CD since Windows Media Player may stop working.

COPY SONGS TO A CD OR PORTABLE DEVICE

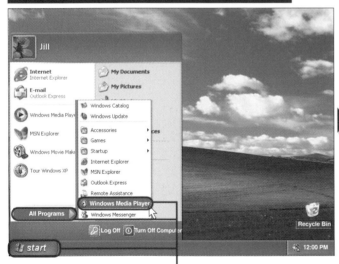

1 To copy songs to a CD, insert a blank CD into your recordable CD drive.

*Note: When you insert a blank CD, a dialog box appears, asking what you want Windows to do. Click **Cancel** to close the dialog box.*

2 Click **start** to display the Start menu.

3 Click **All Programs** to view a list of the programs on your computer.

4 Click **Windows Media Player**.

■ The Windows Media Player window appears.

5 Click the **Copy to CD or Device** tab.

■ If the Copy to CD or Device tab is not displayed, click this arrow (≫) until the tab appears.

6 Click this area to display a list of the categories in the Media Library.

7 Click the category that contains the songs you want to copy.

What hardware do I need to copy songs to a CD?

You will need a recordable CD drive to copy songs to a CD.

CD-R Drive

A CD-R (Compact Disc-Recordable) drive allows you to permanently record data on CD-R discs. You cannot erase the contents of a CD-R disc.

CD-RW Drive

A CD-RW (Compact Disc-ReWritable) drive allows you to record data on CD-RW or CD-R discs. You can erase the contents of a CD-RW disc in order to copy new data to the disc. To erase the contents of a CD-RW disc, see the top of page 93.

Can I copy songs to a CD at different times?

You can copy songs to a CD only once using Windows Media Player. Since you must copy all the songs to a CD at the same time, make sure you carefully select all the songs you want to copy.

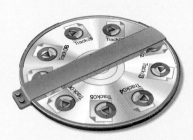

■ This area displays the songs in the category you selected. Windows Media Player will copy each song that displays a check mark (✔).

8 To add (☑) or remove (☐) a check mark, click the box (☐) beside the song.

■ This area displays the device you will copy the songs to. You can click this area to select a different device.

9 Click **Copy Music** to start copying.

■ This column indicates the progress of the copy.

■ To cancel the copy at any time, click **Cancel**.

■ When the copy is complete, this area displays all the songs you copied to the device.

Note: When you copy songs to a CD, Windows automatically ejects the CD from the recordable CD drive when the copy is complete.

10 Click ✖ to close the Windows Media Player window.

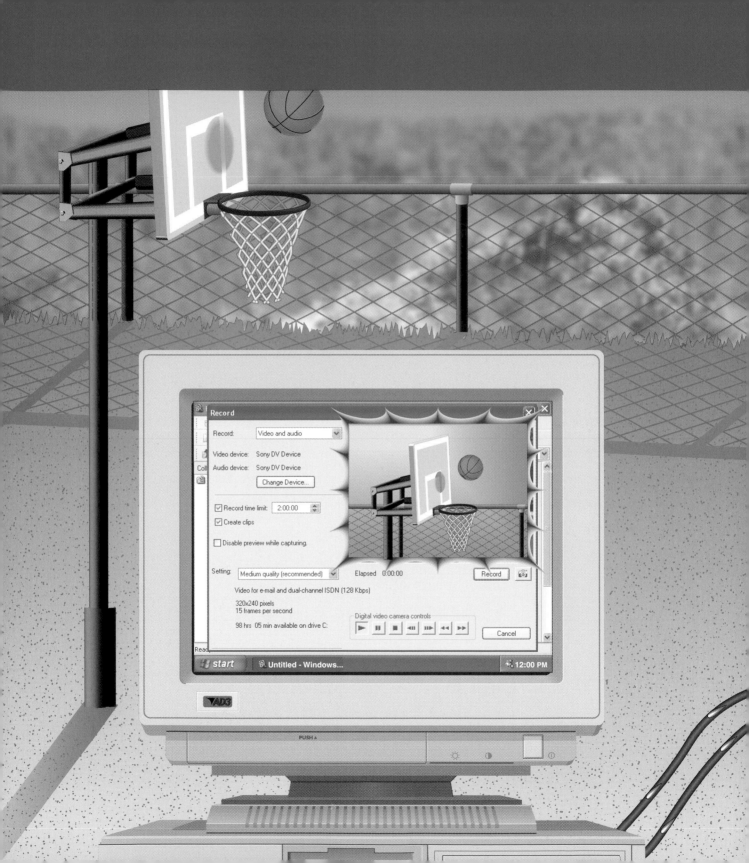

CHAPTER 8

Create Movies

Read this chapter to find out how to use the Windows Movie Maker program. You will learn how to record, play and edit your own home movies.

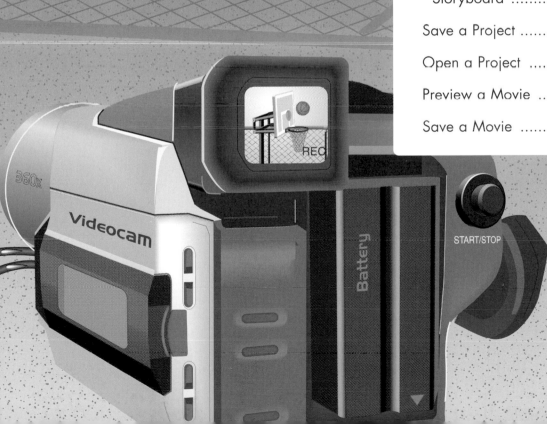

INTRODUCTION TO WINDOWS MOVIE MAKER

You can use Windows Movie Maker to transfer your home movies to your computer. You can then organize and edit the movies before sharing them with friends and family.

Before using Windows Movie Maker, you need to connect and install the equipment needed to transfer your home movies to your computer.

Video Source

You can transfer movies from a video camera onto your computer. You can also transfer movies from a Web camera, television broadcast, VCR or DVD player onto your computer.

Cables

You will need one or more cables to connect the video camera or other video source to your computer. The video source or the card you use to connect the video source to your computer may come with the cables you need. If you do not have the required cables, you can purchase the cables at a computer store.

Connector

You need a specific type of connector to be able to connect a video camera or other video source to your computer. If your computer does not already have the appropriate type of connector, you can purchase the connector at a computer store.

Video Source	Type of Connector Commonly Required
Analog Video Camera	Video Capture Card
Digital Video Camera	FireWire Port or FireWire Card
DVD	TV Tuner Card
Television Broadcast	TV Tuner Card
VCR	TV Tuner Card
Web Camera	USB Port or USB Card

Minimum Computer Requirements

Your computer must have the following minimum requirements for Windows Movie Maker to work properly.

➢ 300 MHz Pentium II or equivalent

➢ 64 MB of RAM

➢ 2 GB of free hard disk space

➢ Sound capabilities

You can start
Windows Movie
Maker to create
and work with
movies on your
computer.

START WINDOWS MOVIE MAKER

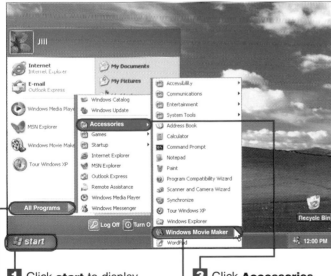

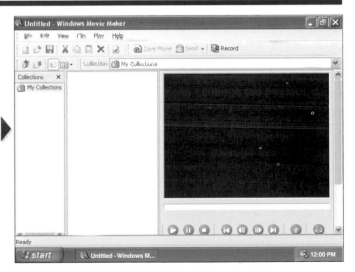

1 Click **start** to display
the Start menu.

2 Click **All Programs** to
view a list of the programs
on your computer.

3 Click **Accessories**.

4 Click **Windows
Movie Maker**.

■ The Windows Movie
Maker window appears.

■ You can now record
video from your video
camera or other video
source onto your computer.
To record video onto your
computer, see page 158.

RECORD A VIDEO

You can record video from your video camera or other video source onto your computer.

Before you start recording video, make sure your video camera or other video source is properly connected to your computer and turned on. Also make sure the tape or other media is at the point where you want to begin recording.

RECORD A VIDEO

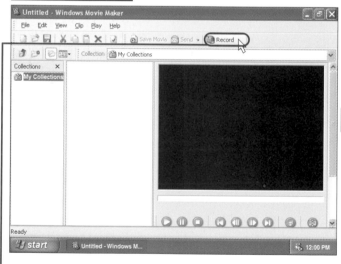

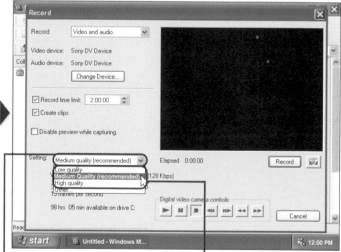

1 Click **Record** to record a video onto your computer.

*Note: A dialog box appears if your computer may not provide acceptable performance when recording from a high-speed device such as a digital video camera. Click **Yes** to record video using the device.*

■ The Record dialog box appears.

2 Click this area to display a list of the available quality settings that you can use to record the video.

3 Click the quality setting you want to use.

Note: For information on selecting a quality setting, see the top of page 159.

Why am I unable to record video from my video camera?

When recording video from a video camera, make sure your camera is in Playback mode and not in Standby mode. You cannot record video when your video camera is in Standby mode.

What should I consider when selecting a quality setting to record my video?

A higher quality setting produces a higher quality video, but results in a larger file size. Videos with a larger file size take up more space on your computer and will take longer to transfer over the Internet. Some computers also may not be able to properly play a higher quality video.

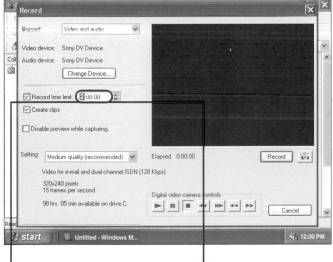

■ This area indicates the time period after which Windows Movie Maker will stop recording the video.

Note: The default recording time is set at two hours. The time may be less, depending on your free hard disk space and the quality setting you selected in step 3.

4 To change the length of time, click the part of the time you want to change and then type a new number.

5 Click ▶ to begin playing the video.

Note: You can also press the play button on your video camera or other video source to begin playing the video.

■ This area displays the video.

6 Click **Record** to start recording the video onto your computer.

CONTINUED ▶

RECORD A VIDEO

Windows automatically stores each video you record in the My Videos folder on your computer.

Windows creates the My Videos folder the first time you start Windows Movie Maker. The My Videos folder is stored within the My Documents folder.

RECORD A VIDEO (CONTINUED)

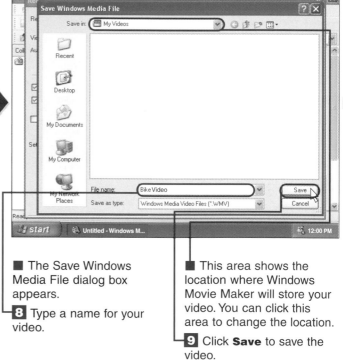

■ The word **Recording** blinks in this area when you are recording.

■ This area displays the time that has passed since you started recording the video.

7 Click **Stop** when you want to stop recording the video.

Note: You may have to press the stop button on your video camera or other video source to stop the video.

■ The Save Windows Media File dialog box appears.

8 Type a name for your video.

■ This area shows the location where Windows Movie Maker will store your video. You can click this area to change the location.

9 Click **Save** to save the video.

How does Windows Movie Maker organize the videos I record?

Collections

Each time you record a video, Windows Movie Maker creates a collection to store all the clips for the video. Each collection appears as a folder (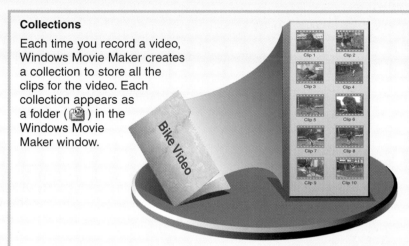) in the Windows Movie Maker window.

Clips

Windows Movie Maker automatically breaks up a video you record into smaller, more manageable segments, called clips. A clip is created each time Windows detects a different sequence in a video, such as when you turn on your video camera or when you switch from pause to once again begin recording.

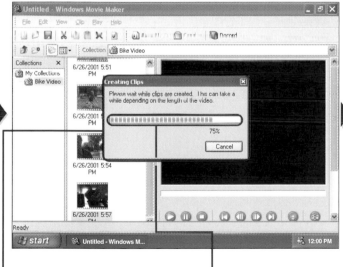

■ The Creating Clips dialog box appears while Windows Movie Maker creates the clips for your video. For information on clips, see the top of this page.

■ This area shows the progress of the creation of the clips.

■ When Windows Movie Maker has finished creating the clips for your video, this area displays a folder that stores the collection of video clips. The name of the collection is the name you specified in step **8**.

■ This area displays the video clips within the collection. To help you identify the video clips, Windows Movie Maker displays the first frame of each clip.

PLAY A VIDEO CLIP

You can play each video clip that you have recorded on your computer.

Playing video clips can help you determine which clips you want to include in your movie.

PLAY A VIDEO CLIP

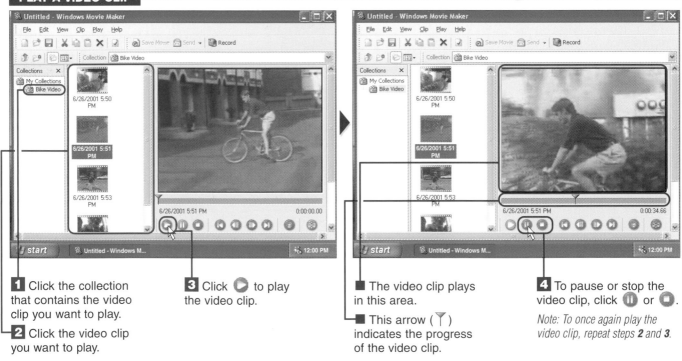

1 Click the collection that contains the video clip you want to play.

2 Click the video clip you want to play.

3 Click ▶ to play the video clip.

■ The video clip plays in this area.

■ This arrow (⊤) indicates the progress of the video clip.

4 To pause or stop the video clip, click ❚❚ or ■.

Note: To once again play the video clip, repeat steps 2 and 3.

ADD A VIDEO CLIP TO THE STORYBOARD

You must add each video clip that you want to include in your movie to the storyboard.

The storyboard displays the order in which video clips will play in your movie.

ADD A VIDEO CLIP TO THE STORYBOARD

1 Click the collection that contains the video clip you want to add to the storyboard.

2 Click the video clip you want to add.

3 Click **Clip**.

4 Click **Add To Storyboard/Timeline**.

■ The video clip appears on the storyboard.

■ You can repeat steps **1** to **4** for each video clip you want to add to the storyboard.

REMOVE A VIDEO CLIP

1 Click the video clip on the storyboard that you want to remove. Then press the Delete key.

Note: Deleting a video clip from the storyboard will not remove the video clip from Windows Movie Maker.

REARRANGE VIDEO CLIPS ON THE STORYBOARD

You can change
the order of the
video clips on
the storyboard to
change the order
in which the clips
will play in your
movie.

REARRANGE VIDEO CLIPS ON THE STORYBOARD

1 Position the mouse
over the video clip on the
storyboard that you want
to move to a different
location.

2 Drag the video clip
to a new location on the
storyboard. A vertical
bar indicates where the
video clip will appear.

■ The video clip appears
in the new location.

■ The surrounding video
clips automatically move
to make room for the
video clip.

You can save
a project so
you can later
review and
make changes
to the project.

A project is a rough
draft of your movie that
contains all the video
clips you added to the
storyboard. You should
regularly save changes
you make to a project to
avoid losing your work.

SAVE A PROJECT

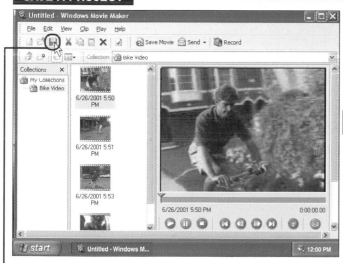

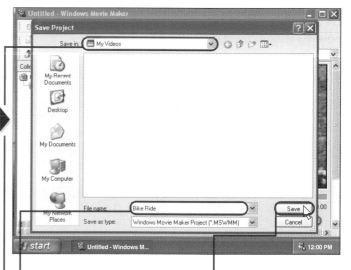

1 Click ▣ to save
your project.

■ The Save Project
dialog box appears.

*Note: If you previously saved
your project, the Save Project
dialog box will not appear
since you have already named
the project.*

2 Type a name for your
project.

■ This area shows the
location where Windows
Movie Maker will store your
project. You can click this
area to change the location.

3 Click **Save** to save
your project.

OPEN A PROJECT

You can open a saved project to display the video clips in the project. Opening a project allows you to review and make changes to the project.

A project is a rough draft of your movie that contains all the video clips you added to the storyboard.

You can work with only one project at a time. If you are currently working with a project, make sure you save the project before opening another project. To save a project, see page 165.

OPEN A PROJECT

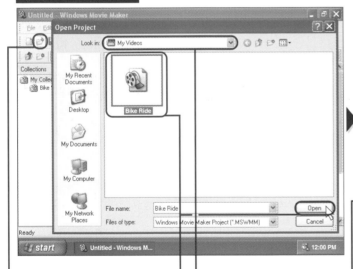

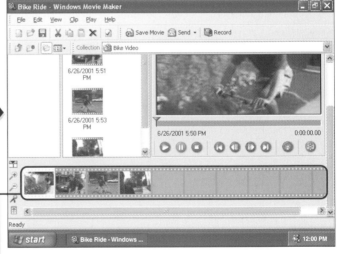

1 Click 📂 to open a project.

■ The Open Project dialog box appears.

■ This area shows the location of the displayed projects. You can click this area to change the location.

2 Click the name of the project you want to open.

3 Click **Open** to open the project.

■ The project opens and the video clips in the project appear on the storyboard. You can now review and make changes to the project.

You can preview
all the video clips
you have added
to the storyboard
as a movie.

PREVIEW A MOVIE

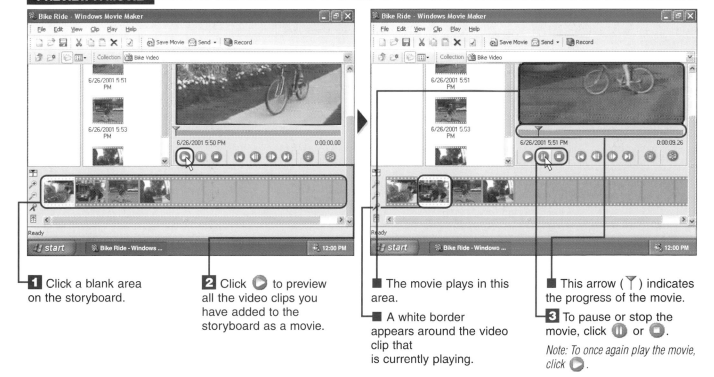

1 Click a blank area
on the storyboard.

2 Click ▶ to preview
all the video clips you
have added to the
storyboard as a movie.

■ The movie plays in this
area.

■ A white border
appears around the video
clip that
is currently playing.

■ This arrow (▽) indicates
the progress of the movie.

3 To pause or stop the
movie, click ⏸ or ⏹.

*Note: To once again play the movie,
click ▶ .*

SAVE A MOVIE

After you add all the video clips that you want to include in your movie to the storyboard, you can save the movie on your computer.

Saving a movie allows you to play the movie at any time and share the movie with friends and family.

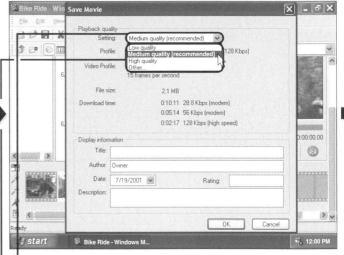

1 Click **Save Movie** to save the video clips on the storyboard as a movie.

■ The Save Movie dialog box appears.

2 Click this area to display a list of the quality settings that you can use for the movie.

3 Click the quality setting you want to use.

Note: Higher quality settings result in larger movie file sizes. Make sure you do not select a higher quality setting than you used to record your video.

r you save
ovie on
computer,
can view
novie in
lows Media
r.

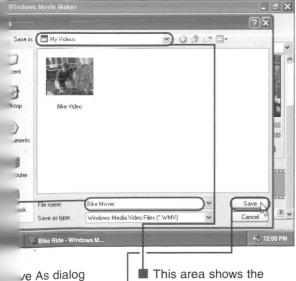

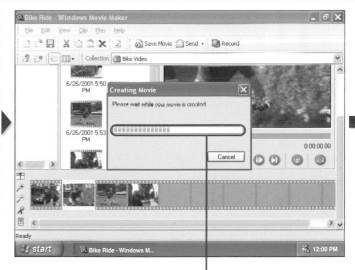

ve As dialog
rs.

name for

■ This area shows the location where Windows Movie Maker will store the movie. You can click this area to change the location.

7 Click **Save** to save the movie.

■ The Creating Movie dialog box appears while Windows Movie Maker creates your movie.

■ This area shows the progress of the creation of the movie.

How can I share a movie with friends and family?

Publish a Movie to the Web

You can publish a movie to the Web to allow people to view the movie. To publish a movie to the Web, see page 72.

Send a Movie in an E-mail Message

You can send a movie in an e-mail message. You should try to keep your movies under 2 MB (2,000 KB) since most companies that provide e-mail accounts limit the size of the messages that you can send and receive over the Internet. To send a movie in an e-mail message, see page 70.

Copy a Movie

If you have a r
drive, you can
from your com
You can then
with other pe
movie to a C

Aft
a n
you
you
the
Win
Play

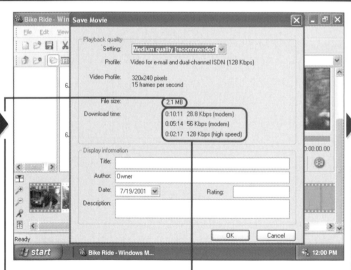

■ This area displays the file size of the movie.

■ This area displays the estimated amount of time the movie will take to transfer over the Internet using three different types of Internet connections.

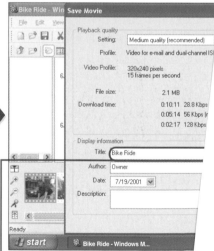

4 Click this area and type a title for the movie.

Note: People who view your movie in Windows Media Player will be able to view the title you enter.

■ The S
box appe

6 Type a
the movie

How can I later play a movie I have saved?

Windows automatically stores your movies in the My Videos folder, which is a subfolder within the My Documents folder. You can double-click a movie in the My Videos folder to play the movie. To view the contents of the My Documents folder, see page 40.

Can I make changes to a movie I have saved?

No. You cannot make changes to a movie you have saved. Windows Movie Maker only allows you to make changes to a project, which is a rough draft of a movie. To open a project, see page 166.

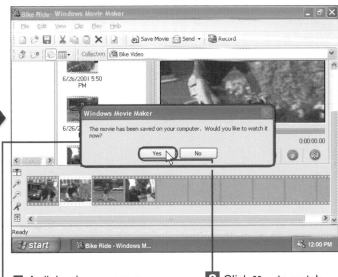

■ A dialog box appears when Windows Movie Maker has finished creating and saving your movie.

8 Click **Yes** to watch the movie now.

*Note: If you do not want to watch the movie now, click **No**.*

■ The Windows Media Player window appears.

■ The movie plays in this area.

9 To pause or stop the movie, click (❙❙) or (■) ((❙❙) changes to (▶)).

Note: To once again play the movie, click (▶).

10 When you finish viewing the movie, click ✖ to close the Windows Media Player window.

CHAPTER 9

Share Your Computer

If you share your computer with one or more people, you can create user accounts so each person can use their own personalized files and settings. In this chapter, you will learn how to create and work with the user accounts on your computer.

CREATE A USER ACCOUNT

If you share your computer with other people, you can create a personalized user account for each person.

You must have a computer administrator account to create a user account. For information on the types of accounts, see page 176.

CREATE A USER ACCOUNT

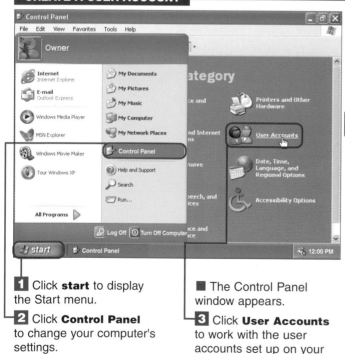

1 Click **start** to display the Start menu.

2 Click **Control Panel** to change your computer's settings.

■ The Control Panel window appears.

3 Click **User Accounts** to work with the user accounts set up on your computer.

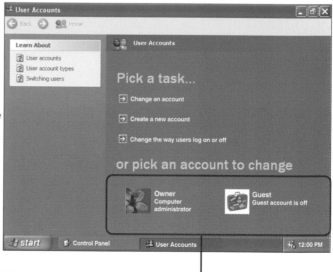

■ The User Accounts window appears.

■ This area displays the user accounts that are currently set up on your computer.

Will Windows keep my personal files separate from the files of other users?

Yes. Windows will keep your personal files separate from the personal files created by other users. For example, your My Documents folder displays only the files you have created. Internet Explorer also keeps your lists of recently visited Web pages and favorite Web pages separate from the lists of other users.

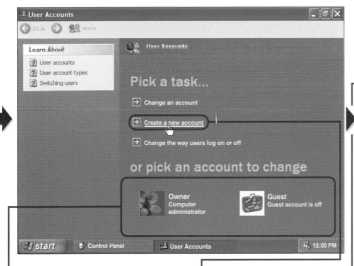

How can I personalize Windows for my user account?

You can personalize the appearance of Windows for your user account by changing the screen saver, desktop background and many other computer settings.

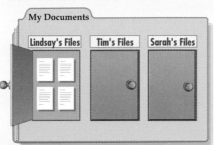

■ Windows automatically creates the Owner and Guest accounts on your computer.

■ The Owner account is a computer administrator account. The Guest account allows a person without a user account to use the computer.

Note: If user accounts were created when Windows was installed on your computer, the first user account created replaced the Owner account.

4 Click **Create a new account**.

5 Type a name for the new account.

Note: The name will appear on the Welcome screen when you log on to Windows and at the top of your Start menu.

6 Click **Next** to continue.

CONTINUED

CREATE A USER ACCOUNT

When you create a user account, you must select the type of account you want to create.

Computer Administrator

The user can perform any task on the computer. For example, the user can create and change all user accounts as well as install programs and hardware.

Limited

The user can perform only certain tasks on the computer. For example, the user can create and change their own password and change some computer settings but cannot delete important files.

CREATE A USER ACCOUNT (CONTINUED)

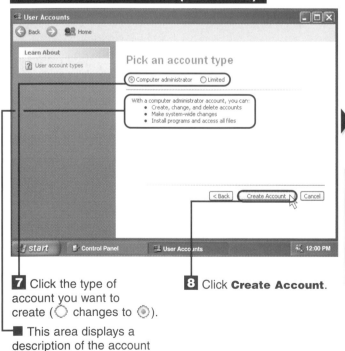

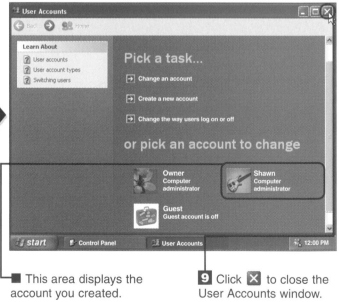

7 Click the type of account you want to create (○ changes to ◉).

■ This area displays a description of the account type you selected.

8 Click **Create Account**.

■ This area displays the account you created.

9 Click ☒ to close the User Accounts window.

DELETE A USER ACCOUNT

If a person no longer uses your computer, you can delete the person's user account from your computer.

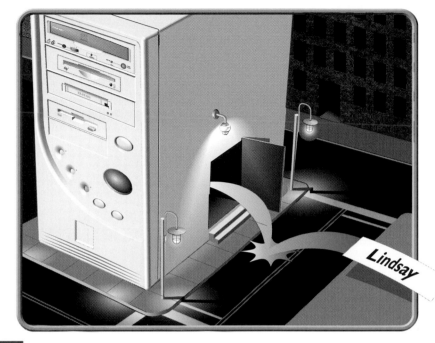

You must have a computer administrator account to delete a user account. For information on the types of accounts, see page 176.

DELETE A USER ACCOUNT

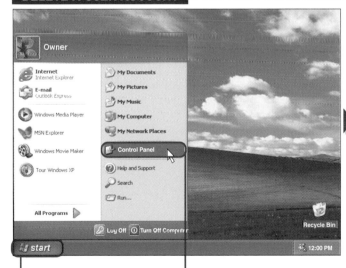

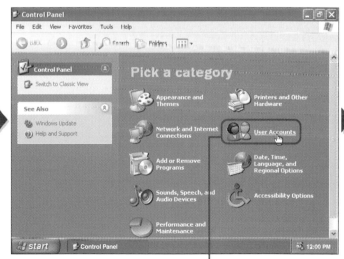

1 Click **start** to display the Start menu.

2 Click **Control Panel** to change your computer's settings.

■ The Control Panel window appears.

3 Click **User Accounts** to work with the user accounts set up on your computer.

CONTINUED

DELETE A USER ACCOUNT

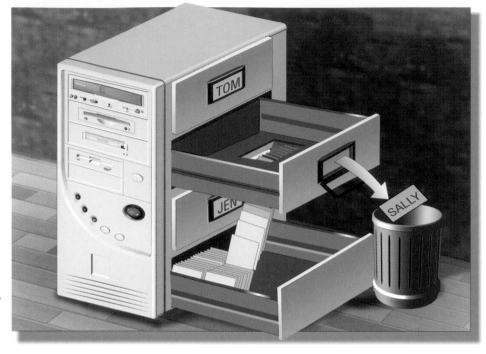

When you delete a user account, you can choose to keep or delete the user's personal files.

If you choose to delete a user's personal files, Windows will permanently delete the files from your computer.

DELETE A USER ACCOUNT (CONTINUED)

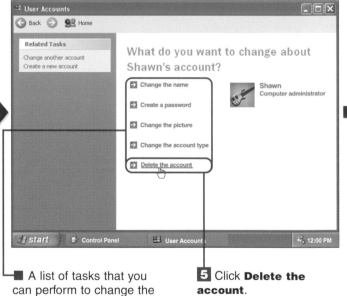

■ The User Accounts window appears.

■ This area displays the accounts that are set up on your computer.

4 Click the account you want to delete.

Note: You cannot delete the Guest account, which allows a person without a user account to use your computer.

■ A list of tasks that you can perform to change the user account appears.

5 Click **Delete the account**.

If I choose to keep the personal files for a deleted user account, which files will Windows save?

Windows will save the user's personal files that are displayed on the desktop and stored in the My Documents folder. The files will be saved on your desktop in a new folder that has the same name as the deleted account. Windows will not save the user's e-mail messages, list of favorite Web pages and other computer settings.

Can I delete a computer administrator account?

Yes. If you have a computer administrator account, you can delete other computer administrator accounts. Windows will not allow you to delete the last computer administrator account on your computer. This ensures that one computer administrator account always exists on the computer.

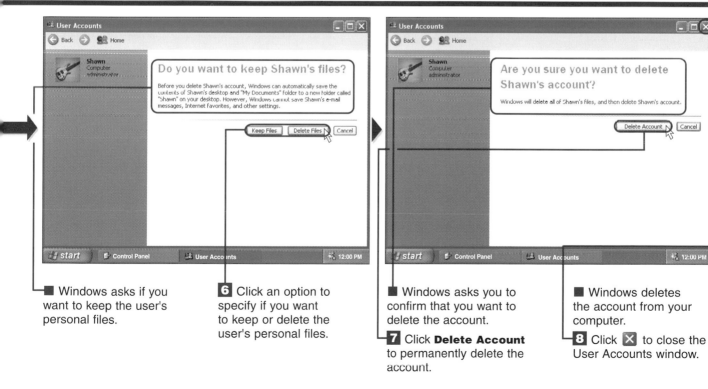

■ Windows asks if you want to keep the user's personal files.

6 Click an option to specify if you want to keep or delete the user's personal files.

■ Windows asks you to confirm that you want to delete the account.

7 Click **Delete Account** to permanently delete the account.

■ Windows deletes the account from your computer.

8 Click ☒ to close the User Accounts window.

ASSIGN A PASSWORD TO A USER ACCOUNT

You can assign a password to your user account to prevent other people from accessing the account. You will need to enter the password each time you want to use Windows.

You should choose a password that is at least seven characters long and contains a random combination of letters, numbers and symbols. Do not use words that people can easily associate with you, such as your name.

If you have a computer administrator account, you can assign passwords to all accounts. If you have a limited account, you can assign a password only to your own account. For information on the types of accounts, see page 176.

ASSIGN A PASSWORD TO A USER ACCOUNT

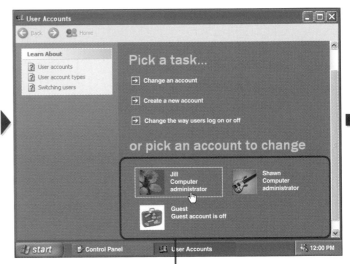

1 Click **start** to display the Start menu.

2 Click **Control Panel** to change your computer's settings.

■ The Control Panel window appears.

3 Click **User Accounts** to work with the user accounts set up on your computer.

■ The User Accounts window appears.

■ If you have a limited account, skip to step **5**.

■ If you have a computer administrator account, this area displays the accounts set up on your computer.

4 Click the account you want to assign a password to.

When assigning a password to my user account, why does Windows ask if I want to make my files and folders private?

When you assign a password to your user account, other users can still access your files and folders. If you do not want other people to have access to your files and folders, you can make your files and folders private. Click **Yes, Make Private** or **No** to specify if you want to make your files and folders private. For more information on making your files and folders private, see page 186.

How can I change the password I assigned to my user account?

To change your password, perform steps **1** to **5** below, except click **Change my password** in step **5**. Then type your current password and perform steps **6** to **9** below, except click **Change Password** in step **9**.

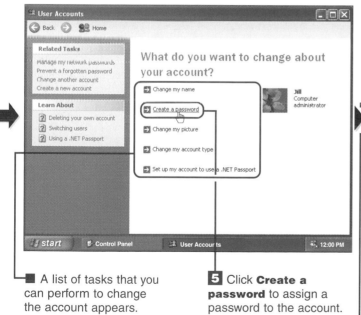

■ A list of tasks that you can perform to change the account appears.

5 Click **Create a password** to assign a password to the account.

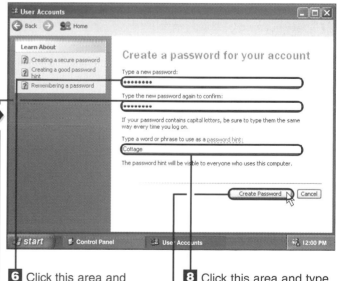

6 Click this area and type a password for the account.

7 Click this area and type the password again to confirm the password.

8 Click this area and type a word or phrase that can help you remember the password. This information will be available to everyone who uses the computer.

9 Click **Create Password**.

LOG OFF WINDOWS

You can log off Windows so another person can log on to Windows to use the computer.

When you log off Windows, you can choose to keep your programs and files open while another person uses the computer. This allows you to quickly return to your programs and files after the other person finishes using the computer.

LOG OFF WINDOWS

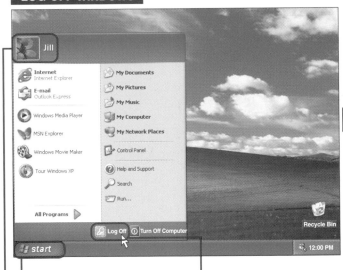

1 Click **start** to display the Start menu.

■ This area displays the name of the current user account.

2 Click **Log Off** to log off Windows.

■ The Log Off Windows dialog box appears.

3 Click one of the following options.

Switch User
Log off Windows, keeping your programs and files open.

Log Off
Log off Windows, closing your open programs and files.

■ The Welcome screen appears, allowing another person to log on to Windows to use the computer. To log on to Windows, see page 183.

If you have set up
user accounts on your
computer, you will
need to log on to
Windows to use the
computer.

You must log on to Windows
each time you turn on your
computer or log off Windows
to switch between user
accounts. For information
on logging off Windows,
see page 182.

LOG ON TO WINDOWS

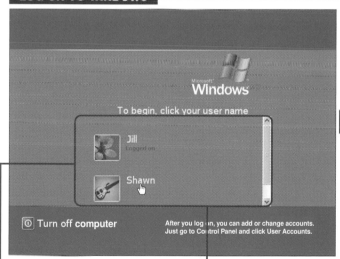

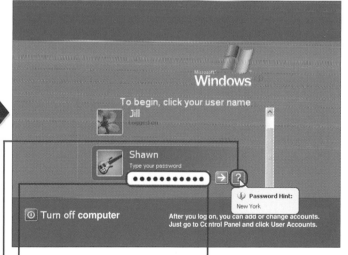

■ When you turn on your
computer or log off Windows
to switch between user
accounts, the Welcome
screen appears.

■ This area displays the
user accounts set up on
your computer.

1 Click the name of
your user account.

■ If you assigned a password
to your user account, a box
appears that allows you to
enter your password.

■ If you cannot remember
your password, click ? to
display the password hint you
entered when you created the
password.

2 Click this area and
type your password. Then
press the Enter key to
log on to Windows.

■ Windows starts,
displaying your own
personalized files and
computer settings.

VIEW SHARED FILES

You can view the personal files of every user set up on your computer.

In most cases, the contents of every user's My Documents folder and its subfolders are available to other users set up on your computer.

If your computer uses the NTFS file system, you cannot view the personal files of other users if you have a limited user account or a user has made their personal folders private. For information on making personal folders private, see page 186.

VIEW SHARED FILES

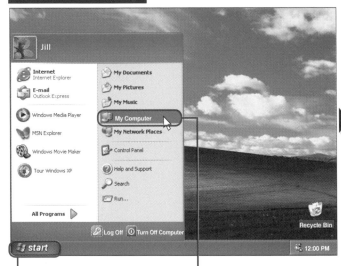

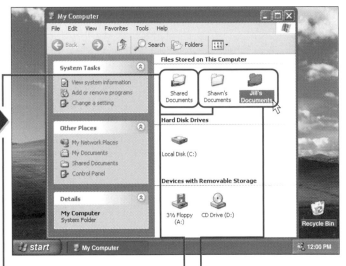

1 Click **start** to display the Start menu.

2 Click **My Computer** to view the contents of your computer.

■ The My Computer window appears.

■ The Shared Documents folder contains files that users have selected to share with all other users set up on your computer.

■ This area displays a folder for each user set up on your computer. Each folder contains a user's personal files.

3 To display the contents of a folder, double-click the folder.

SHARE FILES

If you want to share files with every user set up on your computer, you can copy the files to the Shared Documents folder.

Copying files to the Shared Documents folder is useful when you want to share files that are not stored in the My Documents folder or if your computer uses the NTFS file system and other users are restricted from viewing the contents of your My Documents folder.

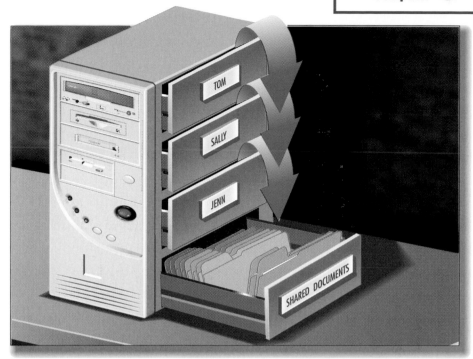

SHARE FILES

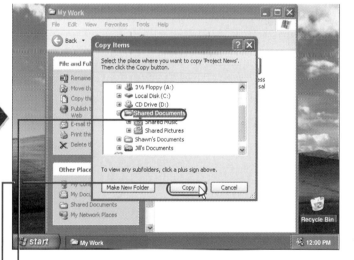

1 Click the file you want to share with every user set up on your computer.

■ To share more than one file, select all the files you want to share. To select multiple files, see page 52.

2 Click **Copy this file**.

*Note: If you selected multiple files, click **Copy the selected items** in step 2.*

■ The Copy Items dialog box appears.

3 Click **Shared Documents**.

4 Click **Copy** to copy the file.

■ Windows places a copy of the file in the Shared Documents folder. The file is now available to every user set up on your computer.

Note: If you no longer want to share a file, delete the file from the Shared Documents folder. To view the contents of the Shared Documents folder, see page 184. To delete a file, see page 62.

MAKE YOUR PERSONAL FOLDERS PRIVATE

You can make the contents of your personal folders private so that only you can access the files within the folders. Your personal folders include the My Documents folder and its subfolders.

You can make your personal folders private only if your computer uses the NTFS file system. The file system is typically determined when you install Windows.

If your computer uses the NTFS file system, the contents of your personal folders are available to every user with an administrator account set up on your computer.

MAKE YOUR PERSONAL FOLDERS PRIVATE

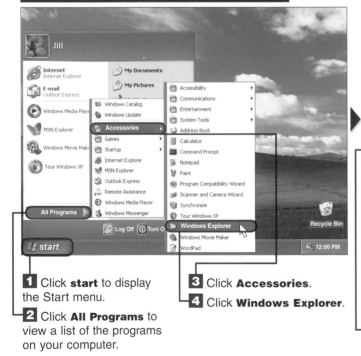

1 Click **start** to display the Start menu.

2 Click **All Programs** to view a list of the programs on your computer.

3 Click **Accessories**.

4 Click **Windows Explorer**.

■ A window appears, allowing you to view the contents of your computer.

■ This area displays the organization of the folders on your computer.

5 Click the **My Documents** folder to specify that you want to make the contents of this folder private.

Note: To make just one subfolder within the My Documents folder private, click the subfolder you want to make private.

What do I need to consider before making my personal folders private?

Before making your personal folders private, you should assign a password to your user account. If you do not assign a password to your user account, anyone will be able to log on to your account and view the contents of your personal folders even if you make the folders private. To assign a password to your user account, see page 180.

After making my personal folders private, can I share just one file in the folders?

Yes. To share a specific file with every user set up on your computer, you need to place a copy of the file in the Shared Documents folder. The Shared Documents folder contains files that every user set up on your computer can access. For information on the Shared Documents folder, see page 185.

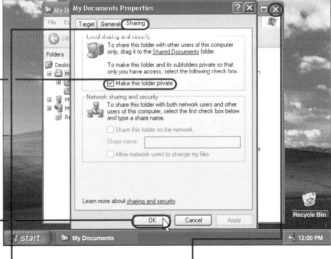

6 Click **File**.

7 Click **Properties**.

■ The My Documents Properties dialog box appears.

8 Click the **Sharing** tab.

9 Click **Make this folder private** to make the My Documents folder and all its files and subfolders private (☐ changes to ☑).

10 Click **OK** to confirm your change.

11 Click ✕ to close the Windows Explorer window.

■ If you no longer want to make your personal folders private, perform steps **1** to **11** (☑ changes to ☐ in step **9**).

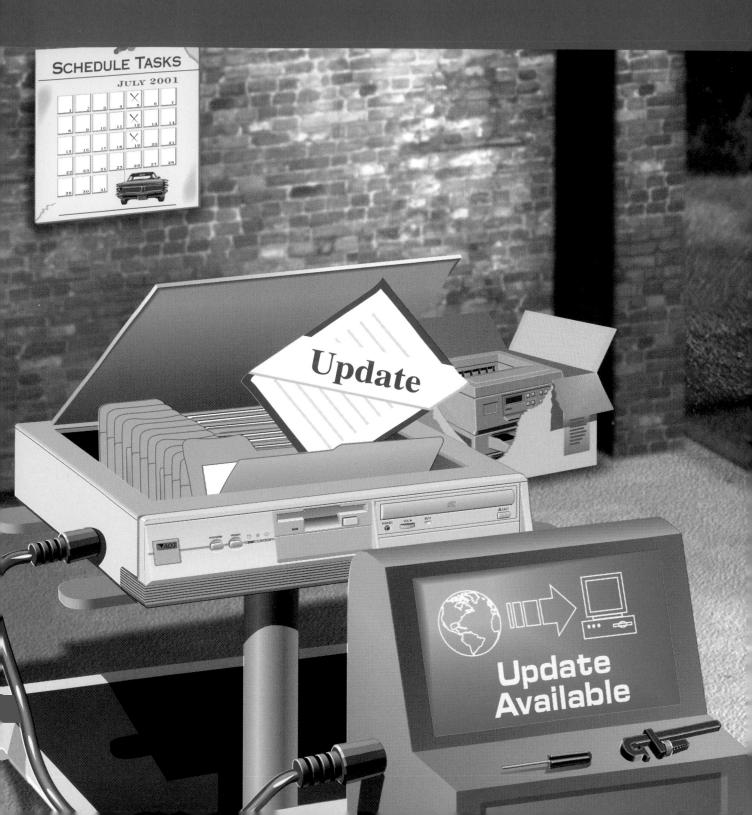

CHAPTER 10

Optimize Computer Performance

Read this chapter to discover several ways to enhance the overall performance of your computer. Learn how to install programs, obtain the latest Windows XP updates, schedule tasks and solve computer problems.

INSTALL A PROGRAM

You can install a
new program on
your computer.
Programs are
available on
CD-ROM discs
and floppy
disks.

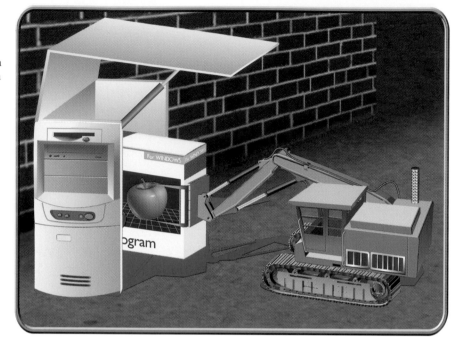

You can only
use the method
below to install
programs
designed for
Windows.

After you install a
new program, make
sure you keep the
program's CD-ROM
disc or floppy disks
in a safe place. If
your computer fails
or you accidentally
erase the program's
files, you may
need to install the
program again.

INSTALL A PROGRAM

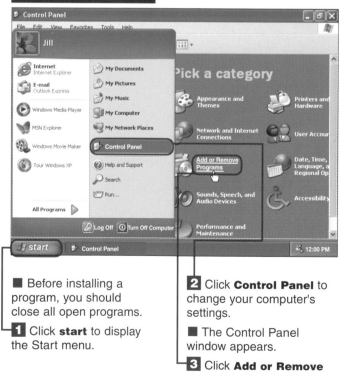

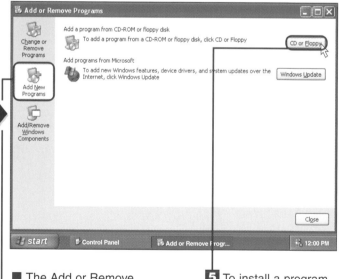

■ Before installing a
program, you should
close all open programs.

1 Click **start** to display
the Start menu.

2 Click **Control Panel** to
change your computer's
settings.

■ The Control Panel
window appears.

3 Click **Add or Remove
Programs**.

■ The Add or Remove
Programs window appears.

4 Click **Add New Programs**
to install a new program.

5 To install a program
from a CD-ROM disc or
floppy disk, click **CD or
Floppy**.

Why did an installation program appear when I inserted a program's CD-ROM disc into my CD-ROM drive?

Most Windows programs available on a CD-ROM disc will automatically start an installation program when you insert the disc into your CD-ROM drive. Follow the instructions on your screen to install the program.

How can I install a program I obtained on the Internet?

You can obtain many useful programs on the Internet, such as at the www.shareware.com Web site. To install a program you obtained on the Internet, locate the program's files on your computer and then double-click the file that allows you to install the program. The file is usually named **install**, **setup** or the name of the program.

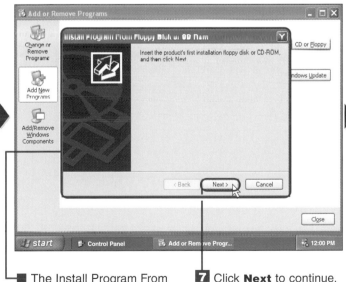

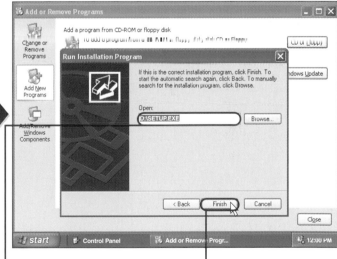

■ The Install Program From Floppy Disk or CD-ROM dialog box appears.

6 Insert the program's first installation floppy disk or CD-ROM disc into the appropriate drive on your computer.

7 Click **Next** to continue.

■ The Run Installation Program dialog box appears.

■ This area displays the location and name of the installation program that Windows will run to install the program.

8 Click **Finish** to install the program.

9 Follow the instructions on your screen. Every program will ask you a different set of questions.

REMOVE A PROGRAM

You can remove a program you no longer use from your computer. Removing a program will free up space on your computer.

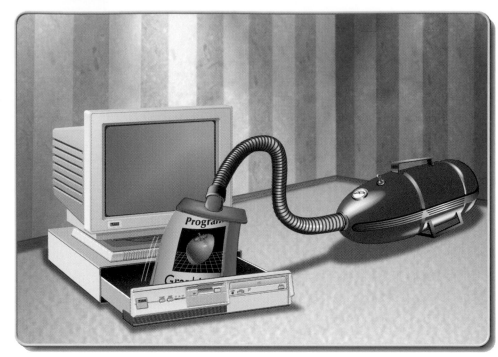

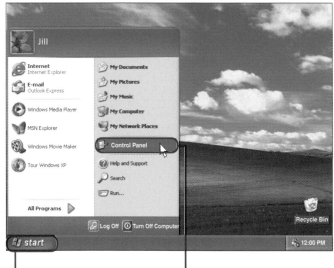

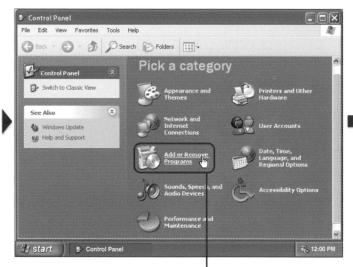

1 Click **start** to display the Start menu.

2 Click **Control Panel** to change your computer's settings.

■ The Control Panel window appears.

3 Click **Add or Remove Programs**.

Why doesn't the program I want to remove appear in the Add or Remove Programs window?

You can only use the Add or Remove Programs window to remove programs designed for Windows. For all other programs, you can check the documentation supplied with the program to determine how to remove the program from your computer. You can also purchase an uninstall program, such as Norton CleanSweep, that will help you delete unwanted programs from your computer.

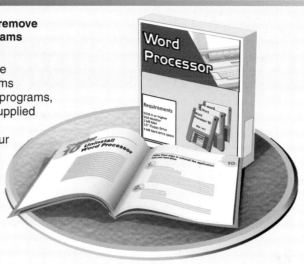

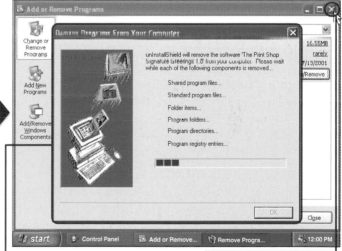

■ The Add or Remove Programs window appears.

■ This area lists the programs installed on your computer.

4 Click the name of the program you want to remove.

5 Click **Change/Remove** or **Remove**.

Note: The name of the button depends on the program you are removing.

■ Windows begins the process of removing the program from your computer.

6 Follow the instructions on your screen. Every program will take you through different steps to remove the program.

7 When Windows has successfully removed the program, click ✕ to close the Add or Remove Programs window.

UPDATE WINDOWS

You can set up Windows to automatically keep your computer up to date with the latest Windows updates available on the Internet.

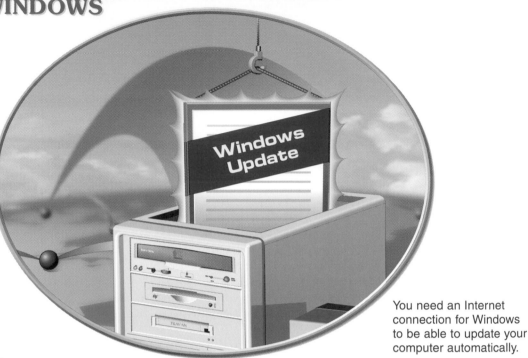

You need an Internet connection for Windows to be able to update your computer automatically.

UPDATE WINDOWS

SET UP AUTOMATIC UPDATES

■ An icon (🌐) and message appear when you can set up Windows to update your computer automatically.

1 Click the icon (🌐) to set up Windows to update your computer automatically.

Note: If 🌐 is hidden, you can click ◀ on the taskbar to display the icon.

■ The Automatic Updates Setup Wizard appears, allowing you to set up Windows to update your computer automatically.

■ This area displays information about updating your computer automatically.

2 Click **Next** to continue.

194

How will Windows update my computer?

Windows will use the latest information available on the Internet to check for outdated Windows software on your computer. To improve the performance of your computer, Windows can update existing software, fix software problems and add new software. Windows can also obtain updated help information and drivers. A driver is software that enables your computer to communicate with a hardware device, such as a printer.

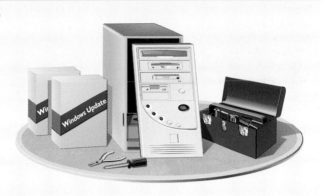

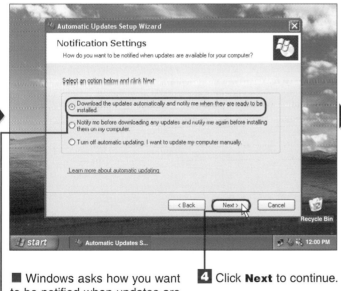

■ Windows asks how you want to be notified when updates are available for your computer.

3 Click this option to have Windows download the updates to your computer automatically and notify you when they are ready to be installed (○ changes to ◉).

4 Click **Next** to continue.

■ This message appears when you have successfully completed the wizard.

5 Click **Finish** to close the wizard.

■ Windows is now set up to update your computer automatically. When you are connected to the Internet, Windows will notify you when updates are available for your computer.

CONTINUED

UPDATE WINDOWS

When you are connected to the Internet, Windows will automatically check for updates that apply to your computer and will notify you when the updates are ready to be installed.

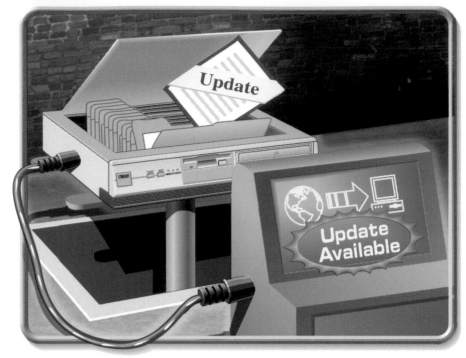

INSTALL UPDATES

■ When you are connected to the Internet, an icon (🌐) and message appear when updates have been downloaded and are ready to be installed on your computer.

1 Click the icon (🌐) to install the recommended updates.

Note: If 🌐 is hidden, you can click 🔽 on the taskbar to display the icon.

■ The Automatic Updates wizard appears, stating that Windows is ready to install the recommended updates for your computer.

■ This area indicates that some updates require you to restart your computer. Before continuing, make sure you save your work and close any open programs.

2 Click **Install** to install the updates.

196

Is there another way that I can update Windows?

You can install specific updates from the Windows Update Web site. The Windows Update Web site can scan your computer to determine which updates you can install to update Windows. To display the Windows Update Web site, perform the following steps.

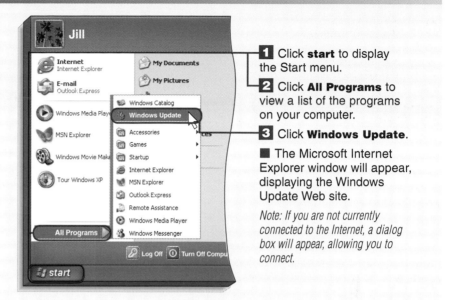

1 Click **start** to display the Start menu.

2 Click **All Programs** to view a list of the programs on your computer.

3 Click **Windows Update**.

■ The Microsoft Internet Explorer window will appear, displaying the Windows Update Web site.

Note: If you are not currently connected to the Internet, a dialog box will appear, allowing you to connect.

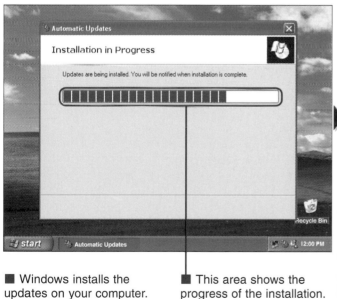

■ Windows installs the updates on your computer.

■ This area shows the progress of the installation.

■ This message appears if you need to restart your computer to complete the installation.

3 Click **Yes** to restart your computer and complete the installation.

*Note: If the "Installation Complete" message appears, you do not need to restart your computer. Click **OK** to complete the installation.*

INSTALL A PRINTER

Before you can use a printer attached to your computer, you need to install the printer on your computer. You need to install a printer only once.

Windows provides a wizard that guides you step by step through the process of installing a printer.

Before installing a printer, make sure you connect the printer to your computer and turn on the printer.

INSTALL A PRINTER

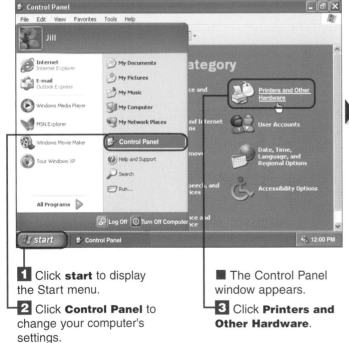

1 Click **start** to display the Start menu.

2 Click **Control Panel** to change your computer's settings.

■ The Control Panel window appears.

3 Click **Printers and Other Hardware**.

■ The Printers and Other Hardware window appears.

4 Click **View installed printers or fax printers**.

Why do I need to install a printer?

Installing a printer allows you to install the printer driver that Windows needs to work with the printer. A printer driver is special software that enables Windows to communicate with a printer.

How do I install a Plug and Play printer?

A Plug and Play printer is a printer that Windows can automatically detect and install. Most new printers are Plug and Play. The first time you connect a Plug and Play printer to your computer and turn on the printer, Windows will usually install the printer without requiring you to make any selections. In some cases, the Found New Hardware Wizard appears, displaying instructions you can follow to install the printer.

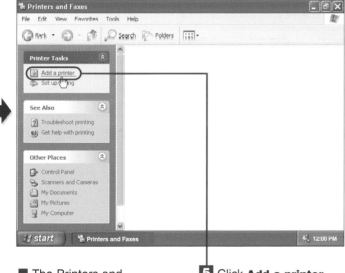

■ The Printers and Faxes window appears.

5 Click **Add a printer** to install a new printer.

■ The Add Printer Wizard appears.

■ This area describes how you can install a Plug and Play printer without using the wizard. For more information on installing a Plug and Play printer, see the top of this page.

6 Click **Next** to continue.

CONTINUED

INSTALL A PRINTER

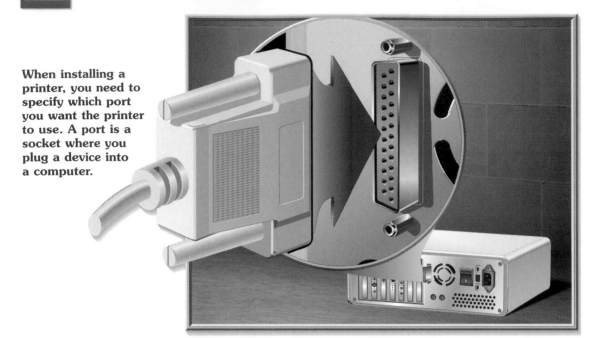

When installing a printer, you need to specify which port you want the printer to use. A port is a socket where you plug a device into a computer.

Ports are usually located at the back of a computer and allow a computer to communicate with the connected devices.

INSTALL A PRINTER (CONTINUED)

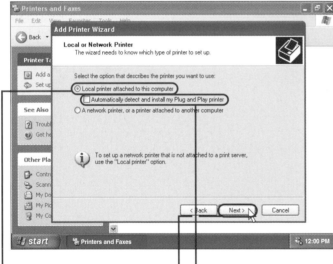

■ The wizard asks how the printer connects to your computer.

7 Click this option to install a printer that connects directly to your computer (○ changes to ◉).

8 If you do not want Windows to automatically detect and install a Plug and Play printer connected to your computer, click this option (☑ changes to ☐).

9 Click **Next** to continue.

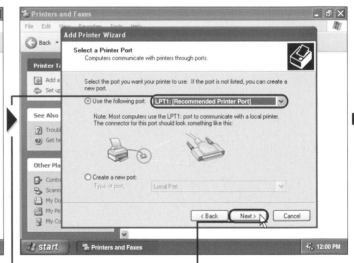

10 This area displays the port your printer will use to communicate with your computer. You can click this area to select a different port.

Note: Most printers use the LPT1 port.

11 Click **Next** to continue.

What should I do if the printer I want to install does not appear in the list?

If the printer you want to install does not appear in the list of printers in step **13** below, you can use the installation disk that came with your printer.

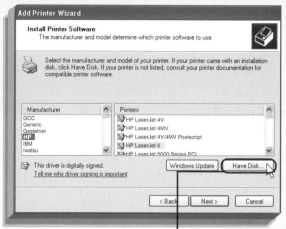

1 Insert the installation floppy disk or CD-ROM disc into the appropriate drive on your computer.

2 Click **Have Disk** to use the installation disk to install the printer.

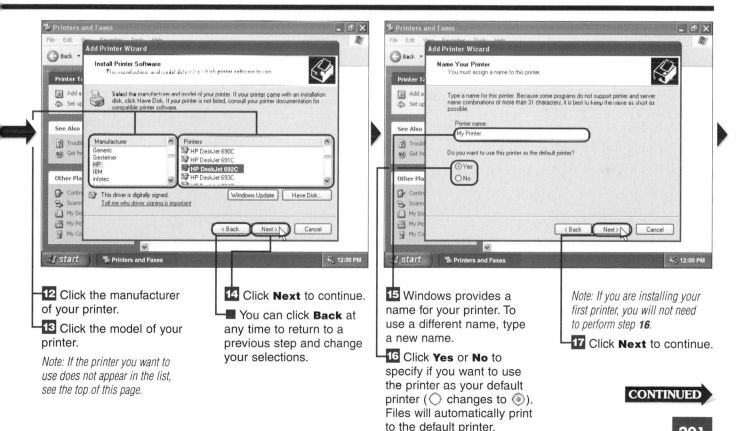

12 Click the manufacturer of your printer.

13 Click the model of your printer.

Note: If the printer you want to use does not appear in the list, see the top of this page.

14 Click **Next** to continue.

■ You can click **Back** at any time to return to a previous step and change your selections.

15 Windows provides a name for your printer. To use a different name, type a new name.

16 Click **Yes** or **No** to specify if you want to use the printer as your default printer (○ changes to ●). Files will automatically print to the default printer.

*Note: If you are installing your first printer, you will not need to perform step **16**.*

17 Click **Next** to continue.

CONTINUED

INSTALL A PRINTER

If your computer is set up on a network, you can share your printer with other people on the network. Sharing a printer allows other people to use your printer to print documents.

Sharing a printer allows individuals and companies to save money since several people on a network can use the same printer.

INSTALL A PRINTER (CONTINUED)

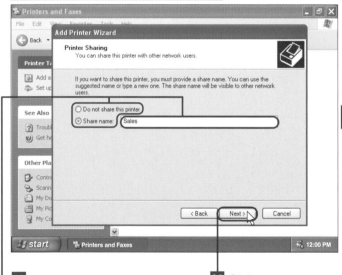

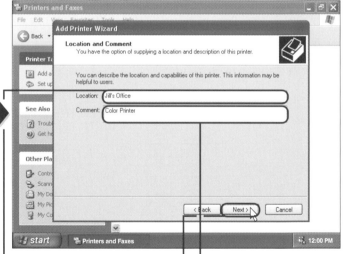

18 Click an option to specify if you want to share the printer on your network (⭕ changes to ◉).

19 If you selected to share the printer, this area displays the printer name people will see on the network. To use a different printer name, type a new name.

20 Click **Next** to continue.

■ If you chose not to share your printer in step **18**, skip to step **24**.

■ Windows allows you to enter information about your printer that can be helpful to other people on your network.

21 Click this area and type the location of your printer.

22 Click this area and type a comment about your printer, such as its capabilities.

23 Click **Next** to continue.

How can I view the printer I installed on my computer?

The Printers and Faxes window displays an icon for the printer you installed on your computer. If you chose to share your printer with other people on your network, a hand (📇) appears in the icon for the shared printer. The Printers and Faxes window may also display an icon for each printer on your network that is available for you to use. To view the Printers and Faxes window, perform steps **1** to **4** on page 198.

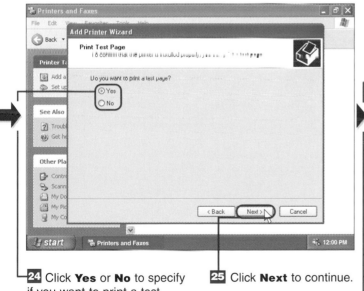

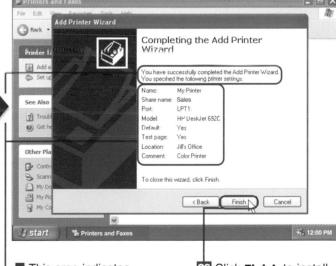

24 Click **Yes** or **No** to specify if you want to print a test page (○ changes to ◉).

Note: A test page will confirm that your printer is installed properly. If you choose to print a test page, make sure your printer is turned on.

25 Click **Next** to continue.

■ This area indicates that you have successfully completed the wizard.

■ This area displays the settings you selected for your printer.

26 Click **Finish** to install the printer.

*Note: If you chose to print a test page in step **24**, a dialog box will appear, confirming that the test page printed correctly. Click **OK** if the test page printed correctly.*

VIEW AMOUNT OF DISK SPACE

You can view the amount of used and free space on a disk.

You should check the amount of free space on your computer's hard disk (C:) at least once a month. Your computer will operate most effectively when at least 20% of your total hard disk space is free.

You may also want to check the amount of free space on your computer's hard disk before installing a program that requires a lot of disk space.

VIEW AMOUNT OF DISK SPACE

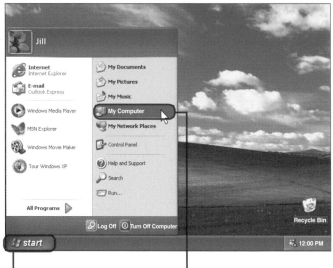

1 Click **start** to display the Start menu.

2 Click **My Computer**.

■ The My Computer window appears.

3 To view the amount of space on a disk, click the disk of interest.

Note: To view the amount of space on a floppy disk or CD-ROM disc, you must insert the disk into the appropriate drive before performing step 3.

4 Click **File**.

5 Click **Properties**.

How can I increase the amount of free space on my hard disk?

Delete Files

Delete files you no longer need from your computer. To delete files, see page 62.

Use Disk Cleanup

Use Disk Cleanup to remove unnecessary files from your computer. To use Disk Cleanup, see page 210.

Remove Programs

Remove programs you no longer use from your computer. To remove programs, see page 192.

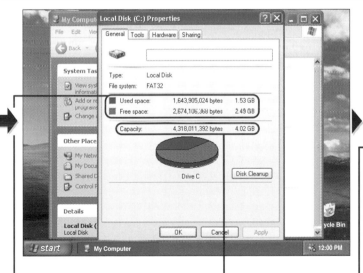

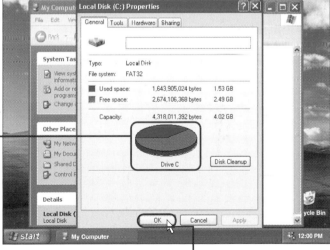

■ The Properties dialog box appears.

■ This area displays the amount of used and free space on the disk, in both bytes and gigabytes (GB).

■ This area displays the total disk storage space, in both bytes and gigabytes (GB).

■ The pie chart displays the amount of used and free space on the disk.

6 When you finish reviewing the information, click **OK** to close the Properties dialog box.

FORMAT A FLOPPY DISK

You must format a floppy disk before you can use the disk to store information.

Floppy disks you buy at computer stores are usually formatted. You may want to later format a floppy disk to erase the information it contains and prepare the disk for storing new information.

FORMAT A FLOPPY DISK

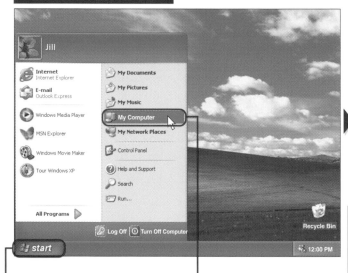

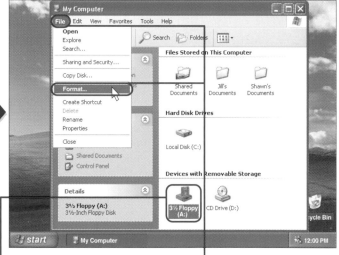

1 Insert the floppy disk you want to format into your floppy drive.

2 Click **start** to display the Start menu.

3 Click **My Computer**.

■ The My Computer window appears.

4 Click the drive that contains the floppy disk you want to format.

5 Click **File**.

6 Click **Format**.

206

How can I tell if a floppy disk is formatted?

Windows will display an error message when you try to view the contents of a floppy disk that is not formatted. The floppy disk may never have been formatted or the disk may have been formatted on a computer that uses a different file system than Windows, such as a Macintosh computer. You cannot tell if a floppy disk is formatted just by looking at the disk. To view the contents of a floppy disk, see page 42.

Why would I want to perform a quick format?

You can choose the Quick Format option if you want to remove all files from a floppy disk, but you do not want to check the disk for damaged areas. You should only use the Quick Format option on a floppy disk that was previously formatted and if you are sure the disk is not damaged.

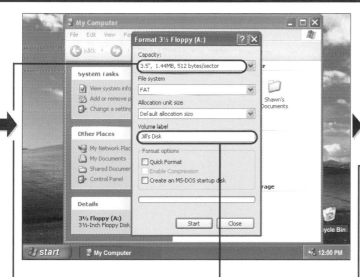

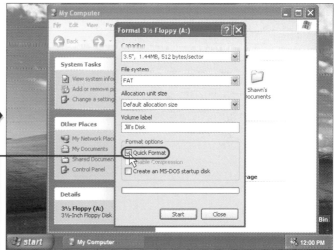

■ The Format dialog box appears.

■ This area displays the amount of information the floppy disk can store.

7 To specify a label for the floppy disk, click this area and type a label.

Note: A label can contain up to 11 characters.

8 If you want to perform a quick format, click this option (□ changes to ☑).

Note: For information on performing a quick format, see the top of this page.

CONTINUED

FORMAT A FLOPPY DISK

Before formatting a floppy disk, make sure the disk does not contain information you want to keep. Formatting a floppy disk will permanently remove all the information on the disk.

FORMAT A FLOPPY DISK (CONTINUED)

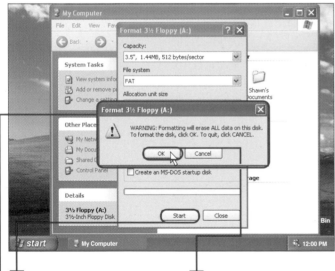

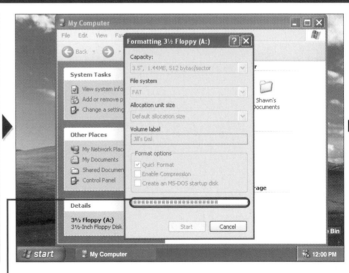

9 Click **Start** to begin formatting the floppy disk.

■ A warning message appears, indicating that formatting the floppy disk will erase all the information on the disk.

10 Click **OK** to continue.

*Note: To cancel the formatting of the floppy disk, click **Cancel**.*

■ This area displays the progress of the format.

Why does an error message appear when I try to format a floppy disk?

An error message will appear if files on the floppy disk are open or if the tab on the disk is in the write-protected position. You cannot change information on a floppy disk when its tab is in the write-protected position. To format the floppy disk, you will need to close any open files on the disk and move the tab on the disk to the non-write-protected position.

write-protected

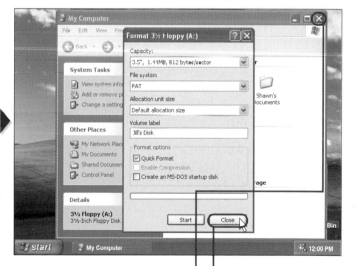

■ A dialog box appears when the format is complete.

11 Click **OK** to close the dialog box.

■ To format another floppy disk, insert the disk and then repeat steps **7** to **11** starting on page 207.

Note: You may want to format several floppy disks at one time so you always have formatted disks available when you need them.

12 Click **Close** to close the Format dialog box.

13 Click ☒ to close the My Computer window.

USING DISK CLEANUP

You can use Disk Cleanup to remove unnecessary files from your computer to free up disk space.

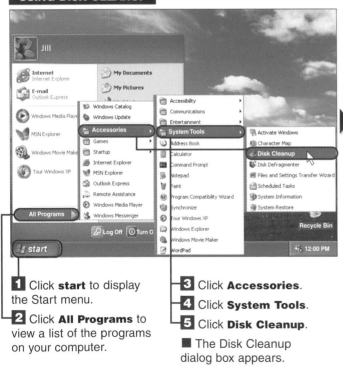

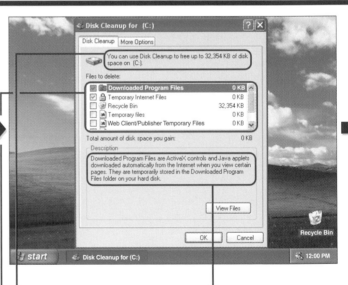

1 Click **start** to display the Start menu.

2 Click **All Programs** to view a list of the programs on your computer.

3 Click **Accessories**.

4 Click **System Tools**.

5 Click **Disk Cleanup**.

■ The Disk Cleanup dialog box appears.

■ This area displays the total amount of disk space you can free up.

■ This area displays the types of files Windows can delete and the amount of disk space each file type uses.

■ This area displays a description of the highlighted file type.

Note: To display a description for a different file type, click the file type.

What are some types of files that Disk Cleanup can remove?

	File Type	Description
	Downloaded Program Files	Program files transferred automatically from the Internet and stored on your computer when you view certain Web pages.
	Temporary Internet Files	Web pages stored on your computer for quick viewing.
	Recycle Bin	Stores files you have deleted from your computer.
	Temporary Files	Files created by programs to store temporary information.
	Web Client/Publisher Temporary Files	Copies of files you have recently accessed on your computer.
	Catalog Files for the Content Indexer	Files previously used to speed up and improve file searches.

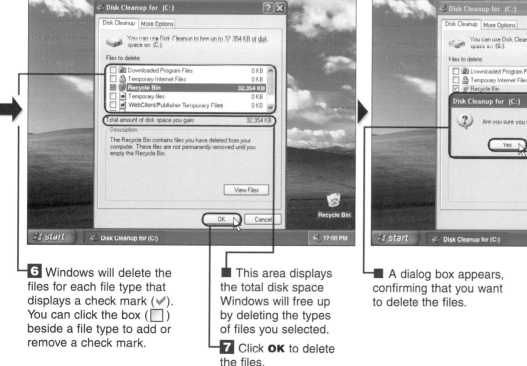

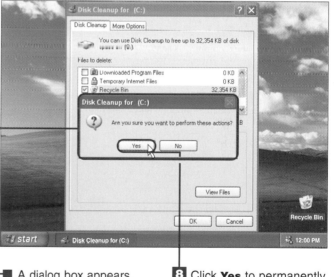

6 Windows will delete the files for each file type that displays a check mark (✔). You can click the box (☐) beside a file type to add or remove a check mark.

■ This area displays the total disk space Windows will free up by deleting the types of files you selected.

7 Click **OK** to delete the files.

■ A dialog box appears, confirming that you want to delete the files.

8 Click **Yes** to permanently delete the files.

DEFRAGMENT YOUR HARD DISK

You can improve the performance of your computer by defragmenting your hard disk. Defragmenting your hard disk will make your programs run faster and your files open more quickly.

Before defragmenting your hard disk, Windows can analyze the disk to determine if you need to defragment the disk. You should have Windows analyze your hard disk at least once a week.

Your hard disk must have at least 15% of free space for Windows to properly defragment the disk. To view the amount of free space on your hard disk, see page 204.

DEFRAGMENT YOUR HARD DISK

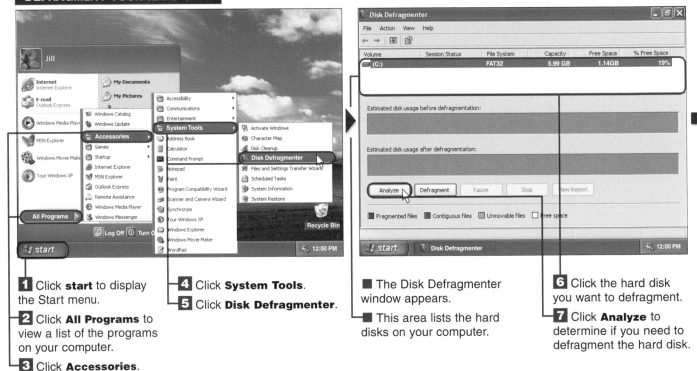

1 Click **start** to display the Start menu.

2 Click **All Programs** to view a list of the programs on your computer.

3 Click **Accessories**.

4 Click **System Tools**.

5 Click **Disk Defragmenter**.

■ The Disk Defragmenter window appears.

■ This area lists the hard disks on your computer.

6 Click the hard disk you want to defragment.

7 Click **Analyze** to determine if you need to defragment the hard disk.

**Why would I need to defragment
my hard disk?**

A fragmented hard disk stores
parts of each file in many different
locations on the disk. Your computer
must search many areas on the disk
to retrieve a file. You can use Disk
Defragmenter to place all the parts
of each file in one location. This
reduces the time your computer
will spend locating files.

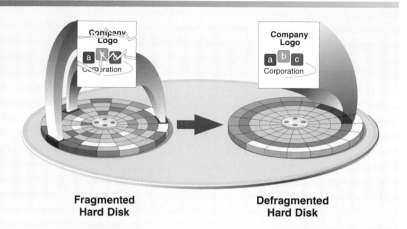

**Fragmented
Hard Disk**

**Defragmented
Hard Disk**

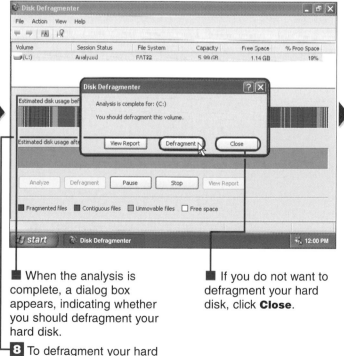

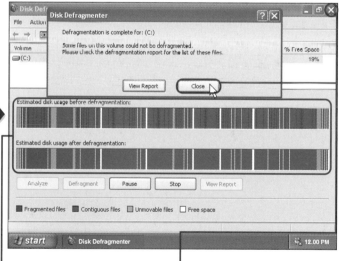

■ When the analysis is
complete, a dialog box
appears, indicating whether
you should defragment your
hard disk.

8 To defragment your hard
disk, click **Defragment**.

■ If you do not want to
defragment your hard
disk, click **Close**.

■ If you selected to
defragment your hard disk,
this area graphically displays
the defragmentation process.

*Note: You can use your computer
during the defragmentation, but
your computer will operate more
slowly and the defragmentation
will take longer to finish.*

■ A dialog box appears
when the defragmentation
is complete.

9 Click **Close** to close
the dialog box.

10 Click **X** to close
the Disk Defragmenter
window.

SCHEDULE TASKS

You can use Task Scheduler to have Windows automatically run specific programs on a regular basis.

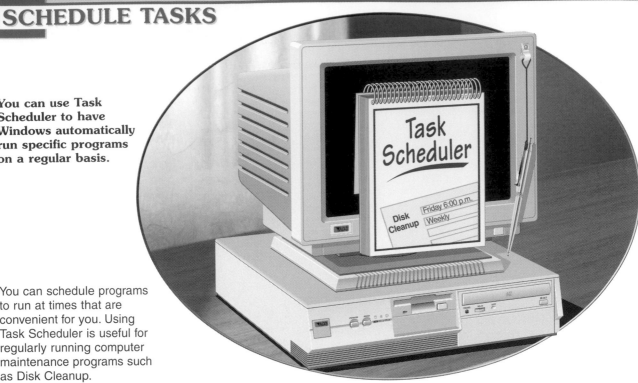

You can schedule programs to run at times that are convenient for you. Using Task Scheduler is useful for regularly running computer maintenance programs such as Disk Cleanup.

SCHEDULE TASKS

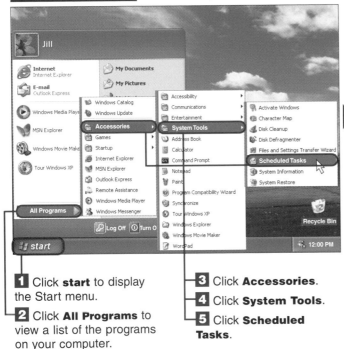

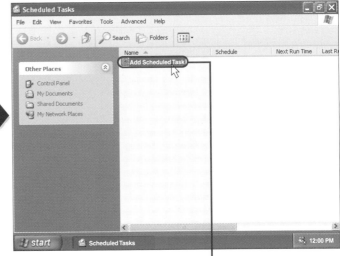

1 Click **start** to display the Start menu.

2 Click **All Programs** to view a list of the programs on your computer.

3 Click **Accessories**.

4 Click **System Tools**.

5 Click **Scheduled Tasks**.

■ The Scheduled Tasks window appears.

6 Double-click **Add Scheduled Task** to schedule a program to run automatically.

What do I need to consider before scheduling a task?

Before scheduling a task, you must assign a password to your user account. To have Windows run a program automatically, you will need to enter the password when scheduling the task. To assign a password to your user account, see page 180.

How does Task Scheduler know when to run a program?

Task Scheduler uses the date and time set in your computer to determine when to run a scheduled program. You should make sure the date and time set in your computer is correct before you schedule a program. To change the date and time set in your computer, see page 110.

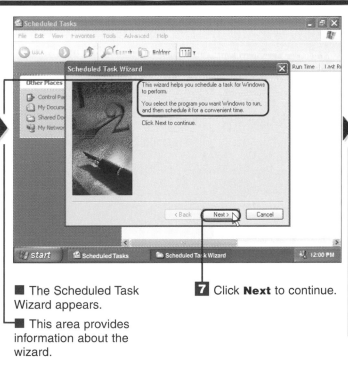

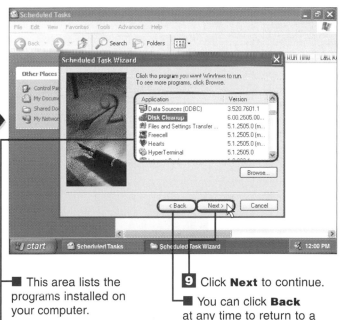

■ The Scheduled Task Wizard appears.

■ This area provides information about the wizard.

7 Click **Next** to continue.

■ This area lists the programs installed on your computer.

8 Click the program you want Windows to run automatically.

9 Click **Next** to continue.

■ You can click **Back** at any time to return to a previous step and change your selections.

CONTINUED

SCHEDULE TASKS

You can specify the
date and time you
want Windows to
run a program.

Make sure you
schedule a program
to run when your
computer will be
turned on.

SCHEDULE TASKS (CONTINUED)

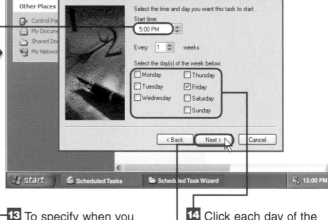

10 Windows provides a
name for the program. To
use a different name, type
a new name.

11 Click an option to specify
when you want the program
to run (○ changes to ◉).

12 Click **Next** to continue.

13 To specify when you
want the program to run,
click the part of the time
you want to change and
then type a new time.

*Note: The options available in
this screen depend on the option
you selected in step 11.*

14 Click each day of the
week you want the program
to run (☐ changes to ☑).

15 Click **Next** to continue.

How do I stop Windows from running a program automatically?

To stop Windows from running a program automatically, you must remove the program from the Scheduled Tasks window. Deleting a program from the Scheduled Tasks window will not remove the program from your computer.

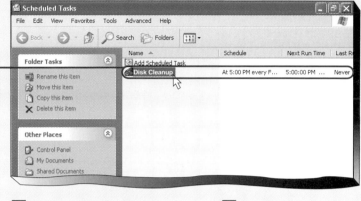

1 Perform steps **1** to **5** on page 214 to display the Scheduled Tasks window.

2 Click the program you no longer want to run automatically and then press the Delete key.

3 A confirmation dialog box will appear. Click **Yes** to delete the program.

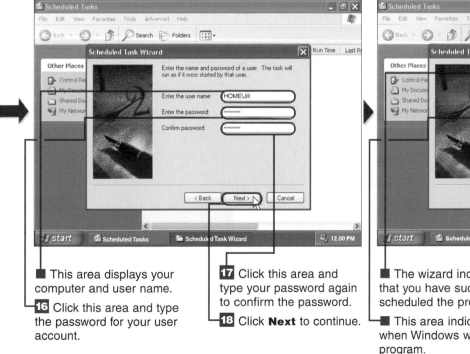

■ This area displays your computer and user name.

16 Click this area and type the password for your user account.

17 Click this area and type your password again to confirm the password.

18 Click **Next** to continue.

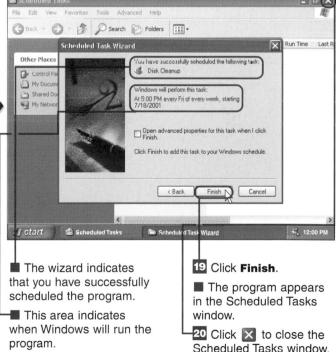

■ The wizard indicates that you have successfully scheduled the program.

■ This area indicates when Windows will run the program.

19 Click **Finish**.

■ The program appears in the Scheduled Tasks window.

20 Click ✕ to close the Scheduled Tasks window.

RESTORE YOUR COMPUTER

If you are experiencing problems with your computer, you can use the System Restore feature to return your computer to a time before the problems occurred.

For example, if your computer does not work properly after you install a program, you can restore your computer to a time before you installed the program.

RESTORE YOUR COMPUTER

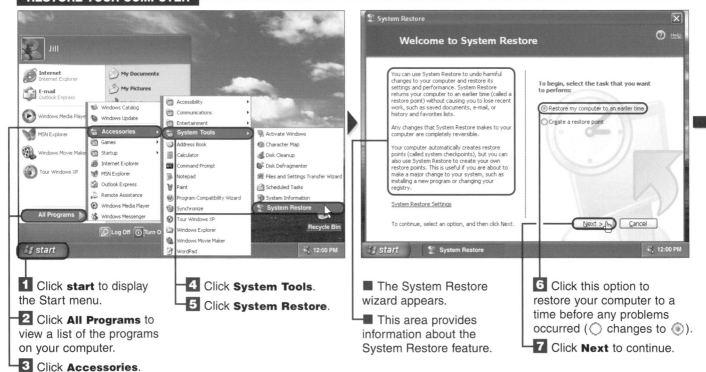

1 Click **start** to display the Start menu.

2 Click **All Programs** to view a list of the programs on your computer.

3 Click **Accessories**.

4 Click **System Tools**.

5 Click **System Restore**.

■ The System Restore wizard appears.

■ This area provides information about the System Restore feature.

6 Click this option to restore your computer to a time before any problems occurred (○ changes to ◉).

7 Click **Next** to continue.

What types of restore points are available?

When restoring your computer, you can select from several types of restore points. A restore point is an earlier, more stable time that you can return your computer to.

Windows can store between one to three weeks of restore points. Here are a few common types of restore points.

System Checkpoint

Restore points created automatically by Windows on a regular basis.

Installed (*Program*)

Restore points created automatically when you install certain programs. The name of the program appears beside the word "Installed."

Automatic Updates Install

Restore points created when you install the recommended updates for Windows. For information on automatically updating Windows, see page 194.

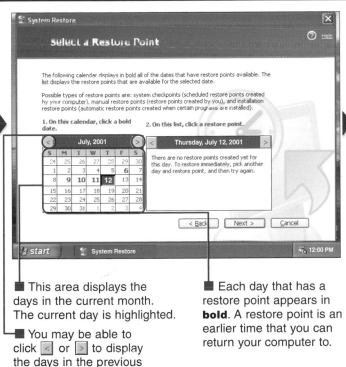

■ This area displays the days in the current month. The current day is highlighted.

■ You may be able to click ◄ or ► to display the days in the previous or next month.

■ Each day that has a restore point appears in **bold**. A restore point is an earlier time that you can return your computer to.

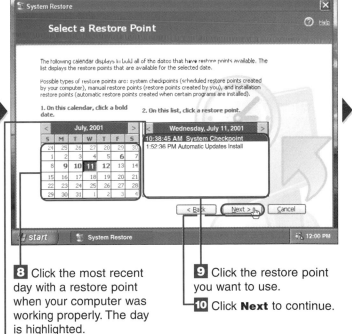

8 Click the most recent day with a restore point when your computer was working properly. The day is highlighted.

■ This area lists the restore points available for the day you selected.

9 Click the restore point you want to use.

10 Click **Next** to continue.

CONTINUED

219

RESTORE YOUR COMPUTER

When you restore your computer to an earlier time, you will not lose any of your recent work, such as documents or e-mail messages.

Before restoring your computer to an earlier time, you should close all open files and programs.

RESTORE YOUR COMPUTER (CONTINUED)

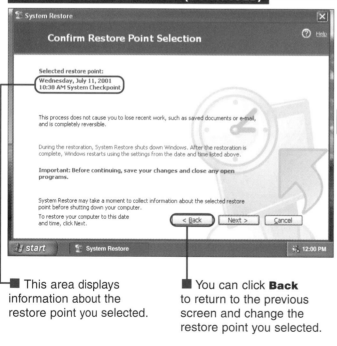

■ This area displays information about the restore point you selected.

■ You can click **Back** to return to the previous screen and change the restore point you selected.

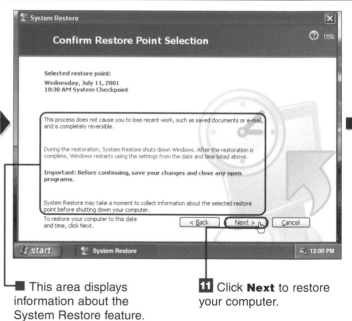

■ This area displays information about the System Restore feature.

11 Click **Next** to restore your computer.

Will I need to re-install any programs after restoring my computer?

When you restore your computer to an earlier time, any programs you installed after that date may be uninstalled. Files you created using the program will not be deleted, but you will need to re-install the program to work with the files again.

Can I reverse the changes made when I restored my computer?

Yes. Any changes that the System Restore feature makes to your computer are completely reversible. To undo your last restoration, perform steps **1** to **7** on page 218, except select **Undo my last restoration** in step **6**. Then perform steps **11** and **12** below.

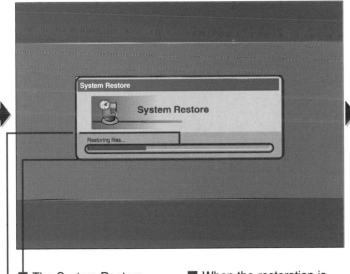

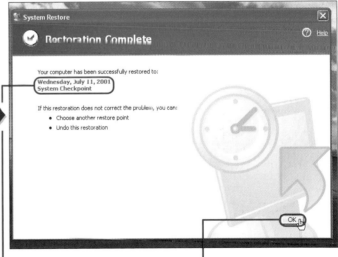

■ The System Restore dialog box appears.

■ This area shows the progress of the restoration.

■ When the restoration is complete, your computer will automatically restart.

■ After your computer restarts, a dialog box appears, indicating that your computer has been successfully restored.

■ This area displays the date to which your computer was restored.

12 Click **OK** to close the dialog box.

GET REMOTE ASSISTANCE

You can allow a person at another computer to view your computer screen and chat with you to help you solve a computer problem.

With your permission, the other person can control your computer to fix the problem.

If either computer is connected to a network, a firewall may prevent you from using Remote Assistance. A firewall protects a network from unauthorized access.

GET REMOTE ASSISTANCE

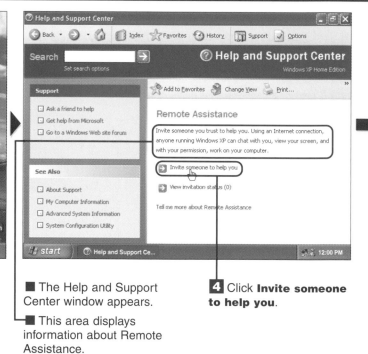

■ You must be connected to the Internet to get remote assistance.

1 Click **start** to display the Start menu.

2 Click **All Programs** to view a list of the programs on your computer.

3 Click **Remote Assistance**.

■ The Help and Support Center window appears.

■ This area displays information about Remote Assistance.

4 Click **Invite someone to help you**.

How can I send an invitation for Remote Assistance to another person?

You can send a Remote Assistance invitation to another person in an e-mail message or by using Windows Messenger.

To use Remote Assistance, both computers must use Windows XP and be connected to the Internet.

E-mail

To send an invitation for Remote Assistance in an e-mail message, both computers must use a compatible e-mail program, such as Outlook Express. For information on Outlook Express, see pages 264 to 285.

Windows Messenger

To send an invitation for Remote Assistance using Windows Messenger, both computers must be signed in to Windows Messenger. The person you want to send an invitation to must also appear in your contact list in Windows Messenger. For information on Windows Messenger, see pages 288 to 297.

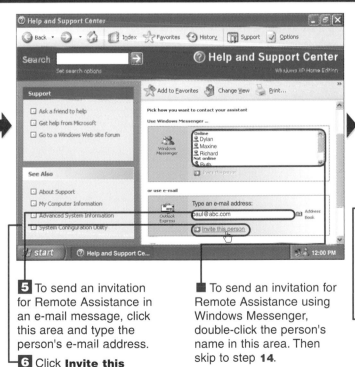

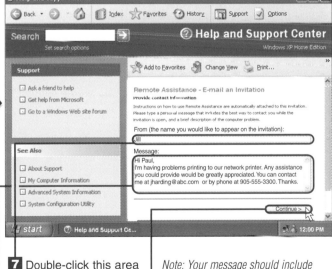

5 To send an invitation for Remote Assistance in an e-mail message, click this area and type the person's e-mail address.

6 Click **Invite this person**.

■ To send an invitation for Remote Assistance using Windows Messenger, double-click the person's name in this area. Then skip to step **14**.

7 Double-click this area and type your name.

8 Click this area and type the message you want to include with the invitation.

Note: Your message should include a brief description of your computer problem and indicate how the other person can contact you. Instructions on how to use Remote Assistance are automatically included with the invitation.

9 Click **Continue**.

GET REMOTE ASSISTANCE

When sending a Remote Assistance invitation in an e-mail message, you can specify when you want the invitation to expire and a password the other person must enter to connect to your computer.

Specifying an expiration time and password for an invitation protects your computer from unauthorized access.

When specifying a password, do not use your name, user name or a common word. Make sure the password contains at least seven characters and contains letters, numbers and symbols. You must tell the other person the password you specified.

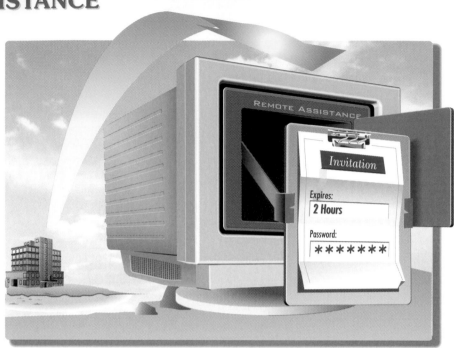

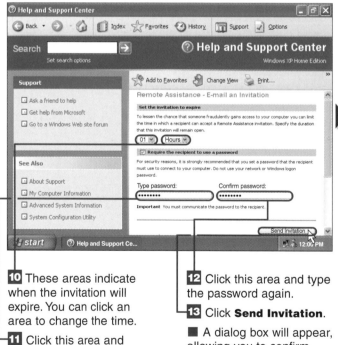

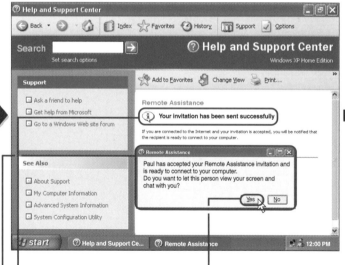

10 These areas indicate when the invitation will expire. You can click an area to change the time.

11 Click this area and type a password the other person must enter to connect to your computer.

12 Click this area and type the password again.

13 Click **Send Invitation**.

■ A dialog box will appear, allowing you to confirm that you want to send the message. Click **Send** to send the message.

■ This message appears when your invitation has been sent successfully.

■ A dialog box appears when the other person accepts your Remote Assistance invitation.

14 Click **Yes** to allow the other person to view your screen and chat with you.

What will the other person's computer screen display?

Once you allow the other person to view your computer screen and chat with you, the Remote Assistance window appears on the person's screen.

Chat

This area displays the ongoing conversation and an area that allows the other person to send you a message.

Your Computer Screen

This area displays your computer screen. The screen shows the tasks that you or the other person perform.

Take Control

The other person can click **Take Control** to ask your permission to control your computer.

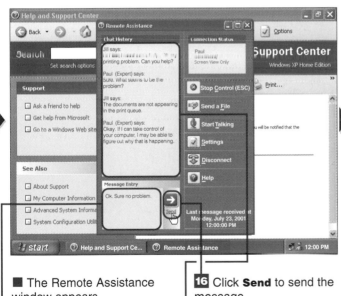

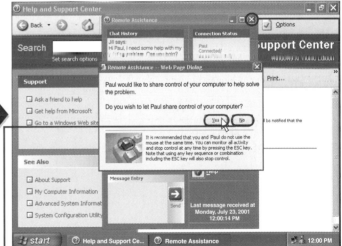

■ The Remote Assistance window appears.

15 To send a message to the other person, click this area and type a message.

16 Click **Send** to send the message.

Note: You can also press the **Enter** *key to send the message.*

■ This area will display the message you sent and the ongoing conversation.

■ A dialog box appears if the other person wants to control your computer.

17 Click **Yes** or **No** to specify if you want the other person to control your computer.

■ To stop the other person from controlling your computer, press the **Esc** key.

*Note: A message appears, indicating that the other person is no longer controlling your computer. Click **OK**.*

18 When you finish using Remote Assistance, click **X** to close the window.

CHAPTER 11

Work on a Network

A network is a group of connected computers. This chapter teaches you how to share information and printers on a network, as well as set up your own home network.

BROWSE THROUGH A NETWORK

You can use My
Network Places to
browse through the
information available
on your network.

You can work with the
files available on your
network as you would
work with files stored
on your own computer.

BROWSE THROUGH A NETWORK

1 Click **start** to display
the Start menu.

2 Click **My Computer**
to view the contents of
your computer.

■ If My Network Places
appears on the Start
menu, click **My Network
Places** and then skip to
step **4**.

■ The My Computer
window appears.

3 Click **My Network
Places** to browse through
the information available
on your network.

Why can I no longer access a folder on my network?

You will not be able to access a folder on your network if the computer that stores the folder is turned off or if the owner of the computer stops sharing the folder.

Can two people on a network work on the same file at once?

Most programs, such as word processors, allow only one person to make changes to a file at one time. Some programs, such as database programs, may allow several people on a network to make changes to a file at the same time.

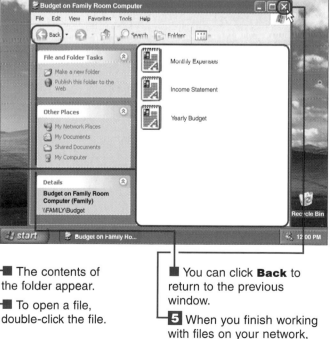

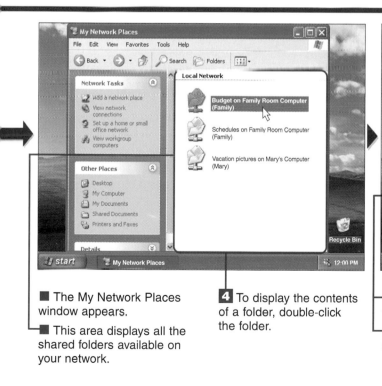

■ The My Network Places window appears.

■ This area displays all the shared folders available on your network.

4 To display the contents of a folder, double-click the folder.

■ The contents of the folder appear.

■ To open a file, double-click the file.

■ You can click **Back** to return to the previous window.

5 When you finish working with files on your network, click ✕ to close the window.

SHARE INFORMATION

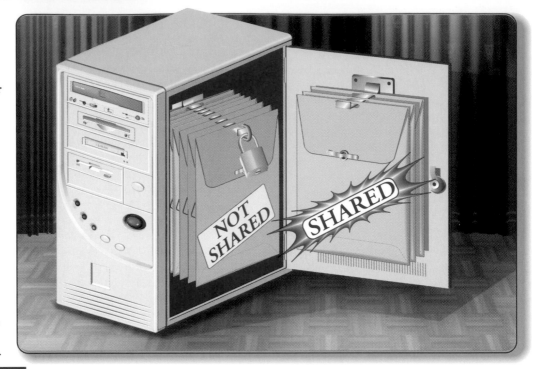

You can specify the information on your computer that you want to share with other people on your network.

Sharing information is useful when people on a network need to access the same files.

SHARE INFORMATION

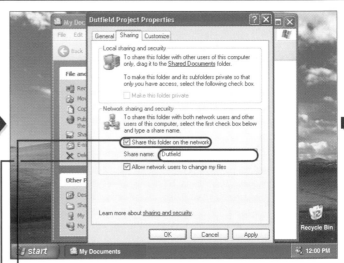

1 Click the folder you want to share with other people on your network.

2 Click **Share this folder**.

■ A Properties dialog box appears.

3 Click this option to share the folder with other people on your network (☐ changes to ☑).

4 This area displays the name of the folder people will see on your network. To change the folder name, drag the mouse ⌶ over the current name and then type a new name.

Note: Changing the name of the folder will not change the name of the folder on your computer.

230

What must I consider before sharing information on my computer?

Before you can share information on your computer with other people on your network, your computer must be set up on the network. To set up your computer on a network, see page 236.

When you set up your computer on a network, Windows automatically shares your Shared Documents folder. For information on the Shared Documents folder, see page 185.

How can I share a folder located on my desktop?

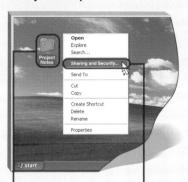

1 To share a folder located on your desktop, right-click the folder. A menu appears.

2 Click **Sharing and Security**. Then perform steps **3** to **6** below to share the folder.

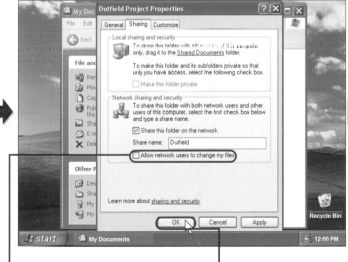

5 If you do not want people on your network to make changes to files in the folder, click this option (☑ changes to ☐).

6 Click **OK** to share the folder.

■ A hand (👌) appears in the icon for the shared folder.

■ Everyone on your network will be able to access all the files within the shared folder.

■ To stop sharing a folder, perform steps **1** to **3** (☑ changes to ☐ in step **3**). Then perform step **6**.

SHARE A PRINTER

You can share your printer with other people on a network. Sharing a printer allows others to use your printer to print documents.

Sharing a printer allows individuals and companies to save money since several people on a network can use the same printer.

To share a printer on a network, your computer must be set up on a network. To set up a computer on a network, see page 236.

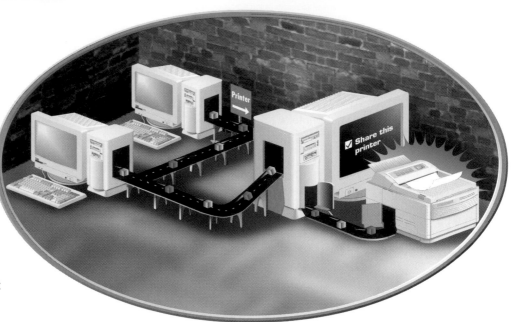

SHARE A PRINTER

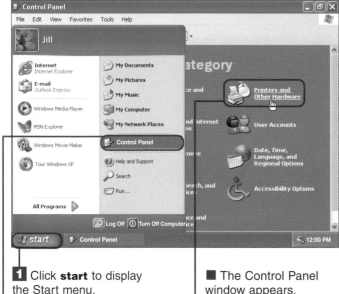

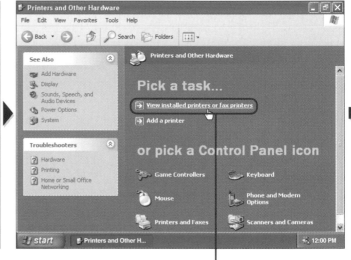

1 Click **start** to display the Start menu.

2 Click **Control Panel** to change your computer's settings.

■ The Control Panel window appears.

3 Click **Printers and Other Hardware**.

■ The Printers and Other Hardware window appears.

4 Click **View installed printers or fax printers**.

How can I tell if my printer is shared?

In the Printers and Faxes window, a hand ( ) appears in the icon for your shared printer. Windows may have already shared your printer when you set up your computer on the network or installed the printer. You should make sure both your computer and the shared printer are turned on and are accessible when other people want to use the printer.

How do I stop sharing a printer?

When you no longer want people on the network to use your printer, you can stop sharing your printer. Perform steps **1** to **10** below, except select **Do not share this printer** in step **7**.

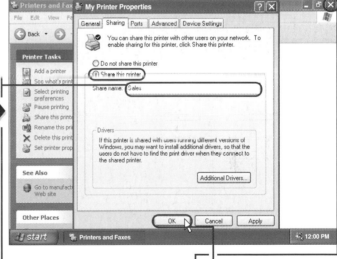

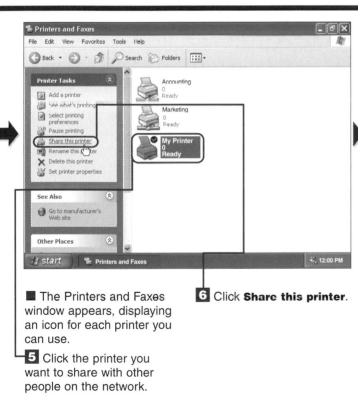

■ The Printers and Faxes window appears, displaying an icon for each printer you can use.

5 Click the printer you want to share with other people on the network.

6 Click **Share this printer**.

■ A Properties dialog box appears.

7 Click **Share this printer** to share the printer with other people on the network (○ changes to ◉).

8 This area displays the name of the printer people will see on the network. To change the printer name, type a new name.

9 Click **OK** to confirm your changes.

10 Click **X** to close the Printers and Faxes window.

CHANGE YOUR DEFAULT PRINTER

If you have access to more than one printer, you can select which printer you want to automatically print your documents. The printer you select is called the default printer.

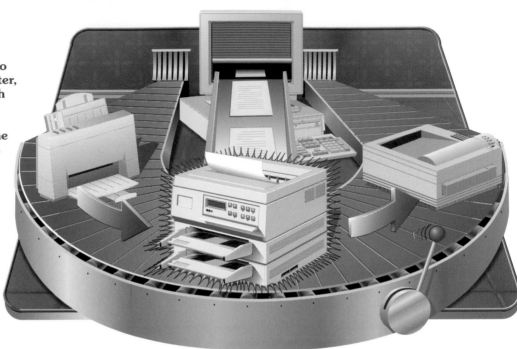

CHANGE YOUR DEFAULT PRINTER

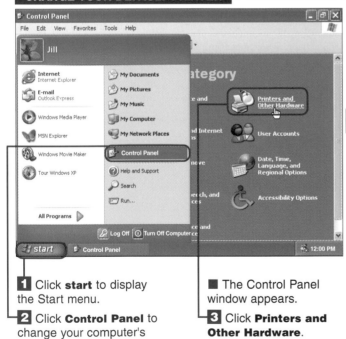

1 Click **start** to display the Start menu.

2 Click **Control Panel** to change your computer's settings.

■ The Control Panel window appears.

3 Click **Printers and Other Hardware**.

■ The Printers and Other Hardware window appears.

4 Click **View installed printers or fax printers**.

234

Which printer should I select as my default printer?

When selecting a default printer, you should select the printer you will use most often. The printer you select should be close to your desk and offer the capabilities you need.

Can I use a printer that is not my default printer?

You may occasionally want to use another printer to print a document, such as when your default printer is not working properly. When you print a document, most programs will display a dialog box that allows you to select the printer you want to use.

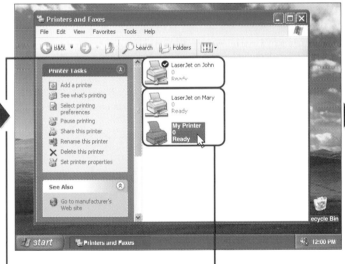

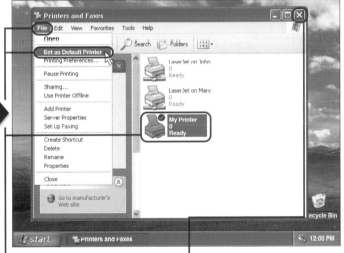

■ The Printers and Faxes window appears, displaying an icon for each printer you can use.

■ Your default printer displays a check mark (◯) in its icon.

5 Click the printer you want to set as your new default printer.

6 Click **File**.

7 Click **Set as Default Printer**.

■ The new default printer displays a check mark (◯) in its icon.

■ Your documents will now automatically print to the new default printer.

8 Click ☒ to close the Printers and Faxes window.

SET UP A HOME NETWORK

If you have more than one computer at home, you can set up a network so the computers can exchange information and share equipment.

Share Information

A network allows you to work with information stored on other computers on the network. Sharing information is useful when people on a network are working together on a project and need to access the same files.

Share Equipment

A network allows several computers to share equipment, such as a printer. Sharing equipment allows you to save money since several people on the network can use the same equipment.

Share an Internet Connection

You can set up a computer to share its Internet connection with other computers on the network. All the computers on the network can use the shared Internet connection to access the Internet at the same time. The computer that shares its Internet connection must be turned on when other computers on the network want to access the Internet.

Your Internet Service Provider (ISP), which is the company that gives you access to the Internet, may charge extra or not allow multiple computers to share a single Internet connection. You can contact your ISP for more information.

Protect Your Network

When you set up a network, Windows will install firewall software on the computer that shares its Internet connection. The firewall software is designed to protect your network from unauthorized access when computers on the network are connected to the Internet.

Play Multi-Player Games

Many games allow several people on a network and the Internet to compete against each other. You can obtain multi-player games at computer stores and on the Internet.

NETWORK HARDWARE

**You need to install and set
up your network hardware to
enable the computers on your
network to communicate.**

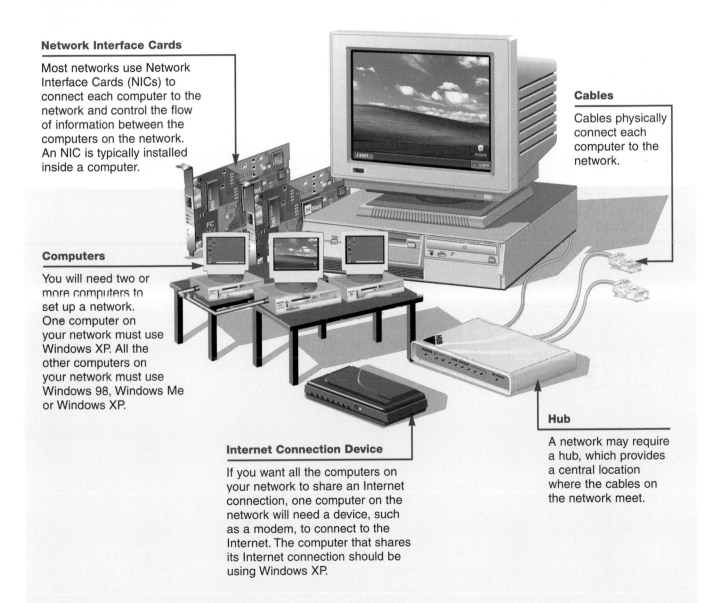

Network Interface Cards

Most networks use Network
Interface Cards (NICs) to
connect each computer to the
network and control the flow
of information between the
computers on the network.
An NIC is typically installed
inside a computer.

Cables

Cables physically
connect each
computer to the
network.

Computers

You will need two or
more computers to
set up a network.
One computer on
your network must use
Windows XP. All the
other computers on
your network must use
Windows 98, Windows Me
or Windows XP.

Internet Connection Device

If you want all the computers on
your network to share an Internet
connection, one computer on the
network will need a device, such
as a modem, to connect to the
Internet. The computer that shares
its Internet connection should be
using Windows XP.

Hub

A network may require
a hub, which provides
a central location
where the cables on
the network meet.

SET UP A HOME NETWORK

Windows provides the Network Setup Wizard that will take you step by step through the process of setting up a computer on your home network.

You must run the Network Setup Wizard on each computer you want to set up on your home network. If the computers on your network will share an Internet connection, you should run the wizard on the computer that has the Internet connection first.

SET UP A HOME NETWORK

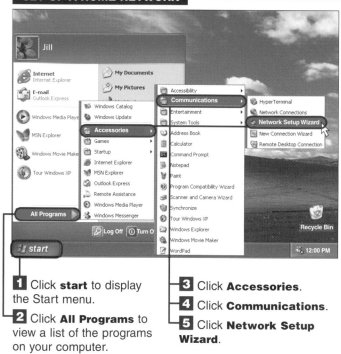

1 Click **start** to display the Start menu.

2 Click **All Programs** to view a list of the programs on your computer.

3 Click **Accessories**.

4 Click **Communications**.

5 Click **Network Setup Wizard**.

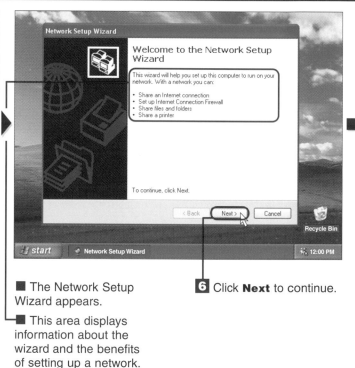

■ The Network Setup Wizard appears.

■ This area displays information about the wizard and the benefits of setting up a network.

6 Click **Next** to continue.

What are the most common ways a computer connects to the Internet on a home network?

You need to select the way a computer connects to the Internet in step **8** below. Here are the two most common ways a computer will connect to the Internet on a home network.

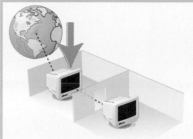
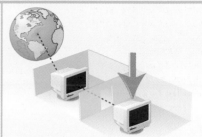

This computer connects directly to the Internet. The other computers on my network connect to the Internet through this computer.

This computer connects to the Internet through another computer on my network or through a residential gateway. A residential gateway is a hardware device that connects a network to the Internet and typically offers a high-speed connection to the Internet.

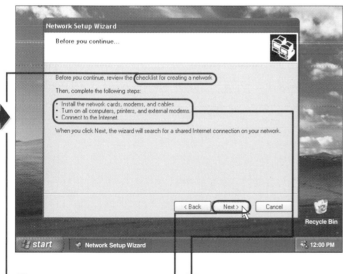
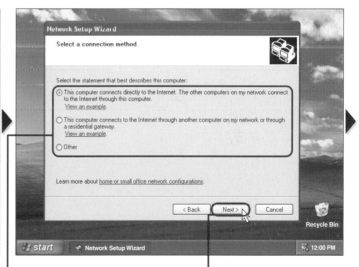

■ You can click this link to review a checklist for creating a network.

Note: If you click the link, the Help and Support Center window appears, displaying the checklist. When you finish reviewing the checklist, click ✖ to close the window.

■ Before continuing, make sure you have completed the steps listed in this area.

7 Click **Next** to continue.

8 Click the option that best describes the way the computer connects to the Internet (◯ changes to ◉).

*Note: You can click **Other** to view additional statements if the displayed statements do not describe the computer.*

9 Click **Next** to continue.

*Note: If you selected **Other** in step **8**, repeat steps **8** and **9**.*

CONTINUED

SET UP A HOME NETWORK

When setting up a computer on your network, you need to provide a description, computer name and workgroup name for the computer.

A computer name identifies the computer on your network. A workgroup name identifies the group of computers on your network that the computer belongs to.

SET UP A HOME NETWORK (CONTINUED)

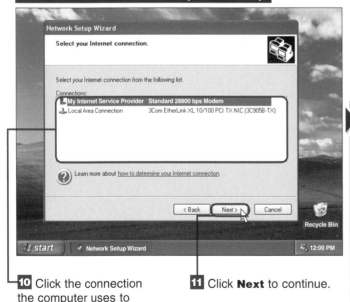

10 Click the connection the computer uses to connect to the Internet.

Note: This screen may not appear, depending on the statement you selected in step 8. If the screen does not appear, skip to step 12.

11 Click **Next** to continue.

12 Type a brief description for the computer.

13 Double-click this area and type a name for the computer.

Note: For information on choosing a computer name, see the top of page 241.

14 Click **Next** to continue.

What should I consider when choosing a computer name?

➤ Each computer on your network must have a different name.

➤ A computer name can contain up to 15 characters.

➤ A computer name cannot contain spaces or special characters, such as ; : , " < > * + = \ | or ?.

➤ Your Internet Service Provider (ISP), which is the company that gives you access to the Internet, may require you to use a specific name for the computer that shares its Internet connection. If this is true for your ISP, make sure you use the name your ISP specifies.

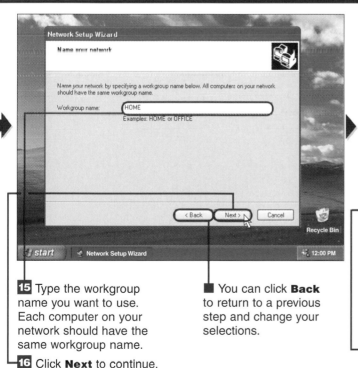

15 Type the workgroup name you want to use. Each computer on your network should have the same workgroup name.

16 Click **Next** to continue.

■ You can click **Back** to return to a previous step and change your selections.

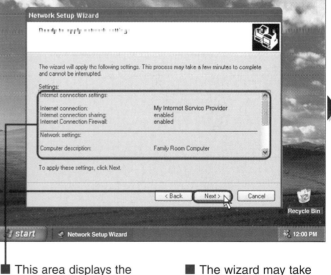

■ This area displays the network settings that the wizard will apply to the computer.

17 Click **Next** to apply the network settings.

■ The wizard may take a few minutes to apply the network settings. This process cannot be interrupted.

CONTINUED

SET UP A HOME NETWORK

You need to specify how you want to set up other computers that use Windows 98 or Windows Me on your home network.

Windows 98

Windows Me

To set up other computers that use Windows 98 or Windows Me, you can create a Network Setup disk or use the CD you used to install Windows XP.

To set up other computers that use Windows XP, perform the steps starting on page 238 on each computer.

SET UP A HOME NETWORK (CONTINUED)

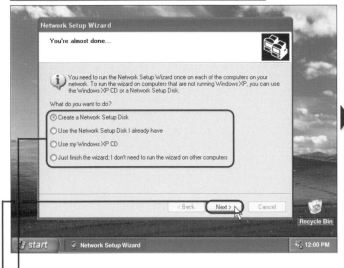

18 Click an option to specify the task you want to perform to set up other computers on your network (○ changes to ◉).

19 Click **Next** to continue.

*Note: If you chose to use the Network Setup disk you already have or the Windows XP CD, skip to step **22**. If you chose to just finish the wizard, skip to step **24**.*

20 Insert a formatted, blank floppy disk into the floppy drive.

■ If you are using an unformatted floppy disk or the disk contains files, you can click **Format Disk** to format the disk.

Note: Formatting a disk will permanently remove all the information on the disk. For more information on formatting a floppy disk, see page 206.

21 Click **Next** to continue.

What resources can I share on my network?

After you set up your network, you can share folders and your printer with other computers on the network. The Network Setup Wizard automatically shares your Shared Documents folder and your printer. For information on the Shared Documents folder, see page 185. For information on sharing folders and printers, see pages 230 and 232.

How can I view all the folders that are shared on my network?

You can use **My Network Places** to access all the folders that are shared by your computer and other computers on your network. To use My Network Places, see page 228.

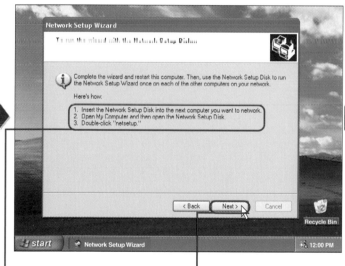

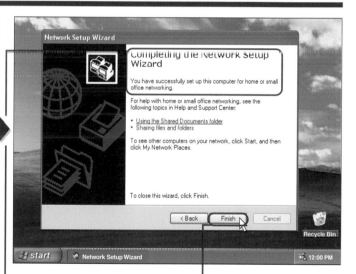

■ The wizard displays the steps you need to perform to set up other computers on your network. The displayed steps depend on the option you selected in step **18**.

22 Click **Next** to continue.

■ This message appears when you have successfully set up the computer on your network.

23 If you created a Network Setup disk, remove the floppy disk from the drive.

24 Click **Finish** to close the wizard.

■ A message may appear, stating that you must restart the computer before the new settings will take effect. Click **Yes** to restart the computer.

CHAPTER 12

Browse the Web

This chapter will explain how the World Wide Web works and how you can use it to transfer information to your computer from Web sites around the world.

INTRODUCTION TO THE WEB

The World Wide Web is part of the Internet and consists of a huge collection of documents stored on computers around the world. The World Wide Web is commonly called the Web.

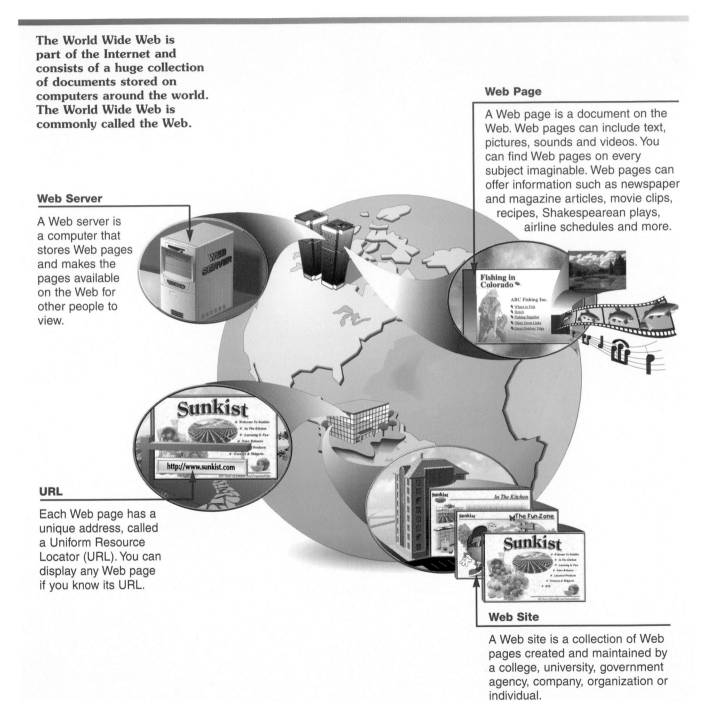

Web Page

A Web page is a document on the Web. Web pages can include text, pictures, sounds and videos. You can find Web pages on every subject imaginable. Web pages can offer information such as newspaper and magazine articles, movie clips, recipes, Shakespearean plays, airline schedules and more.

Web Server

A Web server is a computer that stores Web pages and makes the pages available on the Web for other people to view.

URL

Each Web page has a unique address, called a Uniform Resource Locator (URL). You can display any Web page if you know its URL.

Web Site

A Web site is a collection of Web pages created and maintained by a college, university, government agency, company, organization or individual.

Web Browser

A Web browser is a program that allows you to view and explore information on the Web. Windows XP comes with the Microsoft Internet Explorer Web browser.

Links

Web pages contain links, which are highlighted text or images on a Web page that connect to other pages on the Web. You can select a link to display a Web page located on the same computer or on a computer across the city, country or world. Links are also known as hyperlinks.

Links allow you to easily navigate through a vast amount of information by jumping from one Web page to another. This is known as "browsing the Web."

Connecting to the Internet

Most people connect to the Internet using a company called an Internet Service Provider (ISP). Once you pay your ISP to connect to the Internet, you can view and exchange information on the Internet free of charge.

Most individuals use a modem to connect to the Internet, although cable modems and Digital Subscriber Line (DSL) modems are becoming more popular. Most schools and businesses connect to the Internet through a network connection.

START INTERNET EXPLORER

You can start
Internet Explorer
to browse
through the
information
on the Web.

The first time you
start Internet
Explorer, the New
Connection Wizard
will appear if you have
not yet set up your
connection to the
Internet. Follow the
instructions in the
wizard to set up your
Internet connection.

START INTERNET EXPLORER

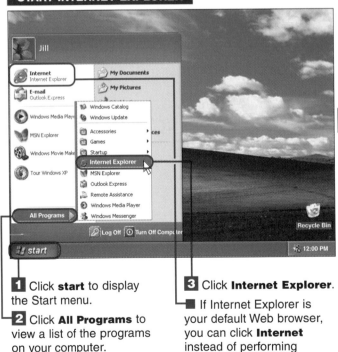

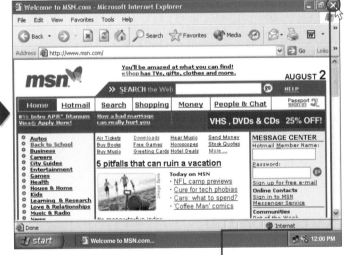

1 Click **start** to display
the Start menu.

2 Click **All Programs** to
view a list of the programs
on your computer.

3 Click **Internet Explorer**.

■ If Internet Explorer is
your default Web browser,
you can click **Internet**
instead of performing
steps **2** and **3**.

■ The Microsoft Internet
Explorer window appears,
displaying your home page.

*Note: If you are not currently
connected to the Internet, a dialog
box will appear that allows you to
connect.*

4 When you finish
browsing through the
information on the
Web, click **X** to close
the Microsoft Internet
Explorer window.

SELECT A LINK

A link connects text or an image on one Web page to another Web page. When you select the text or image, the linked Web page appears.

Links allow you to easily navigate through a vast amount of information by jumping from one Web page to another. Links are also known as hyperlinks.

SELECT A LINK

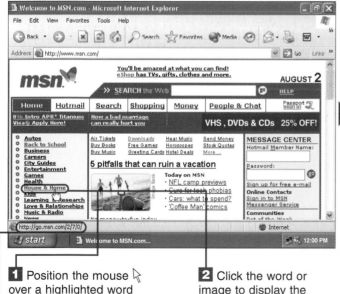

1 Position the mouse ⊾ over a highlighted word or image of interest. The mouse ⊾ changes to a hand ⊖ when over a link.

■ This area displays the address of the Web page that the link will take you to.

2 Click the word or image to display the linked Web page.

■ The linked Web page appears.

■ This area shows the progress of the transfer.

■ This area displays the title of the Web page.

■ This area displays the address of the Web page.

DISPLAY A SPECIFIC WEB PAGE

You can display any page on the Web that you have heard or read about.

You need to know the address of the Web page that you want to view. Each page on the Web has a unique address, called a Uniform Resource Locator (URL).

DISPLAY A SPECIFIC WEB PAGE

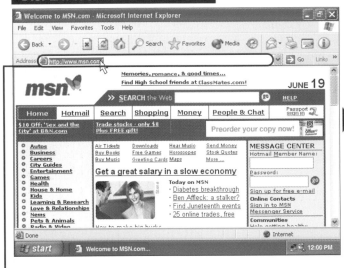

1 Click this area to highlight the current Web page address.

2 Type the address of the Web page you want to display and then press the Enter key.

*Note: You do not need to type **http://** when typing a Web page address. For example, you do not need to type **http://** in front of www.walmart.com.*

■ This area shows the progress of the transfer.

■ The Web page appears on your screen.

What are some popular Web pages that I can display?

Web Page	Web Page Address
Amazon.com	www.amazon.com
CBS SportsLine.com	www.sportsline.com
CNN.com	www.cnn.com
Cooking.com	www.cooking.com
Discovery.com	www.discovery.com
eBay	www.ebay.com
Encyclopedia.com	www.encyclopedia.com
HowStuffWorks	www.howstuffworks.com
Lonely Planet Online	www.lonelyplanet.com
maranGraphics	www.maran.com
Monster.com	www.monster.com
MP3.com	www.mp3.com
NASA	www.nasa.gov
Quote.com	www.quote.com
Weather.com	www.weather.com

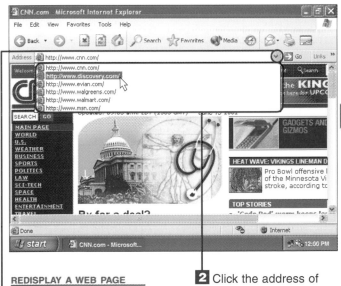

REDISPLAY A WEB PAGE

1 Click ⌄ in this area to display the addresses of the Web pages you have recently displayed.

2 Click the address of the Web page you want to redisplay.

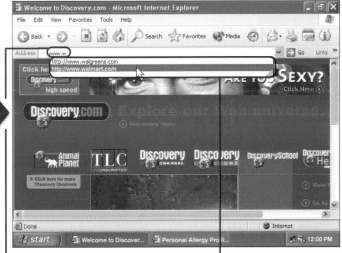

■ The Web page you selected appears on your screen.

QUICKLY REDISPLAY A WEB PAGE

1 If you begin typing the address of a Web page you have recently displayed, a list of matching addresses automatically appears.

2 Click the address of the Web page you want to redisplay.

STOP TRANSFER OF A WEB PAGE

If a Web page is taking a long time to appear on your screen, you can stop the transfer of the page.

You may also want to stop the transfer of a Web page if you realize a page contains information that does not interest you.

STOP TRANSFER OF A WEB PAGE

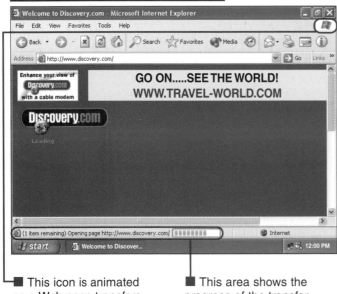

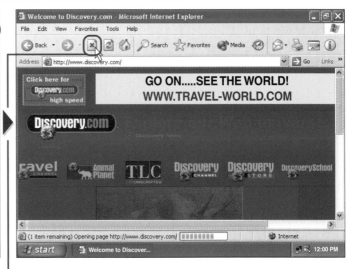

■ This icon is animated as a Web page transfers to your computer.

■ This area shows the progress of the transfer.

1 Click 🗷 to stop the transfer of the Web page.

■ If you stopped the transfer of the Web page because the page was taking too long to appear, you may want to try displaying the page at a later time.

MOVE THROUGH WEB PAGES

You can easily move back and forth through the Web pages you have viewed since you last started Internet Explorer.

MOVE THROUGH WEB PAGES

MOVE BACK

1 Click **Back** to return to the last Web page you viewed.

Note: The Back button is only available if you have viewed more than one Web page since you last started Internet Explorer.

MOVE FORWARD

1 Click 🔘 to move forward through the Web pages you have viewed.

Note: The 🔘 button is only available after you use the Back button to return to a Web page.

DISPLAY AND CHANGE YOUR HOME PAGE

You can display and change the Web page that appears each time you start Internet Explorer. This page is called your home page.

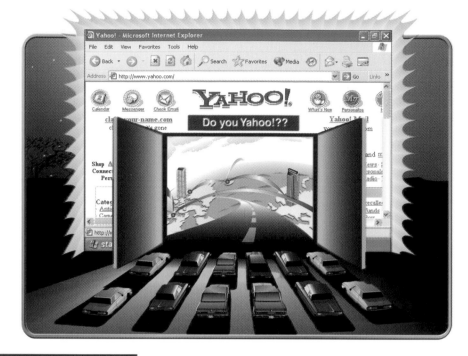

DISPLAY AND CHANGE YOUR HOME PAGE

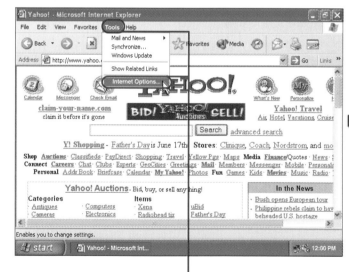

DISPLAY YOUR HOME PAGE

1 Click  to display your home page.

■ Your home page appears.

Note: Your home page may be different than the home page shown above.

CHANGE YOUR HOME PAGE

1 Display the Web page you want to set as your home page.

Note: To display a specific Web page, see page 250.

2 Click **Tools**.

3 Click **Internet Options**.

Which Web page should I set as my home page?

You can set any page on the Web as your home page. The page you choose should be a page you want to frequently visit. You may want to choose a page that provides a good starting point for exploring the Web, such as www.yahoo.com, or a page that provides information about your personal interests or work.

How can I once again use my original home page?

To once again use your original home page, perform steps **1** to **5** starting on page 254, except select **Use Default** in step **4**. In most cases, the www.msn.com Web page is the original home page.

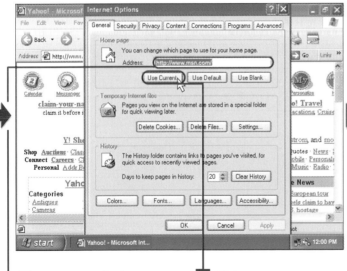

■ The Internet Options dialog box appears.

■ This area displays the address of your current home page.

4 Click **Use Current** to set the Web page displayed on your screen as your new home page.

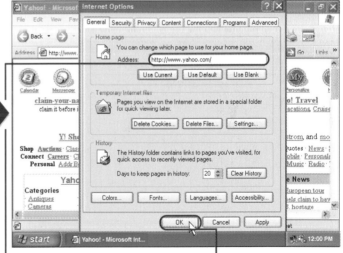

■ This area displays the address of your new home page.

5 Click **OK** to confirm your change.

SEARCH THE WEB

You can search for
Web pages that
discuss topics of
interest to you.

Internet Explorer uses the
MSN search tool to help
you find Web pages. A
search tool is a service
on the Web that catalogs
Web pages to help you
find pages of interest.

SEARCH THE WEB

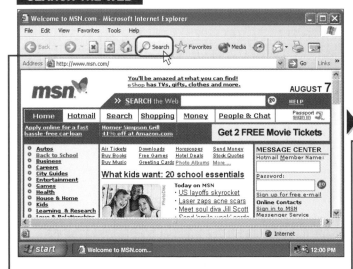

1 Click **Search** to
search for Web pages
of interest.

■ The Search Companion
area appears.

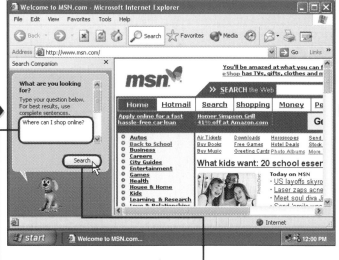

2 Click this area and
then type a question that
describes the information
you want to search for.

3 Click **Search** to start
the search.

Is there another way to search for information on the Web?

Yes. Many Web sites allow you to search for information on the Web. These Web sites can also allow you to browse through categories, such as news, sports and entertainment, to find Web pages of interest. Here are some popular Web sites that allow you to search for information on the Web.

Google

www.google.com

Lycos

www.lycos.com

Yahoo!

www.yahoo.com

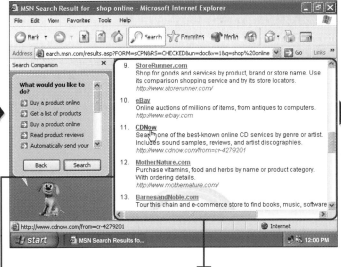

■ A list of matching Web pages and their descriptions appear in this area.

4 To display a Web page, click the Web page of interest.

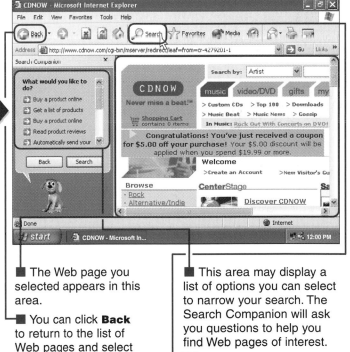

■ The Web page you selected appears in this area.

■ You can click **Back** to return to the list of Web pages and select another Web page.

■ This area may display a list of options you can select to narrow your search. The Search Companion will ask you questions to help you find Web pages of interest.

5 When you finish searching, click **Search** to hide the Search Companion area.

257

DISPLAY HISTORY OF VIEWED WEB PAGES

Internet Explorer uses the History list to keep track of the Web pages you have recently viewed. You can display the History list at any time to redisplay a Web page.

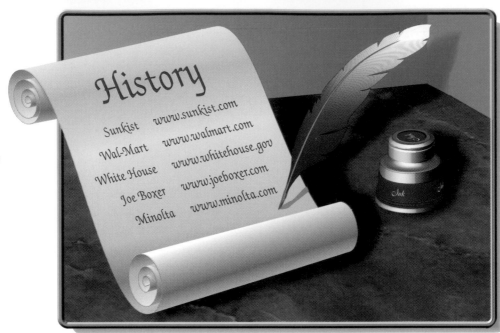

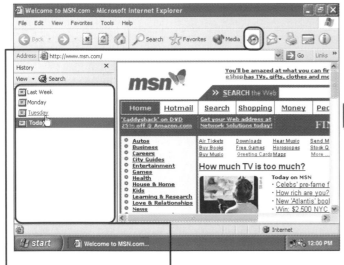

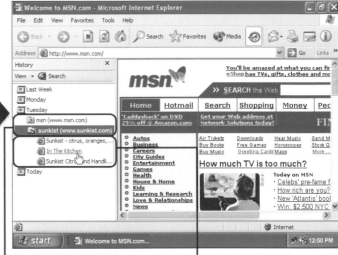

1 Click 🕔 to display a list of the Web pages you have recently viewed.

■ The History list appears, displaying a list of the Web pages you have recently viewed. The list is organized by week and day, with each week and day displaying the 📅 symbol.

2 Click the week or day you viewed the Web page you want to view again.

■ The Web sites (🌐) you viewed during the week or day appear.

Note: If you opened files on your computer during the week or day, the folders that contain the files also appear.

3 Click the Web site of interest.

■ The Web pages (📄) you viewed at the Web site appear.

4 Click the Web page you want to view.

How long does the History list keep track of the Web pages I have viewed?

By default, the History list keeps track of the Web pages you have viewed over the last 20 days.

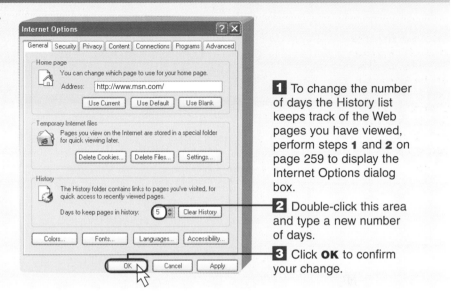

1 To change the number of days the History list keeps track of the Web pages you have viewed, perform steps **1** and **2** on page 259 to display the Internet Options dialog box.

2 Double-click this area and type a new number of days.

3 Click **OK** to confirm your change.

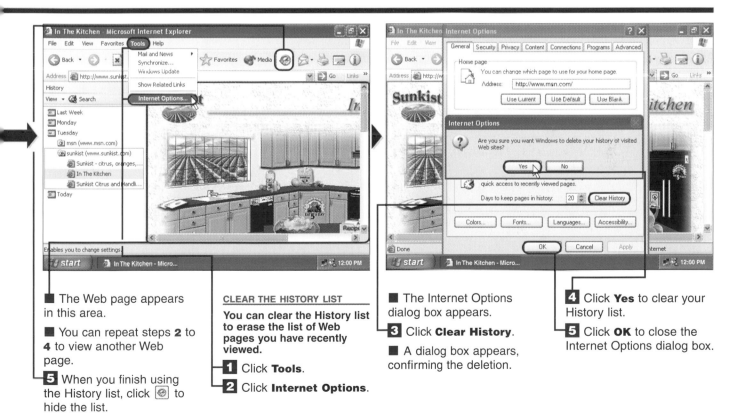

■ The Web page appears in this area.

■ You can repeat steps **2** to **4** to view another Web page.

5 When you finish using the History list, click 🖉 to hide the list.

CLEAR THE HISTORY LIST

You can clear the History list to erase the list of Web pages you have recently viewed.

1 Click **Tools**.

2 Click **Internet Options**.

■ The Internet Options dialog box appears.

3 Click **Clear History**.

■ A dialog box appears, confirming the deletion.

4 Click **Yes** to clear your History list.

5 Click **OK** to close the Internet Options dialog box.

ADD A WEB PAGE TO FAVORITES

You can use the Favorites feature to create a list of Web pages that you frequently visit. The Favorites feature allows you to quickly display a favorite Web page at any time.

Selecting Web pages from your list of favorites saves you from having to remember and constantly retype the same Web page addresses over and over again.

ADD A WEB PAGE TO FAVORITES

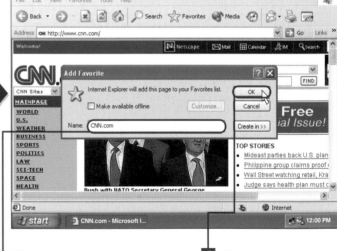

1 Display the Web page you want to add to your list of favorite Web pages.

Note: To display a specific Web page, see page 250.

2 Click **Favorites**.

3 Click **Add to Favorites**.

■ The Add Favorite dialog box appears.

■ The name of the Web page appears in this area.

4 Click **OK** to add the Web page to your list of favorites.

Does Internet Explorer automatically add Web pages to my list of favorites?

Yes. Internet Explorer automatically adds the Links folder and the following Web pages to your list of favorites.

Links folder

Contains several useful Web pages, such as the Free Hotmail page, which allows you to set up and use a free e-mail account.

MSN.com

A Web site provided by Microsoft that offers a great starting point for exploring the Web.

Radio Station Guide

Allows you to listen to radio stations from around the world that broadcast on the Internet.

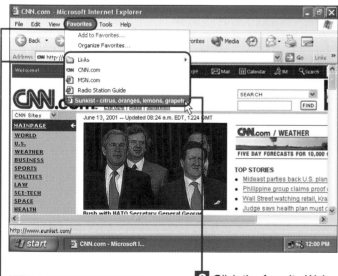

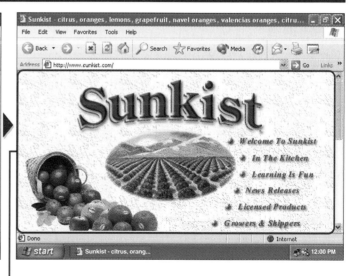

VIEW A FAVORITE WEB PAGE

1 Click **Favorites**.

■ A list of your favorite Web pages appears.

Note: If the entire list does not appear, position the mouse over the bottom of the menu to browse through the entire list.

2 Click the favorite Web page you want to view.

Note: To display the favorite Web pages in a folder, click the folder (📁) before performing step 2.

■ The favorite Web page you selected appears.

■ You can repeat steps **1** and **2** to view another favorite Web page.

CHAPTER 13

Exchange E-mail

You can exchange e-mail messages with friends, family members and colleagues from around the world. In this chapter, you will learn how to read and send messages, use the address book and more.

READ MESSAGES

You can start Outlook Express to open and read the contents of your e-mail messages.

The first time you start Outlook Express, a wizard will appear if you have not yet set up your Internet connection or e-mail account. Follow the instructions in the wizard to set up your Internet connection and/or e-mail account.

READ MESSAGES

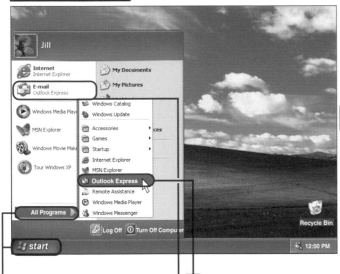

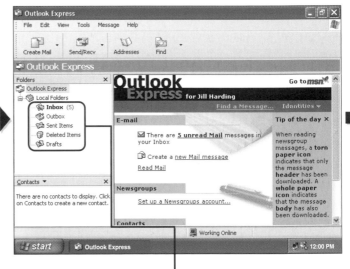

START OUTLOOK EXPRESS

1 Click **start** to display the Start menu.

2 Click **All Programs** to view a list of the programs on your computer.

3 Click **Outlook Express**.

■ If Outlook Express is your default e-mail program, you can click **E-mail** instead of performing steps **2** and **3**.

■ The Outlook Express window appears.

Note: If you are not currently connected to the Internet, a dialog box will appear that allows you to connect.

READ MESSAGES

■ This area displays the folders that contain your messages.

Note: A number in brackets beside a folder indicates how many unread messages the folder contains. The number disappears when you have read all the messages in the folder.

What folders does Outlook Express use to store my messages?

Inbox
Stores messages sent to you.

Outbox
Temporarily stores messages that have not yet been sent.

Sent Items
Stores copies of messages you have sent.

Deleted Items
Stores messages you have deleted.

Drafts
Stores messages you have not yet completed.

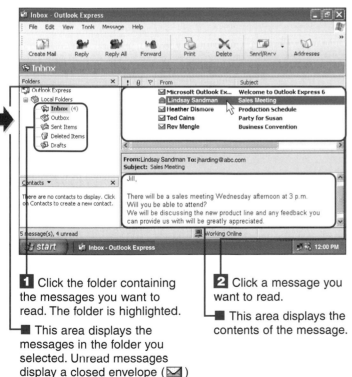

1 Click the folder containing the messages you want to read. The folder is highlighted.

■ This area displays the messages in the folder you selected. Unread messages display a closed envelope (✉) and appear in **bold** type.

2 Click a message you want to read.

■ This area displays the contents of the message.

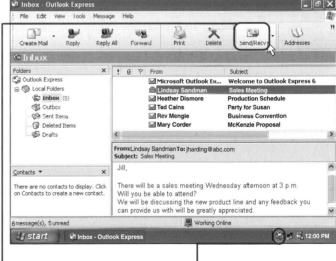

CHECK FOR NEW MESSAGES

When you are connected to the Internet, Outlook Express automatically checks for new messages every 30 minutes.

1 To immediately check for new messages, click **Send/Recv**.

■ When you have new messages, a new e-mail icon (✉) appears in this area.

SEND A MESSAGE

You can send
a message to
express an idea
or request
information.

To practice sending
a message, you can
send a message to
yourself.

SEND A MESSAGE

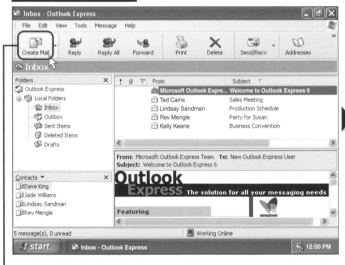

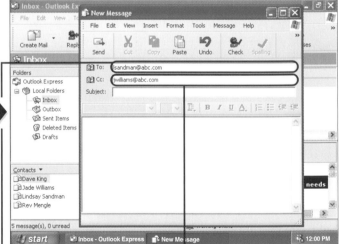

1 Click **Create Mail** to
send a new message.

■ The New Message
window appears.

2 Type the e-mail
address of the person
you want to receive
the message.

3 To send a copy of the
message to a person who
is not directly involved but
would be interested in the
message, click this area and
then type the person's e-mail
address.

*Note: To send the message to more
than one person, separate each
e-mail address with a semicolon (;).*

How can I express emotions in my e-mail messages?

You can use special characters, called smileys, to express emotions in e-mail messages. These characters resemble human faces if you turn them sideways.

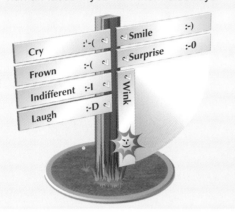

Cry :'-(Smile :-)

Frown :-(Surprise :-0

Indifferent :-I

Laugh :-D   Wink

 What should I consider when sending a message?

A MESSAGE WRITTEN IN CAPITAL LETTERS IS ANNOYING AND DIFFICULT TO READ. THIS IS CALLED SHOUTING. Always use upper and lower case letters when typing e-mail messages.

HOW ARE YOU?

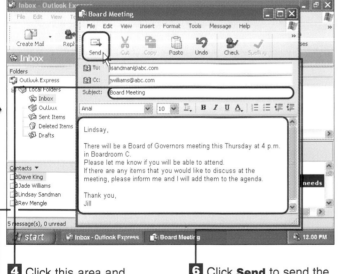

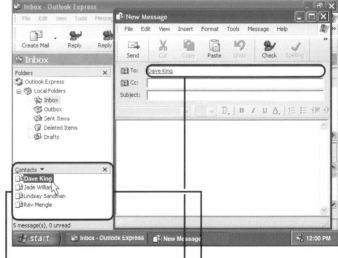

4 Click this area and then type the subject of the message.

5 Click this area and then type the message.

6 Click **Send** to send the message.

■ Outlook Express sends the message and stores a copy of the message in the Sent Items folder.

QUICKLY ADDRESS A MESSAGE

■ The Contacts list displays the name of each person in your address book.

Note: To add names to the address book, see page 278.

1 To quickly send a message to a person in the Contacts list, double-click the name of the person.

■ The New Message window appears.

■ Outlook Express addresses the message for you.

SAVE A DRAFT OF A MESSAGE

You can save a draft of a message so you can send the message at a later time.

Saving a draft of a message allows you to later review and make changes to a message.

SAVE A DRAFT OF A MESSAGE

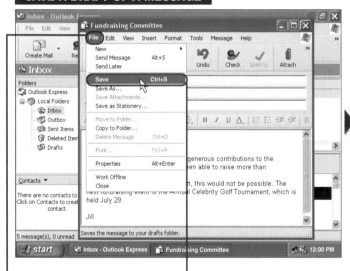

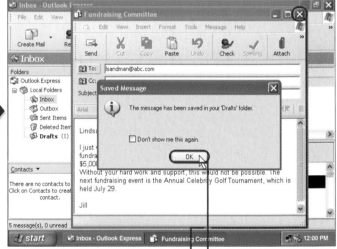

1 To create a message, perform steps **1** to **5** starting on page 266.

2 Click **File**.

3 Click **Save** to save the message as a draft so you can send the message at a later time.

■ The Saved Message dialog box appears, stating that your message was saved in your Drafts folder.

4 Click **OK** to close the dialog box.

5 Click ✕ to close the window that displays the message.

I no longer want to send a message I saved as a draft. How can I delete the message?

If you no longer want to send a message you saved as a draft, you can delete the message from the Drafts folder as you would delete any message. To delete a message, see page 277.

What should I consider before sending a message?

Before you send a message, make sure the message is clear, concise and does not contain any spelling or grammar errors. You should also make sure the person receiving the message will not misinterpret the message. For example, the person may not realize a statement is meant to be sarcastic.

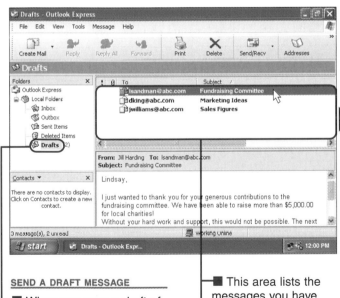

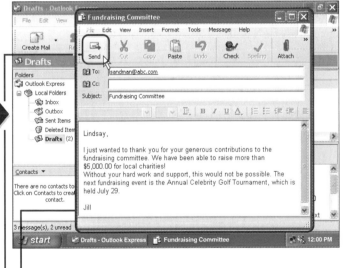

SEND A DRAFT MESSAGE

■ When you save a draft of a message, Outlook Express stores the message in the Drafts folder until you are ready to send the message.

1 Click the **Drafts** folder to display the messages in the folder.

■ This area lists the messages you have saved as drafts.

2 Double-click the message you want to send.

■ A window appears, displaying the contents of the message. You can review and make changes to the message.

3 To send the message, click **Send**.

■ Outlook Express removes the message from the Drafts folder and places a copy of the message in the Sent Items folder.

REPLY TO A MESSAGE

You can reply to a
message to answer
a question, express
an opinion or
supply additional
information.

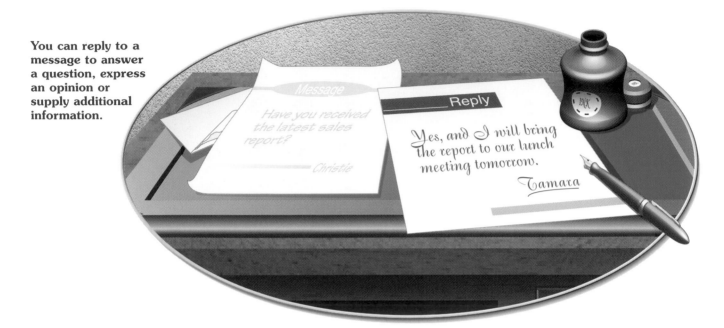

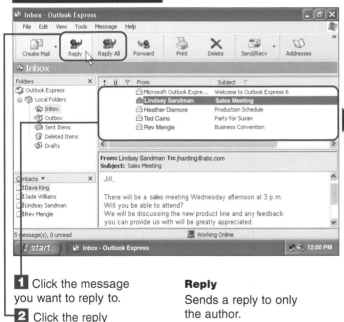

1 Click the message
you want to reply to.

2 Click the reply
option you want to use.

Reply
Sends a reply to only
the author.

Reply All
Sends a reply to the
author and everyone
who received the
original message.

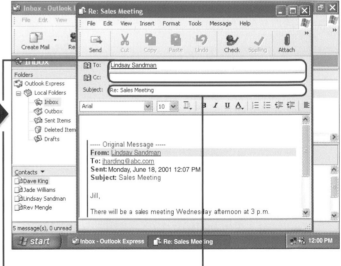

■ A window appears
for you to compose your
reply.

■ Outlook Express fills
in the e-mail address(es)
for you.

■ Outlook Express also
fills in the subject, starting
the subject with **Re:**.

How can I save time when typing a message?

You can use abbreviations for words and phrases to save time when typing messages. Here are some commonly used abbreviations.

Abbreviation	Meaning	Abbreviation	Meaning
BTW	by the way	LOL	laughing out loud
FAQ	frequently asked questions	MOTAS	member of the appropriate sex
FOAF	friend of a friend	MOTOS	member of the opposite sex
FWIW	for what it's worth		
FYI	for your information	MOTSS	member of the same sex
IMHO	in my humble opinion		
IMO	in my opinion	ROTFL	rolling on the floor laughing
IOW	in other words	SO	significant other
L8R	later	WRT	with respect to

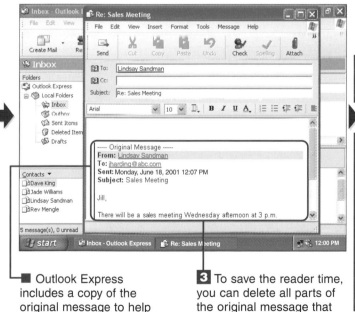

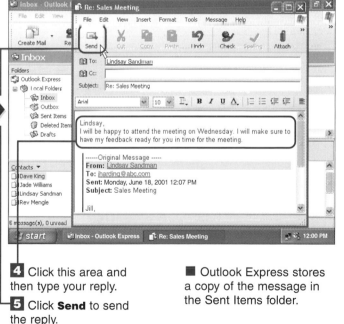

■ Outlook Express includes a copy of the original message to help the reader identify which message you are replying to. This is called quoting.

3 To save the reader time, you can delete all parts of the original message that do not directly relate to your reply.

4 Click this area and then type your reply.

5 Click **Send** to send the reply.

■ Outlook Express stores a copy of the message in the Sent Items folder.

FORWARD A MESSAGE

After reading a message, you can add comments and then forward the message to a friend, family member or colleague.

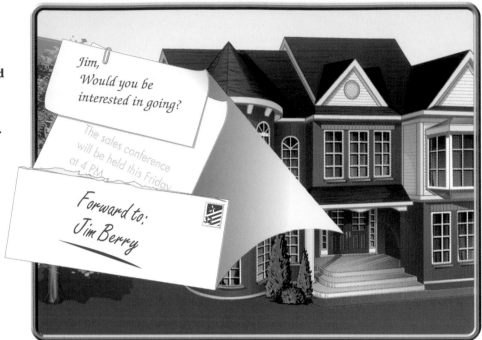

Forwarding a message is useful when you know another person would be interested in the message.

FORWARD A MESSAGE

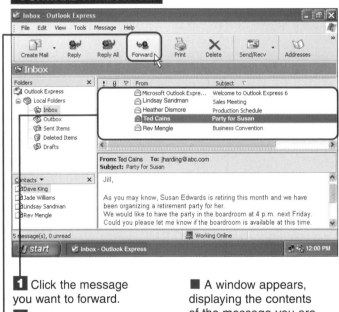

1 Click the message you want to forward.

2 Click **Forward**.

■ A window appears, displaying the contents of the message you are forwarding.

3 Type the e-mail address of the person you want to receive the message.

■ Outlook Express fills in the subject for you, starting the subject with **Fw:**.

4 Click this area and then type any comments about the message you are forwarding.

5 Click **Send** to forward the message.

You can produce
a paper copy of
a message.

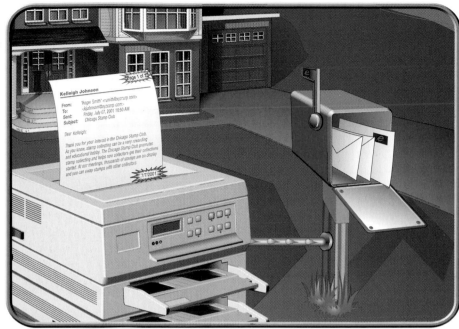

Outlook Express
prints the page
number and total
number of pages
at the top of each
page. The current
date prints at the
bottom of each
page.

PRINT A MESSAGE

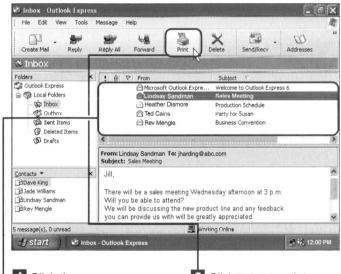

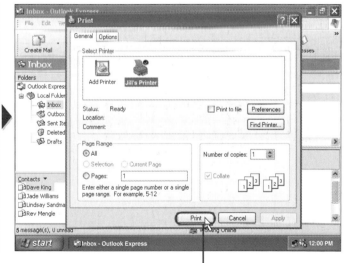

1 Click the message
you want to print.

2 Click **Print** to print
the message.

■ The Print dialog box
appears.

3 Click **Print** to print
the entire message.

ATTACH A FILE TO A MESSAGE

You can attach a file to a message you are sending. Attaching a file to a message is useful when you want to include additional information with a message.

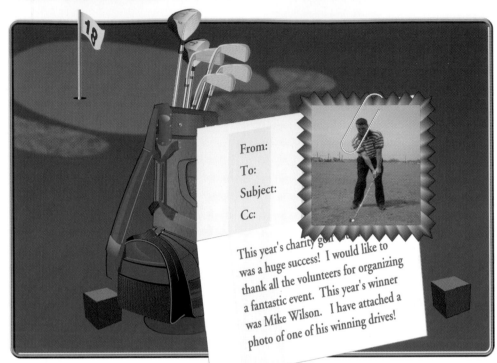

This year's charity golf was a huge success! I would like to thank all the volunteers for organizing a fantastic event. This year's winner was Mike Wilson. I have attached a photo of one of his winning drives!

ATTACH A FILE TO A MESSAGE

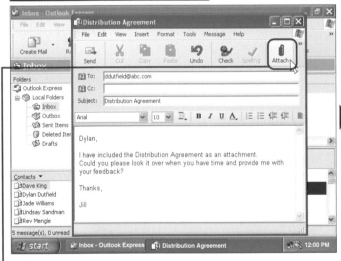

1 To create a message, perform steps **1** to **5** starting on page 266.

2 Click **Attach** to attach a file to the message.

Note: If the Attach button does not appear in the window, you need to enlarge the window to display the button. To resize a window, see page 9.

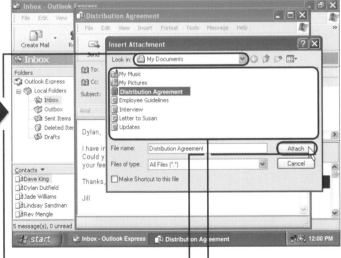

■ The Insert Attachment dialog box appears.

■ This area shows the location of the displayed files. You can click this area to change the location.

3 Click the name of the file you want to attach to the message.

4 Click **Attach** to attach the file to the message.

What types of files can I attach to a message?

You can attach many types of files to a message, including documents, pictures, videos, sounds and programs. The computer receiving the message must have the necessary hardware and software installed to display or play the file you attach.

Can I attach a large file to a message?

The company that provides your e-mail account will usually limit the size of the messages that you can send and receive over the Internet. Most companies do not allow you to send or receive messages larger than 2 MB, which includes all attached files.

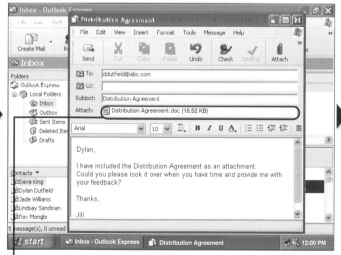

■ This area displays the name and size of the file you selected.

■ To attach additional files to the message, perform steps **2** to **4** for each file you want to attach.

5 Click **Send** to send the message.

■ Outlook Express will send the message and the attached file(s) to the e-mail address(es) you specified.

OPEN AN ATTACHED FILE

You can easily open a file attached to a message you receive.

Before opening an attached file, make sure the file is from a reliable source. Some files can contain viruses, which can damage the information on your computer. You can use an anti-virus program, such as McAfee VirusScan, to check files for viruses.

OPEN AN ATTACHED FILE

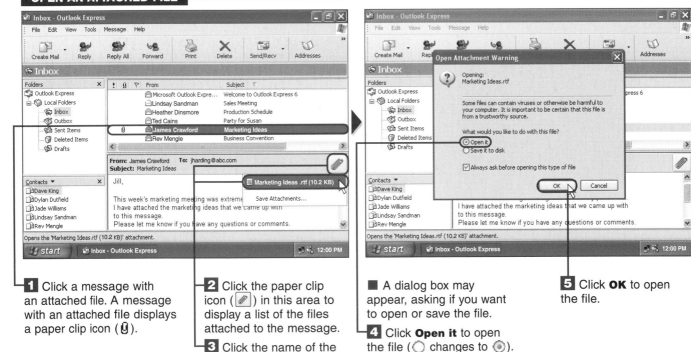

1 Click a message with an attached file. A message with an attached file displays a paper clip icon (📎).

2 Click the paper clip icon (📎) in this area to display a list of the files attached to the message.

3 Click the name of the file you want to open.

■ A dialog box may appear, asking if you want to open or save the file.

4 Click **Open it** to open the file (○ changes to ◉).

5 Click **OK** to open the file.

You can delete a
message you no
longer need. Deleting
messages prevents
your folders from
becoming cluttered
with messages.

DELETE A MESSAGE

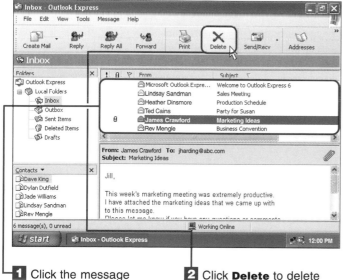

1 Click the message
you want to delete.

2 Click **Delete** to delete
the message.

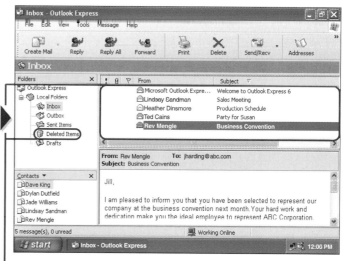

■ Outlook Express removes
the message from the current
folder and places the message
in the Deleted Items folder.

*Note: Deleting a message
from the Deleted Items folder
will permanently remove the
message from your computer.*

ADD A NAME TO THE ADDRESS BOOK

You can use the
address book to
store the e-mail
addresses of
people you
frequently send
messages to.

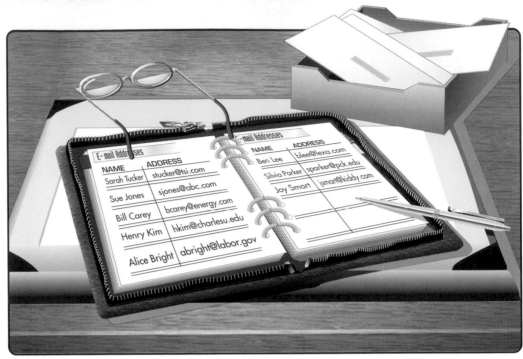

Selecting a name from
the address book helps
you avoid typing mistakes
when entering an e-mail
address. Typing mistakes
can result in a message
being delivered to the
wrong person or being
returned to you.

ADD A NAME TO THE ADDRESS BOOK

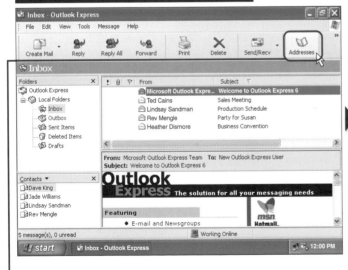

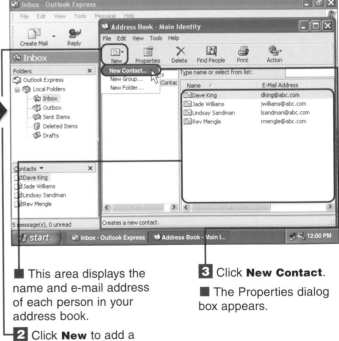

1 Click **Addresses**
to display the address
book.

■ The Address Book
window appears.

■ This area displays the
name and e-mail address
of each person in your
address book.

2 Click **New** to add a
name to the address book.

3 Click **New Contact**.

■ The Properties dialog
box appears.

Can Outlook Express automatically add names to my address book?

Yes. Each time you reply to a message, the name and e-mail address of the person who sent the message is automatically added to your address book.

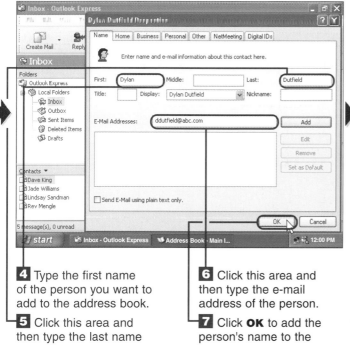

How do I delete a name from the address book?

To delete a person's name from the address book, click their name in the Address Book window and then press the `Delete` key. When a confirmation dialog box appears, click **Yes** to confirm the deletion. Outlook Express permanently removes the person's name from your address book.

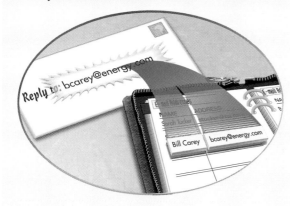

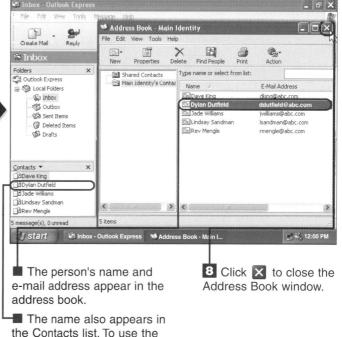

4 Type the first name of the person you want to add to the address book.

5 Click this area and then type the last name of the person.

6 Click this area and then type the e-mail address of the person.

7 Click **OK** to add the person's name to the address book.

■ The person's name and e-mail address appear in the address book.

■ The name also appears in the Contacts list. To use the Contacts list to quickly send a message, see page 267.

8 Click ✕ to close the Address Book window.

ADD A GROUP TO THE ADDRESS BOOK

You can add a group to your address book so you can quickly send the same message to every person in the group.

You can create as many groups as you need. A person can belong to more than one group.

ADD A GROUP TO THE ADDRESS BOOK

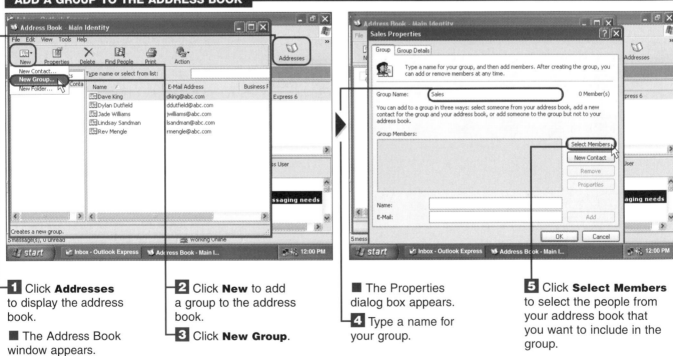

1 Click **Addresses** to display the address book.

■ The Address Book window appears.

2 Click **New** to add a group to the address book.

3 Click **New Group**.

■ The Properties dialog box appears.

4 Type a name for your group.

5 Click **Select Members** to select the people from your address book that you want to include in the group.

How do I send a message to a group?

When composing a message, you can type the name of the group to send the message to every person in the group. To compose and send a message, see page 266.

How do I delete a group from the address book?

To delete a group from the address book, click the name of the group in the Address Book window and then press the Delete key. In the confirmation dialog box that appears, click **Yes** to confirm the deletion. Outlook Express will not remove the people within the group from your address book.

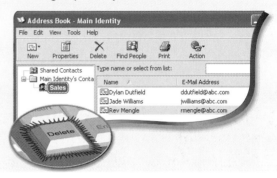

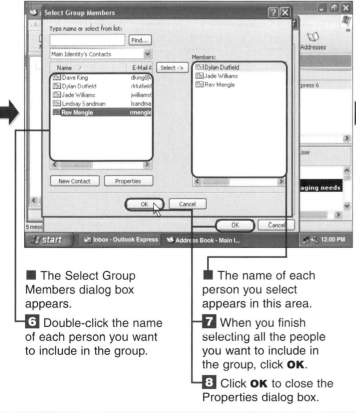

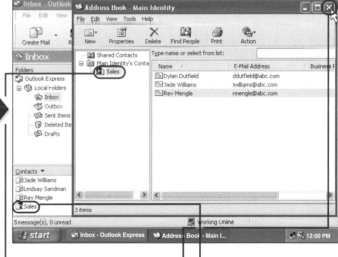

■ The Select Group Members dialog box appears.

6 Double-click the name of each person you want to include in the group.

■ The name of each person you select appears in this area.

7 When you finish selecting all the people you want to include in the group, click **OK**.

8 Click **OK** to close the Properties dialog box.

■ The group appears in the address book. A group displays the 🔛 symbol.

■ The group also appears in the Contacts list. To use the Contacts list to quickly send a message to every person in the group, see page 267.

9 Click **X** to close the Address Book window.

SELECT A NAME FROM THE ADDRESS BOOK

When sending a message, you can select the name of the person you want to receive the message from the address book.

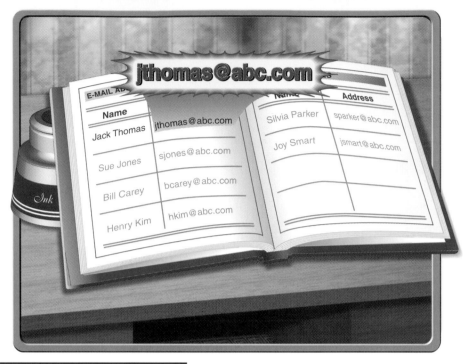

jthomas@abc.com

Name	Address
Jack Thomas	jthomas@abc.com
Sue Jones	sjones@abc.com
Bill Carey	bcarey@abc.com
Henry Kim	hkim@abc.com
Silvia Parker	sparker@abc.com
Joy Smart	jsmart@abc.com

Selecting names from the address book saves you from having to remember the e-mail addresses of people you often send messages to.

SELECT A NAME FROM THE ADDRESS BOOK

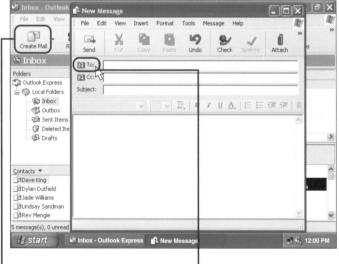

1 Click **Create Mail** to create a new message.

■ The New Message window appears.

2 To select a name from the address book, click **To:**.

■ The Select Recipients dialog box appears.

3 Click the name of the person you want to receive the message.

4 Click **To:**.

■ This area displays the name of the person you selected.

■ You can repeat steps **3** and **4** for each person you want to receive the message.

How can I address a message I want to send?

To

Sends the message to the person you specify.

Carbon Copy (Cc)

Sends an exact copy of the message to a person who is not directly involved, but would be interested in the message.

Blind Carbon Copy (Bcc)

Sends an exact copy of the message to a person without anyone else knowing that the person received the message.

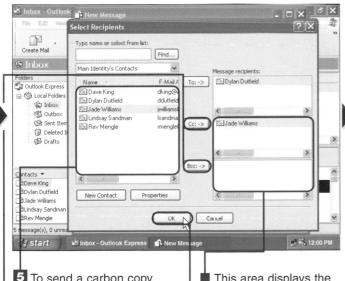

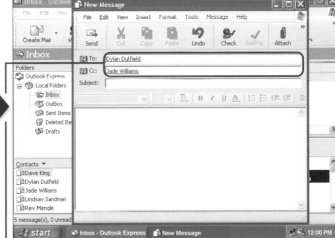

5 To send a carbon copy or blind carbon copy of the message to another person, click the name of the person.

6 Click **Cc:** or **Bcc:**.

■ This area displays the name of the person you selected.

■ You can repeat steps **5** and **6** for each person you want to receive a copy of the message.

7 Click **OK**.

■ This area displays the name of each person you selected from the address book.

■ You can now finish composing the message.

ADD A SIGNATURE TO MESSAGES

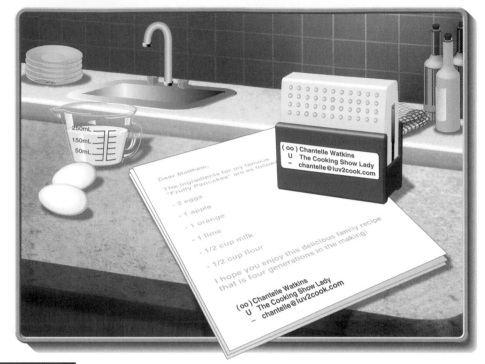

You can have Outlook Express add personal information to the end of every message you send. This information is called a signature.

A signature saves you from having to type the same information every time you send a message.

ADD A SIGNATURE TO MESSAGES

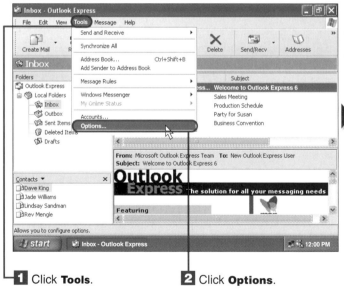

1 Click **Tools**.

2 Click **Options**.

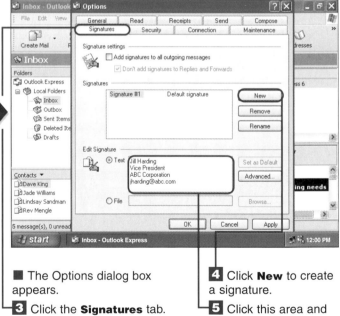

■ The Options dialog box appears.

3 Click the **Signatures** tab.

4 Click **New** to create a signature.

5 Click this area and type the text for your signature.

What can I include in a signature?

A signature can include information such as your name, e-mail address, occupation, favorite quotation or Web page address. You can also use plain characters to display simple pictures in your signature. As a courtesy to people who will receive your messages, you should limit your signature to four or five lines.

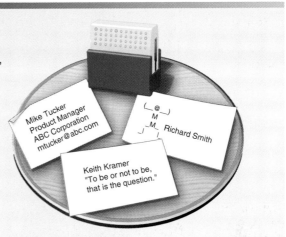

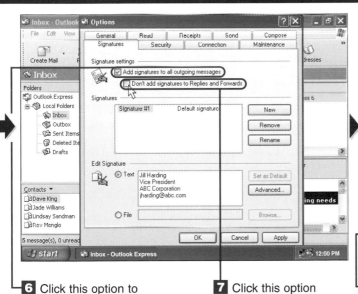

6 Click this option to add your signature to the messages you send (☐ changes to ☑).

7 Click this option to add your signature when you reply to or forward a message (☑ changes to ☐).

8 Click **OK** to confirm your changes.

■ If you no longer want to add a signature to the messages you send, perform steps **1** to **3** and then perform step **6** (☑ changes to ☐). Then press the Enter key.

CHAPTER 14

Exchange Instant Messages

Read this chapter to find out how to exchange instant messages and files with your friends over the Internet using Windows Messenger.

START WINDOWS MESSENGER

You can use Windows Messenger to see when your friends are online and exchange instant messages and files with them.

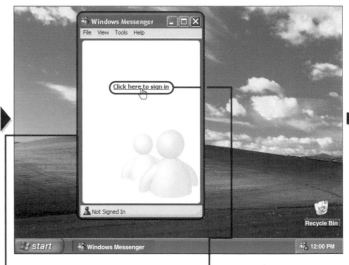

1 Click **start** to display the Start menu.

2 Click **All Programs** to view a list of the programs on your computer.

3 Click **Windows Messenger**.

■ You can also double-click this icon (🐾) to start Windows Messenger.

Note: If 🐾 is hidden, you can click ◀ *on the taskbar to display the icon.*

■ The Windows Messenger window appears.

■ If you are already signed in to Windows Messenger, you do not need to perform steps **4** to **6**.

4 Click this link to sign in to Windows Messenger.

■ The .NET Messenger Service dialog box appears.

288

Why does a wizard appear when I start Windows Messenger?

The first time you start Windows Messenger, a wizard appears to help you add a Passport to your user account. You must add a Passport to your user account to use Windows Messenger. Follow the instructions in the wizard to add a Passport to your user account.

How can I sign out of Windows Messenger?

When you finish using Windows Messenger, you can sign out of the service.

1 In the Windows Messenger window, click **File**.

2 Click **Sign out**.

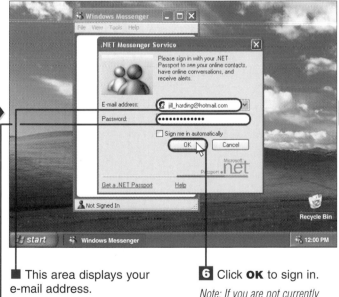

■ This area displays your e-mail address.

5 Type your password. Make sure you type the uppercase and lowercase letters exactly.

6 Click **OK** to sign in.

Note: If you are not currently connected to the Internet, a dialog box may appear, allowing you to connect.

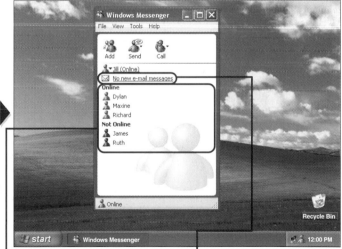

■ If you have added contacts to your list, this area displays the contacts that are currently online and not online.

Note: To add contacts to your list, see page 290.

■ You can click this link to read your e-mail messages. If you have a Hotmail e-mail account, the link displays the number of new e-mail messages you have received.

ADD A CONTACT

You can add a person to your contact list to see when they are online and available to exchange instant messages.

Windows Messenger allows you to add up to 150 people to your contact list.

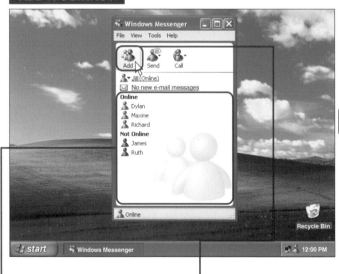

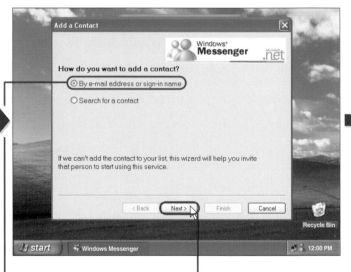

■ This area displays each person you have added to your contact list. You can see the contacts that are currently online and not online.

1 Click **Add** to add a person to your contact list.

■ The Add a Contact wizard appears.

2 Click this option to add a contact by specifying the person's e-mail address (○ changes to ◉).

3 Click **Next** to continue.

Who can I add to my contact list?

Each person you want to add to your contact list requires a Passport. A Passport is obtained when Windows Messenger is set up on a computer. People using a program that is compatible with Windows Messenger can obtain a Passport at the passport.com Web site.

 How do I remove a person from my contact list?

In the Windows Messenger window, click the name of the person you want to remove from your contact list and then press the Delete key. The person will no longer appear in your contact list.

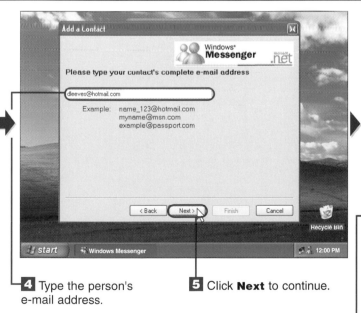

■4 Type the person's e-mail address.

■5 Click **Next** to continue.

■ This message appears if the wizard added the person to your contact list.

■6 Click **Finish** to close the wizard.

■ The person appears in your contact list.

Note: Windows Messenger will notify the person that you added them to your contact list.

SEND AN INSTANT MESSAGE

You can send an instant message to a person in your contact list. The person must be currently signed in to Windows Messenger.

For information on adding a person to your contact list, see page 290.

When sending instant messages, never give out your password or credit card information.

SEND AN INSTANT MESSAGE

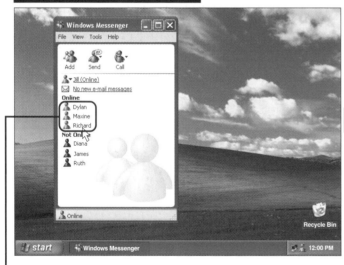

1 Double-click the name of the person you want to send an instant message to.

■ The Conversation window appears.

2 Click this area and type your message.

Note: A message can be up to 400 characters long.

3 Click **Send** to send the message.

Note: You can also press the **Enter** *key to send the message.*

How can I express emotions in my instant messages?

If you type one of the following sets of characters, Windows Messenger will automatically replace the characters with an image, called an emoticon. Emoticons allow you to express emotions in your instant messages.

Type	Windows Messenger Sends	Type	Windows Messenger Sends
:p	😀	(d)	🍸
(y)	👍	(i)	💡
(g)	🎁	(S)	🌙
(f)	🌷	(*)	⭐

What should I consider when sending an instant message?

A MESSAGE WRITTEN IN CAPITAL LETTERS IS ANNOYING AND DIFFICULT TO READ. THIS IS CALLED SHOUTING. Always use upper and lower case letters when typing an instant message.

■ This area displays the message you sent and the ongoing conversation.

■ This area displays the date and time the other person last sent you a message. If the other person is typing a message, this area indicates that the person is typing.

4 When you finish exchanging messages, click ✕ to close the Conversation window.

RECEIVE AN INSTANT MESSAGE

■ When you receive an instant message that is not part of an ongoing conversation, your computer makes a sound and briefly displays a box containing the first part of the message.

1 To display the entire message, click inside the box.

Note: You can also click the Conversation button on the taskbar to display the entire message.

■ The Conversation window appears, displaying the message.

SEND A FILE

While exchanging instant messages with another person, you can send the person a file.

SENDING...

RECEIVING...

If your computer is connected to a network with a firewall, you may not be able to send a file.

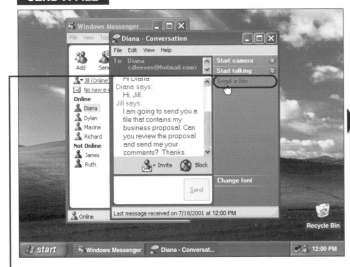

1 While exchanging instant messages with another person, click **Send a file**.

Note: For information on sending instant messages, see page 292.

■ The Send a File dialog box appears.

■ This area shows the location of the displayed files. You can click this area to change the location.

2 Click the file you want to send.

3 Click **Open** to send the file.

What types of files can I send?

You can send many types of files, including documents, pictures, sounds, videos and programs. The computer receiving the file must have the necessary hardware and software installed to display or play the file.

Is there another way that I can send a file?

You can also send a file by attaching the file to an e-mail message. This is useful when you want to send a file to a person who is not currently signed in to Windows Messenger. To attach a file to an e-mail message, see page 274.

■ This area displays the status of the file transfer. The other person must accept the file before the file will transfer.

■ If you no longer want to send the file, you can click **Cancel** to stop the transfer of the file.

*Note: After the other person accepts the file, the **Cancel** option is no longer available.*

■ This message appears when the other person accepts the file.

■ This message appears when the file transfer is complete.

RECEIVE A FILE

While exchanging instant messages with another person, you can receive a file from the other person.

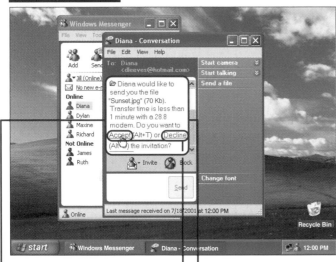

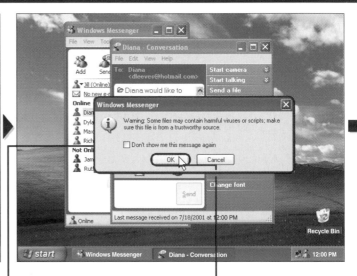

■ While exchanging instant messages with another person, a message appears when the other person sends you a file.

Note: For information on sending instant messages, see page 292.

■ The message displays information about the file, including the file name, file size and transfer time.

1 Click **Accept** or **Decline** to accept or decline the file.

■ If you chose to accept the file, a dialog box appears, warning that some files may contain harmful viruses that can damage the information on your computer.

2 Click **OK** to receive the file.

What should I consider before opening a file I received?

Before opening a file you received, you should use an anti-virus program, such as McAfee VirusScan, to check the file for viruses. Some files may contain viruses, which can damage the information on your computer. You should be very cautious of files you receive from people you do not know.

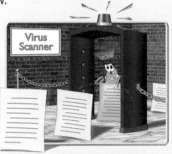

How can I later open a file I received?

Windows automatically saves files you received in the My Received Files folder, which is a subfolder within your My Documents folder. You can open the files in this folder at any time. To view the contents of your My Documents folder, see page 40.

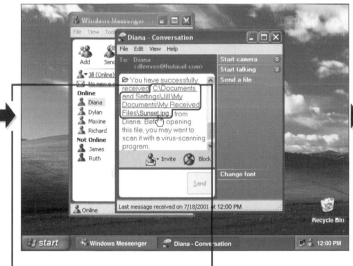

■ When the file finishes transferring to your computer, the location and name of the file appear as a link.

3 To open the file, click the link.

■ The file opens.

4 When you finish viewing the file, click ☒ to close the file.

INDEX

INDEX

INDEX

INDEX

Read Less – Learn More™
Visual

Simplified®

Simply the Easiest Way to Learn

For visual learners who are brand-new to a topic and want to be shown, not told, how to solve a problem in a friendly, approachable way.

All *Simplified*® books feature friendly Disk characters who demonstrate and explain the purpose of each task.

Title	ISBN	U.S. Price
America Online Simplified, 3rd Ed. (Version 7.0)	0-7645-3673-7	$24.99
Computers Simplified, 5th Ed.	0-7645-3524-2	$27.99
Creating Web Pages with HTML Simplified, 2nd Ed.	0-7645-6067-0	$27.99
Excel 97 Simplified	0-7645-6022-0	$27.99
Excel 2002 Simplified	0-7645-3589-7	$27.99
FrontPage 2000 Simplified	0-7645-3450-5	$27.99
FrontPage 2002 Simplified	0-7645-3612-5	$27.99
Internet and World Wide Web Simplified, 3rd Ed.	0-7645-3409-2	$27.99
Microsoft Excel 2000 Simplified	0-7645-6053-0	$27.99
Microsoft Office 2000 Simplified	0-7645-6052-2	$29.99
Microsoft Word 2000 Simplified	0-7645-6054-9	$27.99
More Windows 98 Simplified	0-7645-6037-9	$27.99
Office 97 Simplified	0-7645-6009-3	$29.99
Office XP Simplified	0-7645-0850-4	$29.99
PC Upgrade and Repair Simplified, 2nd Ed.	0-7645-3560-9	$27.99
Windows 98 Simplified	0-7645-6030-1	$27.99
Windows Me Millennium Edition Simplified	0-7645-3494-7	$27.99
Windows XP Simplified	0-7645-3618-4	$27.99
Word 2002 Simplified	0-7645-3588-9	$27.99

Over 10 million *Visual* books in print!

with these full-color Visual™ guides

The Fast and Easy Way to Learn

Title	ISBN	U.S. Price
Teach Yourself Access 97 VISUALLY	0-7645-6026-3	$29.99
Teach Yourself FrontPage 2000 VISUALLY	0-7645-3451-3	$29.99
Teach Yourself HTML VISUALLY	0-7645-3423-8	$29.99
Teach Yourself the Internet and World Wide Web VISUALLY, 2nd Ed.	0-7645-3410-6	$29.99
Teach Yourself Microsoft Access 2000 VISUALLY	0-7645-6059-X	$29.99
Teach Yourself Microsoft Excel 97 VISUALLY	0-7645-6063-8	$29.99
Teach Yourself Microsoft Excel 2000 VISUALLY	0-7645-6056-5	$29.99
Teach Yourself Microsoft Office 2000 VISUALLY	0-7645-6051-4	$29.99
Teach Yourself Microsoft Word 2000 VISUALLY	0-7645-6055-7	$29.99
Teach Yourself VISUALLY Access 2002	0-7645-3591-9	$29.99
Teach Yourself VISUALLY Adobe Acrobat 5 PDF	0-7645-3667-2	$29.99
Teach Yourself VISUALLY Adobe Photoshop Elements	0-7645-3678-8	$29.99
Teach Yourself VISUALLY Adobe Premiere 6	0-7645-3664-8	$29.99
Teach Yourself VISUALLY Computers, 3rd Ed.	0-7645-3525-0	$29.99
Teach Yourself VISUALLY Digital Photography	0-7645-3565-X	$29.99
Teach Yourself VISUALLY Digital Video	0-7645-3688-5	$29.99
Teach Yourself VISUALLY Dreamweaver 3	0-7645-3470-X	$29.99
Teach Yourself VISUALLY Dreamweaver 4	0-7645-0851-2	$29.99
Teach Yourself VISUALLY Dreamweaver MX	0-7645-3697-4	$29.99
Teach Yourself VISUALLY E-commerce with FrontPage	0-7645-3579-X	$29.99
Teach Yourself VISUALLY Excel 2002	0-7645-3594-3	$29.99
Teach Yourself VISUALLY Fireworks 4	0-7645-3566-8	$29.99
Teach Yourself VISUALLY Flash 5	0-7645-3540-4	$29.99
Teach Yourself VISUALLY Flash MX	0-7645-3661-3	$29.99
Teach Yourself VISUALLY FrontPage 2002	0-7645-3590-0	$29.99
Teach Yourself VISUALLY Illustrator 10	0-7645-3654-0	$29.99
Teach Yourself VISUALLY iMac	0-7645-3453-X	$29.99
Teach Yourself VISUALLY Investing Online	0-7645-3459-9	$29.99
Teach Yourself VISUALLY Macromedia Web Collection	0-7645-3648-6	$29.99
Teach Yourself VISUALLY Networking, 2nd Ed.	0-7645-3534-X	$29.99
Teach Yourself VISUALLY Office XP	0-7645-0854-7	$29.99
Teach Yourself VISUALLY Photoshop 6	0-7645-3513-7	$29.99
Teach Yourself VISUALLY Photoshop 7	0-7645-3682-6	$29.99
Teach Yourself VISUALLY PowerPoint 2002	0-7645-3660-5	$29.99
Teach Yourself VISUALLY Quicken 2001	0-7645-3526-9	$29.99
Teach Yourself VISUALLY Windows 2000 Server	0-7645-3428-9	$29.99
Teach Yourself VISUALLY Windows Me Millennium Edition	0-7645-3495-5	$29.99
Teach Yourself VISUALLY Windows XP	0-7645-3619-2	$29.99
Teach Yourself VISUALLY MORE Windows XP	0-7645-3698-2	$29.99
Teach Yourself VISUALLY Word 2002	0-7645-3587-0	$29.99
Teach Yourself Windows 95 VISUALLY	0-7645-6001-8	$29.99
Teach Yourself Windows 98 VISUALLY	0-7645-6025-5	$29.99
Teach Yourself Windows 2000 Professional VISUALLY	0-7645-6040-9	$29.99